FAITH LACKING
UNDERSTANDING

"While at first glance Rauser's claim that major doctrines of the Christian faith appear problematic – to violate logic or our moral sense, or to lack minimal plausibility in light of current scientific ways of viewing the world – seems to be an attempt to undermine those doctrines, in truth *Rauser is seeking to preserve them*. He reminds us that merely repeating something is not the same as understanding it. He thus forces us back to the scriptures in order to maintain the biblical paradoxes. Rauser will not allow us to be intellectually lazy, but calls us to pursue rigorous orthodoxy from a position of humility. There is enough here to provoke, prod, and delight Christians from all traditions – and everyone will have their moment of discomfort. But I believe that Rauser is correct: facing difficult questions is actually for all our good since, in the end, it takes us back to faith. One more thing should be said: rarely have I read a theological book and found myself laughing out loud as I read it, but I did with this text. Rauser's blend of humor and logic makes reading this book not only insightful, but really enjoyable."

Kelly M. Kapic,
Associate Professor of Theological Studies, Covenant College

"This exciting volume should be read and pondered by all who care about the nature and content of constructive theology. Bring it on!"

Oliver Crisp, *Reader in Theology, University of Bristol.*

"When it comes to the central beliefs of Christianity, we so often either possess our own interpretation of them with too much certainty, or remain ignorant and intimidated by them. Randal Rauser guides us toward an alternative approach to thinking about doctrine. Using one of the earliest formulations of Christian faith – the Apostles' Creed – Rauser leads us on a stimulating journey that is both unsettling and yet simultaneously faith-affirming.'"

Jason Clark, *founding pastor of Sutton Vineyard, London*

"One of the many strengths of this tour of the Apostles' Creed is its reminder that the central beliefs of Christian faith are also mysteries that are beyond our comprehension. Randal Rauser proves to be an excellent guide for this journey to the heights and depths of Christian teaching. He knows the well trodden ways as well as some interesting trails that are off of the beaten path. And all along the trek he helps us to see through the eyes of faith that which we cannot understand.'

John R. Franke,
Clemens Professor of Missional Theology, Biblical Seminary, USA

"Randal Rauser probes our understanding of central Christian beliefs, not letting us get away with sloppy thinking or too-easy answers. He has a deep knowledge of Christian teaching through the ages, and particularly of recent philosophical probings of the claims of the Christian faith, but he makes the difficult arguments accessible, and guides us through them with a sure hand, and a delightfully humorous touch. Most importantly, he doesn't try to tell us what is right, but shows us the options fairly and openly, and invites us to do our own thinking. This is not a technical book, but it is a thought-provoking one. No thoughtful Christian will regret reading it."

Steve Holmes,
Lecturer in Theology, University of St Andrews, Scotland

FAITH LACKING UNDERSTANDING

Theology "Through a Glass, Darkly"

Randal Rauser

MILTON KEYNES ● COLORADO SPRINGS ● HYDERABAD

14 13 12 11 10 09 08   7 6 5 4 3 2 1

First published in 2008 by Paternoster
Paternoster is an imprint of Authentic Media
9 Holdom Avenue, Bletchley, Milton Keynes, Bucks, MK1 1QR
1820 Jet Stream Drive, Colorado Springs, CO 80921, USA
OM Authentic Media, Medchal Road, Jeedimetla Village,
Secunderabad 500 055, A.P., India
www.authenticmedia.co.uk
Authentic Media is a division of IBS-STL U.K., limited by guarantee, with its
Registered Office at Kingstown Broadway, Carlisle, Cumbria CA3 0HA.
Registered in England & Wales No. 1216232. Registered charity 27016

British Library Cataloguing in Publication Data

A catalogue record for this book is available from
the British Library.

ISBN-13: 978-1-84227-547-4

Cover design by James Kessell for Scratch the Sky Ltd.
(www.scratchthesky.com)
Printed in the USA by Versa Press

To Abeonim and Eomeonim

Contents

Acknowledgements

As most readers are aware, books do not write themselves; that, alas, is the job of the author. But while the author may tend to monopolize the credit, many people impact the composition of any work. Sometimes that impact is so subtle as to be undetectable, like that of the mythical butterfly whose fluttering wings eventually launch a thunderstorm halfway around the world. On this page we are concerned with contributions to the work that are detectable, and indeed are substantial enough to merit special (albeit modest) recognition. If you need a context, think of this page as my modest equivalent of an Academy Awards acceptance speech. On this score, thanks go first to Robin Parry who was supportive of the project from the beginning and provided much helpful feedback throughout the process, including his inspired suggestions for the book's title and subtitle. Thanks also go to Taylor Seminary for granting me a course reduction that provided some needed extra time in the research and writing. Next up are Kelly Kapic and Ryan Murphy who provided helpful comments on early drafts of a couple chapters. I am also very appreciative of the work of Tony Graham, Peter Little, and all the helpful staff at Paternoster. Finally, thanks go to my wife Jasper and daughter Jamie who grounded the work in reality by interrupting my lofty ivory tower musings with eminently practical questions like "When are you going to take out the garbage?"

It is not for us to stop believing because we lack understanding, or to postone believing till we can get understanding, but to believe in order that we may understand; as Augustine said, "unless you believe you will not understand."
Faith first, sight afterwards, is God's order, not *vice versa*; and the proof of the sincerity of our faith is our willingness to have it so.

J.I.Packer, *Fundamentalism and the Word of God*, 109

1

On Not Understanding Belief

I believe . . .

Many grammar schools include a "career day" when students invite their parents to come and share about their vocations. At such times the more exciting and dangerous vocations typically move to the center of attention, careers like lion tamer, international spy, and race car driver. One that is not likely to stir the interests of a seven year old is theologian. One can picture the scene: as his son beams with pride, the race car driver finishes an edge-of-your-seat retelling of how he won the F1 race at San Marino. Then, after a thunderous applause, up comes the balding theologian in his tweed jacket, fumbling with his papers. As an uncomfortable silence settles over the room, he attempts to break the ice with a faltering joke: "Why did the Calvinist cross the road?" (The children begin to look around puzzled.) "Because he was elected to from eternity!" (Silence.) Then as nervous beads of perspiration form on his balding head, he abandons attempts at humor and begins to pontificate on the concept of *hypokeimenon* in relation to Augustine's *De Trinitate*. Well there's theology for you: dry, irrelevant, boring, and delivered with all the flair of an accountant. Unfortunately, such images of the awkward, irrelevant theologian are difficult to dispel from the popular consciousness. William Placher has observed, "Several times, introducing me to a church group, a well meaning person has said, 'Bill Placher is a theologian, but I think you'll find what he has to say very interesting.' That *but* always worries me, yet it captures something honest about contemporary attitudes to

Christian   theology."[1] As a theologian myself, I have felt the sting
of this prejudice and I must strongly protest it. Exciting though it
may be to slam into a hairpin turn at 150 mph, for the most profound excitement and danger there is no better discipline than
theology. Granted, the excitement and danger of theology may
not be as visceral as racing or as palpable as espionage, but trust
me: the precincts of the theological library conceal unimaginable
peril and inestimable reward.

In order to defend this bold (if implausible) claim, allow me
to develop a parallel between the theologian and another intrepid adventurer, the mountaineer, beginning with the following
illustration. There once was a man who lived in a city nestled
deep in a towering mountain range. After years of living in the
city, the awesome snow-capped peaks that once amazed the
man had faded into the background of his busy life. No longer
did they startle, amaze or shock him with their grandeur and
spectacle. Having lived there for so long, the mountains had
become overly familiar . . . or so it seemed. But in fact, were the
man ever to venture out of the city and climb up into the mountains, his perspective would rapidly change. On the one hand,
he would be awestruck by the awesome beauty of the mountains and the breathtaking range of their vistas. On the other
hand, he would discover the great danger of the mountains as
the change in altitude would induce dizziness, disorientation,
and fatigue, while peril would threaten from rock slides and
blizzards, wild animals and hidden crevices. Slowly he would
realize that in his busy life in the city, inured to the excitement
and danger all around him, he had hardly known the mountains
at all.

I want to suggest that this story describes the relationship
that many Christians today have to the doctrines (that is, teach-
ings) of their faith: the familiarity we have with the central doctrines of faith, like that of the mountains, is illusory. And so,
once we begin to pursue theology as a self-reflective endeavor
to understand the meaning of and systematic relationship
between doctrines, we will similarly appreciate the beauty and
danger of our beliefs. Consider, for instance, the theological
mountain peaks in our midst that are on display in the ancient
Apostles' Creed:

I believe in God, the Father Almighty,
Maker of heaven and earth.

And in Jesus Christ his only (begotten) Son our Lord;
who was conceived by the Holy Ghost,
born of the Virgin Mary,
suffered under Pontius Pilate,
was crucified, dead, and buried; he descended into hell;
the third day he rose from the dead; he ascended into heaven;
and sitteth at the right hand of God the Father Almighty;
from thence he shall come to judge the quick and the dead.

I believe in the Holy Ghost; the holy catholic Church;
the communion of saints; the forgiveness of sins;
the resurrection of the body; and the life everlasting.
Amen.[2]

If you have been a Christian for any length of time, there is a good chance that you have heard this creed before. Indeed, if you are from a liturgical background, it may be that you have recited it every Sunday for years. But be careful, for rote memorization of the Creed does not mean that one truly *understands and appreciates* it. In order to test your understanding, reflect on your reaction upon reading the Creed. Does it strike you as the mountains strike the man, perhaps as comfortable and prosaic? Perhaps like bland Muzak buried in the chaos of a busy life? If this characterizes your response to the Creed then beware for that is a danger sign that you too have fallen for the illusion of the overly familiar, when in fact you have not yet begun to contemplate the excitement and peril of those ancient confessions.

When it comes to the Apostles' Creed, there is no place for the comfortable, prosaic, or bland. Instead, the proper response is one that appreciates the unique nature of these claims. Some will be astounded by these claims, and so may feel a longing or hope welling up upon the reading of those words (*This is too good to be true!*). To others, the creed may elicit a snort of incredulity or a stare of disbelief (*Bah! Humbug!*). Though the former is obviously preferable, both responses at least recognize that these claims are truly extraordinary and thus warrant a passionate response. But what we cannot countenance is that devastating apathy, that mythic over-familiarity that besets many who think they know something simply because it has been long marginalized to the backdrop of their lives. The very importance of the *creed* should be clear, for it encompasses an account of the most unprecedented divine actions: God's creation and reconciliation of all things! All this is to say that I don't require you to accept the *creed* before we begin, but at least appreciate that it makes claims which are of inestimable import. E.L. Mascall put it particularly well: "Now if anyone says that he finds this difficult to believe, I shall respect his incredulity, though I shall try to resolve it. But if he says that it is too dull to interest him or too trivial to be worth investigating, I shall be at a loss to imagine what in heaven or earth he would consider to be exciting or important."[3] Admittedly the excitement of the *creed* is quite different from an F1 race. But though it may not cause quite the same increase in one's pulse rate, it promises not simply a momentary thrill, but rather the deep, abiding joy and satisfaction of discovering one's true purpose, a transforming realization that touches every aspect of one's being. And so there is no underestimating its significance; as Millard Erickson put it, "Far from being dry or abstract, Christian doctrine deals with the most fundamental issues of life: who am I, what is the ultimate meaning of the universe, where am I going? Christian doctrine is, then, the answers that the Christian gives to those questions that all human beings ask."[4]

Not only is the story told by the Creed exciting, but it is dangerous as well. Now I admit, this claim may be a harder sell, but I am not the first individual to make it. G.K. Chesterton for one warned in his great book *Orthodoxy*: "People have fallen into a foolish habit of speaking of orthodoxy as something heavy, humdrum, and safe. There never was anything so perilous or so exciting as orthodoxy."[5] Well okay, you say, that's what Chesterton thinks. But why think that it is true? What's so "dangerous" about the doctrines of the Creed? Well for one thing, the Creed makes claims that are not only incredibly important, but just plain incredible. What is more, when we take a closer look at six major doctrines of the Creed—the Trinity, creation, incarnation, atonement, ascension, and final judgment—we must admit that we lack even a basic understanding of them. The problem here, so I will argue, is that every one of these doctrines violates the basic dictates of logic, or our moral sense, or minimal plausibility in light of our scientific understanding of the world. To put it in mountaineering terms, our attempts to understand each of these core doctrines of faith is blocked by a seemingly insurmountable cliff of mystery be it illogicality, immorality, or implausibility. And as such, we have no *theory* of any of these doctrines any more than the mountaineer has a clear path to the top of the mountain. This places us in a most difficult position for while none of these peaks has ever been climbed, faithfulness to the Creed demands nonetheless that we embark on these most daunting ascents.

Before continuing it is important to clarify more fully what each of these problems entails, beginning with the charge of illogicality. This charge arises when a teaching of the faith appears to entail a logical contradiction, that is, a set of logically inconsistent statements. Since no contradiction can be true, our initial response may be to reject at least one of the statements so as to remove the inconsistency, and yet this orthodoxy will not allow. Instead, the Creed demands that in the absence of a resolution to the contradiction, we still embrace it as a logical paradox. In order to appreciate the nature of the challenge this presents, we need to distinguish the logical paradox[6] from rhetorical paradoxes like the following:

> [Anyone] who believes in me will live, even though they die . . . (Jn. 11:25).
>
> known, yet regarded as unknown; dying, and yet we live on; beaten, and yet not killed; sorrowful, yet always rejoicing; poor, yet making many rich; having nothing, and yet possessing everything (2 Cor. 6:9–10).
>
> For when I am weak, then I am strong (2 Cor. 12:10).

It is easy to see why these statements might be confused with logical paradoxes since taken literally, they appear to be contradictory (e.g. by definition if a person is weak then that person cannot be strong). However, these statements are *not* intended literally, but rather rhetorically. Saying that one must die to live

means something like "in surrendering authority over our physical life to Christ we gain spiritual life." And claiming that we find
strength in our weakness means something like "we can do more
when we depend upon God than on our own" and so on. Since
these statements can be translated into non-contradictory form
they are not true paradoxes, but rather are literary and pedagogi-
cal tools. But the situation is very different with a formal logical
paradox which involves a truly inconsistent set of statements.

As such, while we are free to pepper our discourse with
rhetorical paradoxes, we should only accept a logical paradox
(henceforth simply paradox) after every other avenue has been
closed. As Nicholas Rescher warns, "inconsistency tolerance
should be viewed as a position of last resort, to be adopted only
after all else has failed us."[7] One concern with accepting paradoxes, as Donald Baillie points out, is their corrosive impact
upon reasoning: "There is a great danger in the habit of falling
back too easily upon paradox in our religious thinking, and it
would ultimately make all theological argument impossible."[8]
Argument would become impossible because the very process of
argument depends on the ability to analyze the logical relationship between beliefs, and this is undermined every time we
accept a paradox. What is more, it is far from clear that we *can*
embrace a paradox. Logician Wilfrid Hodges asserts that "It
seems we are obliged to believe only what we think is consistent,
without having any real choice in the matter. In this way we are
all logicians, simply because we are human."[9] The admission of
paradox thus places one in an uncomfortable position of believing that a doctrine *really* is consistent, even though for all
appearances it seems not to be. In this book we shall consider
paradoxes in two doctrines, beginning with the doctrine of the
Trinity's assertion that God is both one and three (chapter two).
Although Christians have often glossed over this problem, we
really need some sort of explanation as to why this is not contradictory. We shall next return to the challenge of paradox when
we consider the doctrine of the incarnation (chapter four). Here
the problem is rooted in the apparent contradiction that arises by
predicating both divine and human attributes of the single individual Christ, as when we affirm that Christ was omniscient (as
divine) and not omniscient (as human).

Troubling though a logical contradiction is, existentially many people are likely to experience a greater struggle with doctrines that appear to violate our deepest sense of morality. We all have a deep moral sense that certain actions are abhorrent. Among our deepest seated beliefs are morals encapsulated in such general maxims as "Good is to be done and evil to be avoided" and such specific mandates as "It is always wrong to torture infants". As such, it can be devastating to realize that certain religious beliefs appear to violate these basic moral dictates. Consider for instance the Hindu doctrine of karma. Logically speaking, karma may well be the most complete answer to the problem of evil ever devised, for it wholly reconciles apparently undeserved suffering with the justice of the universe by positing such suffering as punishment for one's past sins: despite the apparent inequity in the world *everyone* gets their just desserts. And yet, impeccable though karma's logical credentials may be, at a moral level I find utterly abhorrent the implication that a lowly Dalit who is forced to work waist deep in the city sewer is getting just what he deserves. As such, I reject the doctrine of karma for what I perceive to be its evil implications (e.g. the justification of systemic abuse and class oppression). And yet even as I denounce karma I feel the weight of Christian doctrines that appear to be saddled with moral baggage no less onerous beginning with the doctrine of the atonement (chapter five). The shock here is found in the claim, central to the Christian "good news", that a loving and merciful God demands blood for sin and then kills his sinless son to get it. While the problem of atonement is difficult, if anything the problem with the doctrine of hell (chapter seven) is even more wrenching. Am I to believe that the God who is supremely love shall cast the unregenerate into a lake of eternal fiery torment while the elect enjoy the most incredible bliss? How could a loving God do this? And how could perfectly redeemed people accept it?

Interestingly, the greatest obstacle to faith may be not the logical or moral difficulties with Christian doctrine but rather the difficulties with its basic plausibility. In the view of many skeptics the whole set of doctrines in the Apostles' Creed represents an obsolete, ancient Near Eastern worldview that would be absurd to take seriously in light of our scientific understanding of the universe.

Christians are not likely to appreciate the full weight of these objections given that they are part of a community of shared belief that serves to reinforce the plausibility of those beliefs for its members. In short, one often doesn't reflect critically upon (let alone doubt) beliefs widely accepted as true within one's doxastic community. It is only when one encounters others who reject those beliefs that one realizes they may not be quite as obvious as one thought. The Hindu raised in India may never question the basic plausibility of karma as a system until she studies at a secular western university where most people dismiss the claim as false if not absurd. The sheltered Christian who attends that same secular western university will have a very similar experience. But what precisely is it about Christianity that strikes many as implausible? Not surprisingly, the areas that invoke the greatest incredulity are those that seem to conflict with the received deliverances of science. The first we shall consider is the doctrine of creation, in particular the subordinate claim to God's divine action in the world (chapter three). The problem here is that the invocation of divine causes to explain events in the world runs straight into the (overwhelmingly successful) methods of science which seek natural explanations rooted in natural laws. Thus, to the skeptic, invoking God's action to explain events in the world smacks of an inexcusable regression as if we were to return to explaining a bolt of lightning by invoking the arm of Zeus. In short, while science has successfully disenchanted the forest, religion threatens to fill it again with pixies and sprites. But things are even worse yet, for the doctrine of Christ's ascension (chapter six) appears to commit us to a patently false three-storied view of the universe (heaven above, hell below) that was definitively undermined close to five hundred years ago. As such, these doctrines are met with skepticism so deep that, as C.S. Lewis observed, responding to it with a conventional, piecemeal apologetic may even *exacerbate* the problem:

> When once a man is convinced that Christianity in *general* implies a local "Heaven", a flat earth, and a God who can have children, he naturally listens with impatience to our solutions of particular difficulties and our defences against particular objections. The more ingenious we are in such solutions and defences the more perverse we seem to him.[10]

And so to return the plausibility to Christian faith, we shall have to defuse the charge of perversity. To put it briefly, if we are to convince the skeptic that the Christian faith could be true, we shall first have to show them that it is a serious contender for the truth.

Together, the illogicality, immorality, and implausibility objections provide a serious cumulative challenge to Christianity. Indeed, such are the difficulties we face that one might conclude the Apostles' Creed is little more than a laundry list of problems. And it must be admitted that more than a few theologians (professional and amateur) have had their faith severely shaken once they have come to grapple with these problems. Indeed, in a few cases, would-be mountaineers have lost their faith altogether. Unable to cope with a doctrine that appears to be irredeemably incoherent, immoral or implausible, their faith stumbled and died and now lies like so many bleached bones littered among the rocky crags. Occasionally Christians have invoked these tragic losses of faith as an argument against embarking on an excursion into the mountains at all. (When my mother was preparing for university she was warned by well-meaning Christians: "Better to be a fool on fire than a scholar on ice.") However, one need not take this extreme response if one observes that in the vast majority of cases, one's shipwrecked faith traced back to inadequate preparation for the journey. Like the mountaineer who set out for a quick day hike in shorts only to end up in a blizzard, many a theological novice has set out for a quick enquiry into a key doctrine (perhaps prompted by a skeptic's critical question) only to be lost in the swirling snows of confusion or doubt. But then the way to avoid that danger is not to pre-empt the trip, but rather to prepare adequately for it.

In addition to the warning for adequate preparation, we might add the following three points. First, we should think of the problems with Christianity as analogous to the problems with an important scientific theory. A successful scientific theory is a broad explanatory framework that evinces the quality of consilience, a "jumping together" of facts from various disciplines within a single, unified explanation.[11] For instance, the theory of plate tectonics provides a framework in which to understand the varied geological features of volcanoes, seafloor spreading, earthquakes, and mountain ranges. Given that every comprehensive theory will have its problems, limitations and anomalies, these challenges must be balanced against the comprehensive scope of explanation offered by the theory. If its explanatory assets are greater than its liabilities then one has good reason to maintain it. The same goes for Christianity. Before it is ever a problem it is a profound solution to many of the greatest mysteries of life from the universal (e.g. why is there something rather than nothing? What is the source of moral obligation?) to the concrete and specific (e.g. who raised Jesus from the dead? Why did Grandma's cancer immediately lapse into remission following that prayer service?). C.S. Lewis put it especially well when he said: "I believe in Christianity as I believe that the sun has risen; not only because I can see it, but because by it I see everything else."[12] So while the points of darkness that Christianity does not yet illumine are serious, they must always be gauged against the light it sheds on countless other areas.

While Christianity parallels a scientific theory in important respects, our second point is to observe that it is also strikingly different because its object of study is unique in the universe precisely by not being *in* the universe at all. Of course that object of study is God, and Christians understand God to be the ultimate source of all being who is himself the greatest possible being there could be. Should it thus surprise us that we experience certain limitations in our understanding of God? The man who has spent his life climbing dirt piles should not be surprised when he finds Mount Everest more than a test of his limits. How much more should we who, in our daily lives, study minute aspects of a finite created world, expect some frustration when we shift our enquiry to the transcendent source of all things? If we are to be tolerant of limitations anywhere in our understanding, it should be here. J.I. Packer puts the limitations of our theological labors into proper perspective:

> The highest wisdom of the theological theorist, even when working under divine inspiration as Paul did, is to recognize that he is, as it were, gazing into the sun, whose very brightness makes it impossible for him fully to see it; so that at the end of the day he has to admit that God has much more to him than theories can

ever contain, and to humble himself in adoration before the one whom he can never fully analyse.[13]

To that I can only add a hearty "Amen!"

Our third (and most critical) rejoinder has unfortunately been reduced to a cliché, but I shall invoke it nonetheless: Christianity is not ultimately a religion, but rather a relationship. Cliché or not, the point is profoundly important. Just imagine a newly married scientist who determined that the best way to a happy marriage is to learn as many facts about his spouse as possible. And so he insisted on dutifully studying his spouse in a laboratory, compiling an ever-growing list of facts derived through meticulous research. What a bizarre picture of the happy marriage this would be! No less bizarre would be a Christian faith that left God in the laboratory, reducing the invitation to relationship to assent to a set of doctrines. The point here is not to marginalize doctrinal statements like the Apostles' Creed but rather to place them within an appropriate context, as tools to deepen our relationship with the Almighty.

While our vertical relationship with God stands at the center of theological enquiry, the only proper way to pursue that relationship is in horizontal community with others. We do not embark on these excursions alone but always with the support and guidance of others. And that's where I come in as a rather modest Sherpa guide to journey with you through some potentially dangerous terrain. As we begin we should keep one final point in mind. While our goal is to understand the doctrines of our faith more deeply, as I suggested above, that goal only finds its fulfillment in light of the relationship with God, and thus the transformation not merely our minds, but our lives as well. So I hope you are ready, for with the Apostles' Creed we truly are in the Himalayas of theology, a dizzying range of doctrinal peaks that are as beautiful as they are dangerous. And in the flush of those first few steps out of the city and onto the green grass of the lower meadows, the adventure begins.

2

On Not Understanding the Trinity

in God the Father Almighty . . .

There are few things I relish as much as a lively theological debate. As such, it was with a good deal of anticipation that I peered through the drapes and saw two unsuspecting Jehovah's Witnesses standing on our front step. Upon learning that I was a Christian, the elder Witness began to cross-examine me on the doctrine of the Trinity: "You believe that Jesus is God?" "Yes," I replied. "*And* you believe that the Father is God?" "Yes." "And Jesus prayed to God in the Garden of Gethsemane?" "*Yes.*" Apparently satisfied that he had cornered his quarry, the Witness then moved in for the kill: "So then, Jesus prayed to . . . *himself?*" Judging by his cool and confident attitude, I could tell that this line of questioning had trapped many unsuspecting Christians, and it was easy to see why. After all, if the Father is God, and Jesus is God, then it seems to follow that Jesus is the Father. And yet no orthodox Christian could confess this. As such, the Witness was noticeably surprised when, instead of conceding defeat or lapsing into confused silence, I fought back by refusing to accept the consequent: while Jesus is God and the Father is God, I insisted that Jesus is *not* the Father. The Witness clearly had not anticipated receiving such a calm and concise response to what he obviously deemed an intractable dilemma. Having deflated his argument, our conversation then moved on to other issues. But truth be known, I had not really dealt with his argument at all, and if I may be honest, my cool attitude was a bit of a bluff. That is not to say that my reply was disingenuous: on the contrary, it was precisely what an orthodox Christian *should* say. Rather, the bluff came in my posture of confidence, implying as it did that the orthodox response somehow defused the dilemma. In fact, it had not and thus I had given no reason to deny the logical conclusion that Christ is the Father.

So how can I confess with the Creed belief in God the Father Almighty . . . and then add the Son and Spirit? Indeed, what do I even *mean* when I make this confession? Christians are often unaware of this tension, no doubt in large part because the doctrine of the Trinity has become so unconnected to their lives. As Karl Rahner observed some decades ago, "Despite their orthodox confession of the Trinity, Christians are, in their practical life, almost mere 'monotheists.' We must be willing to admit that, should the doctrine of the Trinity have to be dropped as false, the major part of religious literature could well remain virtually unchanged."[1] One can test Rahner's observation in the following way: picture a Baptist pastor who, while praying for the communion elements, thanks the Father for dying for us. Chances are that *nobody will even flinch*. Now imagine the explosion if that same Baptist pastor were to perform an infant baptism! And yet, which doctrine is more essential to Christian identity? Perhaps you find that I am being unfair: after all, the communion prayer could be just an honest mistake. But consider for analogy a football referee who occasionally makes an erroneous call because he is not wholly clear on the game's rules. Surely we wouldn't excuse his errors with the quip that people make mistakes. But then why do we tolerate this confusion from our pastors and about a matter of inestimably greater importance than football? Not surprisingly, congregants are ill-equipped to hold their pastors to account. Paul Fiddes illustrates the confusion by citing the responses of churchgoers who were asked to explain the Trinity:

> the answers of about a third of the sample group showed that they understood the last word in the sense of "one person," one respondent affirming typically that "the three are one person: they're all one person." The willingness to accept a pious puzzle was well illustrated by the church member who remarked that "two are hardly enough and four are too many. But if God decides to make one more it's all right with me."[2]

Yikes! It should hardly surprise us that when Christians are this confused, they are easy targets for every Jehovah's Witness knocking at their door. But difficult though a Witness cross-examination could be, it pales in comparison with the contemptuous sneer of nineteenth-century skeptic Robert Ingersoll:

> According to the celestial multiplication table, once one is three and three times one is one; and, according to heavenly subtraction, if we take two from three, three are left. The addition is equally peculiar: if we add two to one, we have but one. Each one is equal to himself and the other two. Nothing ever was, nothing ever can be, more perfectly idiotic and absurd than the dogma of the Trinity.[3]

While it may be jarring to hear someone refer to the revered doctrine of the Trinity as "perfectly idiotic and absurd," Christian theologians have long conceded that the doctrine confounds (and confuses) human wisdom. As William Placher admits, "the old question remains as to whether Christians are just shockingly bad at arithmetic and unable to realize that three does not equal one."[4] Interestingly, while recent decades have seen an explosion of writing on the Trinity,[5] the logical one/three problem (that is, the question that concerns which sense God is one and three) has rarely been addressed.[6] (On the upside, many Christian philosophers have taken on the one/three problem, and we will engage with some of their work below.) I suspect that one of the reasons for this avoidance is that the problem has proven to be notoriously difficult. As Fergus Kerr warns, "even the soundest theologian or the most orthodox bishop will have to settle for the truth that may be held only by denying the alternative heresies."[7] But we cannot let that deter us. So no matter how difficult the road ahead, no matter how thankless we perceive the task, no matter how hopelessly distant the summit of understanding appears, we must begin our ascent of this most perplexing of doctrines: that of the triune God.

As we begin our hike up the lower regions of the slope, we see a sign of warning emerge out of the mist. Signed "A.W. Tozer" it reads: "Love and faith are at home in the mystery of the Godhead. Let reason kneel in reverence outside."[8] While it provides a familiar temptation to turn back, we cannot take the advice for two reasons. First, while this claim that reason stops when we get to God is presented as pious humility, it looks suspiciously like an arbitrary, ad hoc move to indemnify human theological constructions from critical scrutiny. The cost of such special pleading is that our fiercest critics dismiss Christian theology as irrelevant and irrational. (And it surely is special pleading, for the Christian would hardly tolerate such a response proffered by Jehovah's Witnesses or atheists to excuse their contradictions.) Second, this warning against reducing God to our reason misunderstands what is at issue. Our mission is not a grandiose endeavor to explain everything about God but rather a very modest attempt to understand how a minimal set of trinitarian claims can be understood in a way that is not contradictory! And as Richard Cartwright warns, we cannot simply drape a contradiction in the cloak of mystery since "a mystery [is not] supposed to be unintelligible, in the sense that the words in which it is expressed simply cannot be understood."[9] Hence, taking Tozer's advice will not protect us from the idolatry of reason, but it will inhibit our ability to understand the basic meaning of core trinitarian confessions.

With that task before us we can now turn to lay out the road ahead. It seems appropriate to begin by seeking a more precise clarification of the problem, and we will do this by identifying more closely the biblical support for three central confessions of trinitarian doctrine and then noting the logical tension that results. Then we will consider three attempts to resolve that logical tension.

The Biblical Trinitarian Paradox

As my debate with the Jehovah's Witnesses progressed, the elder Witness iterated a common charge that trinitarian doctrine is a corruption of scripture drawn from pagan religion and philosophy.[10] But the claim is erroneous;[11] in fact, the doctrine arose from the experience of the risen Christ as recorded in the New Testament. To be sure, as with many Christian doctrines, the doctrine of the Trinity is not *explicitly* in scripture. The word *trias* first appears in the writings of Theophilus of Antioch (ca. 180) while the Latin equivalent *trinitas* was coined by Tertullian a couple of decades later. Nonetheless, the doctrine is faithful to the scriptural witness summarized in the following three propositions:

(1) There is one God.
(2) The Father is God, the Son is God, and the Spirit is God.
(3) The Father is not the Son, the Father is not the Spirit, and the Son is not the Spirit.

In a moment we will take a closer look at the logical dilemma that arises from these three propositions, but first we will establish the biblical support for each.

Our treatment of (1) shall be relatively brief, for this fundamental monotheistic confession stands at the core of both Christianity and Judaism. While the statement is implied in the Jewish Shema, "Hear O Israel, the LORD our God, the LORD is One" (Deut. 6:4), it does not become explicit until deutero-Isaiah: "I am the first and I am the last; and beside me there is no God" (Isa. 44:6).[12] Christians retained this revolutionary concept of monotheism as we see in James 2:19: "You believe that there is one God. Good! Even the demons believe that—and shudder."[13] It cannot be emphasized too strongly that, whatever their other beliefs, Christians remained uncompromising monotheists.

This brings us to the confession in (2) concerning the divinity of the three persons. One can establish the deity of the Father by noting that the New Testament frequently uses the titles "God" and "the Father" interchangeably. For instance, Jesus taught his disciples to pray to God with the address "our Father" while Paul referred to the one God of Christian worship as the Father (1 Cor. 8:6). The path to establishing the deity of the Son and Spirit is more indirect. Some years ago a friend of mine spent the summer working with a fellow whom he later discovered moonlighted as a professional Muslim apologist. At one point this man challenged my friend to identify *one passage* in the New Testament where Jesus says he is God. Irritated, my friend took up the challenge and spent several tense minutes flipping through the pages of his New Testament, but to his great frustration, he was unable to produce even one text! Unbeknownst to my friend, the problem lay with the Muslim's narrow criteria for what constitutes relevant evidence. The first sign of Jesus' identity is found in the significance of his own actions. Consider for instance that he placed himself in a parallel role to God when he reconstituted a new Israel by calling twelve apostles. In addition, he assumed the divine prerogative to forgive sins, the significance of which was not lost on the Pharisees (Mk. 2:5–11). (In condemning Jesus as a blasphemer, they overlooked the other possibility that he was God.) Further, Jesus distinguished himself from all other Jewish teachers by repeatedly referring to God exclusively as *his* Father in a jarring contrast with the derivative sense that other human beings call God Father (e.g. Mt. 11:27; Mk. 12:1–12; Jn. 5:18). As Gerald O'Collins observes, "Jesus evidently spoke of and with God as his Father in a direct, familial way that was unique, or at least highly unusual, in Palestinian Judaism."[14] The early Christians attributed even more suggestive roles to Christ including creator (Jn. 1:3; Col. 1:16; Heb. 1:2) and sustainer (Jn. 1:3; 1 Cor. 8:6; Col. 1:17; Heb. 1:3) of all things! What is more, while the scriptures do not record Jesus uttering the proposition "I am God" in so many words, he did claim God's name—"I AM"—for himself (Jn. 8:58; cf. Ex. 3:14), a move sufficiently provocative to prompt Jewish leaders to attempt to stone him. And in Revelation 22:13 Jesus Christ claims the divine title "First and the Last" for himself.[15] What is more, early Christians applied to Jesus the theologically loaded title of Lord (*kurios*, which is the Septuagint's translation of *adonai*).[16] And they were not tentative in doing so. Arthur Wainwright observes that one finds it *24 times* in 1 Thessalonians alone, and a grand total of 230 times in all of Paul's letters![17]

Arguably the most powerful evidence for the church's belief in Christ's deity is found in a number of explicit references in scripture including John 1:1 and 1:18, which form an *inclusio* for the introduction to John's Gospel, and John 20:28 which, with John 1:1, forms an *inclusio* for the entire gospel.[18] Jesus' reply to this astounding confession is no less significant: "Because you have seen me, you have believed; blessed are those who have not seen and yet have believed" (Jn. 20:29). While Jesus does not explicitly affirm his own deity, this affirmation of Thomas' statement has the same effect.[19] While the Johannine testimony may represent the highest Christology, Paul also explicitly refers to Christ as God (Rom. 9:5; Titus 2:13) and the author of Hebrews applies a number of Old Testament Yahweh texts to Jesus (e.g. 1:10–12, cf. Ps. 102:25–27). In light of this cascade of evidence, we can appreciate how deftly the Muslim apologist's demand cleverly filters out all the *relevant* data. When we take in the full weight of evidence we come to the conclusion that the early church was convinced that Jesus Christ is God.[20]

We may have belabored the point on the divinity of Jesus, but there is a good strategic reason for doing so: conceptually the primary challenge is to recognize that the one God can be more than one. Once we have admitted the possibility of binitarianism (two in one), it is comparatively straightforward to expand that conception to trinitarianism should the evidence require postulation of a third person. Interestingly, while the main point of contention in Christology is divinity rather than personhood, when we come to pneumatology (the doctrine of the Spirit) the debate is reversed. The scriptures seem unambiguous in their treatment of the Spirit as divine: while God alone is holy, the Spirit is the *Holy* Spirit, Spirit of God, Spirit of Christ, Spirit of Wisdom and Spirit of Truth. Hence, to blaspheme the Spirit is to blaspheme God (Mt. 12:31) and to lie to the Spirit is to lie to God (Acts 5:3–4). In addition, the Spirit exemplifies divine attributes including eternality (Heb. 9:14) and omniscience (1 Cor. 2:10–12). As such, the Spirit's deity is not in real doubt; the more controversial question is whether the evidence supports inferring that the Spirit is a distinct person (*hypostasis*) rather than a *personification* of God's actions or character. In defense of the Spirit's personhood, we can note that personal attributes and actions are attributed to the Spirit: he can be insulted and grieved (Heb. 10:29; Eph. 4:30), he searches and knows (1 Cor. 2:10–11) and he teaches and reminds (Jn. 14:25–26). However, it must be admitted that the Old Testament employs similar language while never inferring the Spirit's personhood. As such, the inference is justified by three novel advances in the New Testament. First, we have references to the Spirit speaking (Acts 10:19–20; 13:2), a striking datum since, as Thomas Oden observes, "None but a person can say 'I.' "[21] Second, Jesus refers to the Spirit with the personal pronoun "He" (Jn. 14:15–17) instead of the neuter pronoun which would be natural in Greek. Thus when

Jesus prepares his disciples for his departure he promises another comforter in his place: "I tell you the truth: It is for your good that I am going away. Unless I go away, the Counselor will not come to you; but if I go, I will send him to you" (Jn. 16:7). To illustrate the significance of the point, imagine that you are on vacation in Europe with European travel guru Rick Steves as your personal tour-guide. One evening he informs you that he has to leave unexpectedly, but he is sending another tour-guide in his place and the concierge will introduce you in the morning. With great expectations, you come down to the hotel lobby the next morning and walk over to the concierge . . . only to discover that your new "tour-guide" is a copy of Rick Steves' *Europe Through the Back Door!* No doubt you would be surprised and more than a little put off, feeling that Steves misled you by referring to the book as if it were a person. By the same token, Jesus could hardly have spoken of the Spirit as a personal replacement (*another* comforter) were the Spirit not a person. Third, the three are commonly juxtaposed in the New Testament (see the examples below). Again, to list a non-personal Spirit with the personal Father and Son would be as misleading as listing Steves and his book together as two tour guides.

Our final point brings us to consider (3) the distinction of the three persons. I was reminded of the need to stress this final premise a few years ago when I gave a public lecture in which I discussed how the doctrine of the Trinity was essential to Christian identity. Afterwards a lady came up, thanked me for the talk, and then politely informed me that not *all* Christians are trinitarians. As it turned out, she was an adherent of Oneness Pentecostalism, a sect which accepts (1) and (2) but denies (3), claiming instead that the Father and Spirit are but manifestations of the person of Christ. The primary reason that we judge Oneness Pentecostalism to be a deep theological error is found in the pivotal texts that juxtapose the Father, Son, and Spirit as distinct personal identities. This is apparent at the beginning of Jesus' ministry when he was baptized, the Father spoke and the Spirit descended as a dove (Mt. 3:16–17; Mk. 1:9–11; Lk. 3:21–22). In addition, in the Matthean baptismal formula (28:19–20) Jesus commands the church to baptize in the *name* (singular) of the Father, Son, and Holy Spirit. In recognizing the significance of this passage, Gregory Nazianzen noted: "The history of Christian theology is best understood as an extended commentary on the baptismal formula."[22] One finds a number of other "triune" passages in scripture which juxtapose the three (e.g. Eph. 2:18; 1 Cor. 12:3–6; 2 Cor. 13:14; 1 Pet. 1:2–12; Jude 20–1; Rev. 1:4;). And then there are those passages that distinguish two of the persons including John 1:1 and 1 Corinthians 8:6 (Jesus and the Father) and John 14:15–17 and 16:7 (Jesus and the Spirit). In light of such texts, it is wholly implausible to suggest as Oneness Pentecostals do, that the three might be manifestations of the same individual. Surely the Jehovah's Witness was correct here: it would indeed be very implausible to posit Jesus praying to himself in the Garden. Or to have Jesus declaring himself his own beloved Son. Or to have Jesus promise that he would send *another* comforter . . . and then send himself!

Consequently, the church was unflinching in its endorsement of (1), (2) and (3). One finds an excellent summary statement in the Athanasian Creed (ca. 500), a document which elicits strong reactions: while some laud it as a perspicuously clear and authoritative statement of correct doctrine, others decry it as obtuse if not incoherent. Consider the following three propositions:

3. And the Catholic Faith is this: That we worship one God in Trinity and Trinity in Unity;
4. Neither confounding the Persons: nor dividing the Substance [Essence].
5. For there is one Person of the Father: another of the Son: and another of the Holy Ghost. But the Godhead of the Father, of the Son, and of the Holy Ghost, is all one : the Glory equal, the Majesty eternal.[23]

The Creed is unapologetically orthodox as it confesses three equally divine persons who, though distinct, "add up" to one God. The potential incoherence will take a bit more effort to define precisely. To do so we will have to return to one crucially important word that appears in each of our propositions: is. The word "is" requires special attention because the logical dilemma depends upon which of three possible meanings is intended in each proposition. The first meaning, the "is of existence," involves a substitution of "is" for "exists." (E.g. "There is a book on the table"="There exists a book on the table.") The is of existence is operative in (1) ("There is one God"="There exists one God"). In the second and third propositions the is functions as a copula joining together the two parts of the statement. However, that copula has two possible meanings: the "is of attribution" (or "is of predication") and the "is of identity." The is of attribution functions to predicate a property of an object. For instance, if I say "My horse is brown and fast" I am attributing the properties of brownness and fastness to my horse. By contrast, in the is of identity the copula functions as an identity claim which abbreviates the more unwieldy phrase *"is the same as"* or *"is identical to."* (E.g. "That is my book"="That is the same book as my book.") Discerning which copula is intended can clear up all sorts of possible confusion. To illustrate, imagine that we are at the Kentucky Derby and I point at a lean grey stallion in the stable and proudly say "That horse is brown and fat." Assuming that I was intending to predicate the properties of brownness and fatness of the horse (the is of attribution) you would judge my statement false. But later when you discover that that grey stallion is *named* Brown and Fat you would realize that I made a true statement with the is of identity. As such, the entire meaning of the sentence changes based on the intended meaning of the copula.

This distinction is crucially important as we seek to understand the second and third trinitarian statements. In the case of (3) the copula clearly functions as the is of identity for the intent is to assert that "the Father *is not the same as* the Son" et cetera. The real question concerns whether (2) should be understood as a property predication or an assertion of strict identity. These two possibilities can be put as follows:

(2a) The Father is divine, the Son is divine, and the Spirit is divine.

(2b) The Father is identical with God, the Son is identical with God, and the Spirit is identical with God.

(2a) interprets the statement as the is of attribution (predicating the property of divinity) while (2b) interprets it as the is of identity. Unfortunately, each interpretation places us in logical conflict with one of our other affirmations. If we adopt (2a) and (3), then it follows that there are three gods which contradicts (1). Conversely, if we adopt (2b) and (1), then we contradict (3) because it follows that each person is identical to the others. As a result, we find ourselves mired in the one/three problem which Richard Cartwright summarizes as follows:

> If each Person is identical with the essence, there cannot be more than one Person. And if, on the other hand, the Persons are to be thought of as sharing a common nature, in the manner of Paul, Silvanus, and Timothy, there cannot be fewer than three Gods. How, in short, can there be three divine Persons and yet only one God?[24]

And with that we are back in the dilemma raised in inchoate form by the Jehovah's Witness.

Each of the following three proposals offers a different resolution to the one/three problem. The first approach, the psychological analogy (PA), is an ancient model which argues that the subject/object distinction that exists within self-conscious individuals illumines the triune distinctions within the one God. The PA takes as its starting point the unity of the single mind (that is, the triune God is like a single mind), and then seeks to establish a diversity of persons within that one mind. The second approach, the whole/part analogy (WPA), responds to the one/three problem by arguing that there is one God proper (the Trinity) which has three divine parts (the Father, Son, and Spirit). Finally, we will turn to the social analogy (SA) which begins with the plurality of persons and then seeks to explain the one/three relation in terms of the unity of an intimate social group.[25] While each analogy offers some limited insight, it remains to be seen whether any one offers a final resolution to restore coherence to this fundamental doctrine.[26]

Me, Myself, and I: The Psychological Analogy

I still recall the first time the Trinity "made sense" for me. I was in a Sunday school class and the teacher told us that the Trinity is like the same man being a husband, father, and . . . firefighter! I suppose I remember that illustration for two reasons. First, I was intrigued by the fact that the guy was a *firefighter* rather than, say, an accountant. (It helps when the illustration comes replete with an impressive firefighter on the flannel graph board.) Second, this was the first time I began to think about the scattered references I heard in church to Father, Son, and Spirit in something like a systematic sense. Unfortunately, as it turns out, this first, halting step toward trinitarian theology was, well, *heretical*. To explain the Trinity as one divine being who fulfils three roles is a form of modalism which, like Oneness Pentecostalism, collapses the distinctions of the persons. The special challenge of any analogy that seeks to explain the Trinity from the divine unity is to establish a sense of plurality sufficient to prevent a collapse into modalism. In a moment we will turn to consider the most influential analogy that begins with oneness: the PA. But first we will consider the theology of the Trinity that lies behind this analogy.

In his recent monograph on the Trinity John Thompson writes: "we stand before the triune God *himself* as worshippers."[27] What makes Thompson's statement interesting is that he uses a single personal pronoun to refer not to any particular triune person, but rather to the entire Trinity. Similarly, A.W. Tozer refers to the one God as distinct from the three persons with a personal pronoun: "God cannot so divide *Himself* that one Person works while another is inactive."[28] Thompson and Tozer are hardly unique in this practice; indeed, Christians regularly refer to the one God with a single personal pronoun. But is this practice appropriate? One danger is that it will lead to a quaternity by adding the Trinity as a fourth person. In recognition of this danger, many theologians have adopted (2b) for if each person is identical with the one God, then the one God does not constitute an *additional* person. With its ability to defuse both tritheism and a quaternity, (2b) has had a large influence through theologians like St. Augustine and Thomas Aquinas as well as the Athanasian Creed and Fourth Lateran Council.[29] Brian Leftow refers to this tradition's approach as the "Latin Trinity" due to its particular influence on western, Latin Christianity.[30]

On the downside, (2b) is in danger of collapsing into modalism. David Brown illustrates the problem by quoting and then commenting on the Fourth Lateran Council:

"We . . . believe and confess . . . that there is one supreme reality . . . which is truly Father, Son and Holy Spirit, at once the three persons taken together and each of them singly." There is no doubt in my mind that this is the doctrine of the Trinity at its most incoherent. Theologically, one can of course understand the motivation behind it, the desire to preserve the claim that in any situation in which divinity is present the entire Godhead is present. But, logically, total nonsense is the result.[31]

Brown's charge of "total nonsense" is rooted in the law of the transitivity of identity which states: if A is identical to B and B is identical to C then, necessarily, A is identical to C. Though this law might initially appear strange, in fact we assume it all the time without even thinking about it. To illustrate, consider the following two propositions:

(4) Stanley Hauerwas is the author of *The Peaceable Kingdom*.
(5) The author of *The Peaceable Kingdom* is the Duke Divinity School theologian most likely to swear during an academic presentation.

Based on (4) and (5) you can logically conclude:

(6) Stanley Hauerwas is the Duke Divinity School theologian most likely to swear during an academic presentation.

Far from being a contentious claim, the inference to (6) based on (4) and (5) is rock solid. So how can it be that when we consider the Trinity the law no longer applies? This is Brown's point: such special pleading is "total nonsense."

Let's say that the theologian replies by playing the mystery card: that which applies to Stanley Hauerwas does not apply to God since God is a great mystery. However, if we use this response to indemnify our transcendent religious claims, then it can be invoked for others as well. Consider the Advaita Vedanta Hindu claim that "Atman is Brahman," that is every single thing is identical with everything that exists. Now consider two examples of "Atman is Brahman":

(7) I am identical with the totality of what exists.
(8) My favorite Tom Jones record is identical with the totality of what exists.

From these two statements we can infer

(9) I am identical with my favorite Tom Jones record.

Clearly (9) is false, for my favorite Tom Jones record has properties that I do not have, such as playing "What's New Pussycat?" when placed on a turntable. Place *me* on a turntable and not much at all will happen. But then the claim that Atman is Brahman is necessarily false,[32] and no lame appeal to the mystery of Brahman can redeem such incoherence. If we find the mystery defense of Brahman unjustified, why do we invoke it for the Trinity?

This is where the analogy comes in. Perhaps we can defend (2b) by identifying something in the world that manifests an analogous logical structure of identity and distinction. As such, the PA claims that the subject-object relation within the self-conscious human individual is relevantly analogous to the internal plurality of the Trinity: God is like the single, self-conscious, reasoning subject. The argument was initially developed by the North African theologian Tertullian. He begins by noting that human beings often reason with themselves, working out their thoughts on a particular issue in a sort of internal monologue. And incredibly we find that in reasoning with ourselves we reason with another:

> So in a sort of way you have in you as a second [person] discourse by which you speak by thinking and by means of which you think by speaking: discourse itself is another [than you]. How much more completely therefore does this action take place in God whose image and similitude you are authoritatively declared to be, that even while silent he has in himself reason, and in <that> reason discourse.[33]

I would suspect that we have all had experiences of speaking with ourselves, soliloquizing as it were. (And we have perhaps also experienced the embarrassment of someone coming upon us unexpectedly and asking to whom we are talking!) This shows that within the self-conscious individual there is a subject/object distinction such that one can have a conversation with oneself. Tertullian then argues that this phenomenon serves as an analogue for the plurality of the one God.

The profundity of Tertullian's insight hit me one day while walking alone across a university campus. In geeky fashion, I was verbally working through a theological dilemma when it occurred to me that I was reasoning *with myself*. Then it occurred to me that if I can reason with myself, then it follows that *I am not alone*. But how can I be *with* myself when I *am* myself? This puzzle is evident in our ability to surprise ourselves. Think of a time where you shocked yourself by saying something utterly stupid or insensitive to another person. Or, on a lighter note, perhaps you surprised yourself with your own wit or even made yourself laugh. This type of phenomenon is fascinating for humor amuses precisely as it introduces an unforeseen incongruity which captures the listener off-guard. A fascinating example is found in Leo Rosten's recollection of the time he was invited to give the first speech at a celebrity roast of W.C. Fields. Rosten—an unknown comedian among towering Hollywood celebrities—mounted the stage to give the first roast. Unfortunately he froze and stood horrified in front of a puzzled—and increasingly impatient—audience:

> I prayed for a trap door to open beneath me, or for lightning to strike me dead. Neither happened. Instead, I heard George Burns' hoarse *sotto voce*: "Say *some*thin'!" with unmistakable disgust.
> I gulped—then someone who was hiding in my throat uttered these words: "The only thing I can say about Mr. W.C. Fields, whom I have admired since the day he advanced upon Baby LeRoy with an icepick, is this: Any man who hates dogs and babies can't be all bad."[34]

The audience immediately erupted in laughter and explosive applause (I'm assuming it is funny for those who knew Fields), thereby saving Rosten's dignity. But the really fascinating fact is that *Rosten was as surprised as anybody by his witticism.* (As he puts it, someone hiding in his throat made the quip.) How do we surprise ourselves with our own wit? From where does this complex subject/object relationship within the individual derive?

Limited though the analogy may be, we might still hope to grasp something of the internal divine distinctions through it. The exploration of divine triunity in terms of human self-consciousness and reason proved suggestive enough to be taken up by a number of theologians after Tertullian including Origen and Gregory Nazianzen.[35] Within the ancient church, the most developed form of the argument comes from Augustine who explicitly sought to move the psychological parallel beyond a binitarian subject/object opposition to a distinctively triadic structure. In his classic study of the Trinity Augustine explores a number of psychological triads, settling in book 9 upon the mind that knows and loves itself. As the mind knows itself, self-knowledge emerges as a second, while the love of self-acceptance then completes the triad. As Augustine put it, these three are the same substance (for "mind is not being loved or known by any other thing"[36]) and yet they are also distinct: "these three are inseparable from each other, and yet each one of them is substance, and all together they are one substance or being."[37] Following Augustine's lead, many other theologians have developed a tripartite psychological analogy, most notably Thomas Aquinas.

So is the psychological analogy successful? Admittedly the subject/object relationship of self-consciousness is itself fascinating.[38] And yet, the worry remains that a consistent application of the analogy will collapse into modalism. For instance, David Brown critiques Augustine's analogy by pointing out that "there is no clear sense in which mind, knowledge, and love are or could be three fundamentally distinct entities; rather what we have is one entity, the mind, together with two of its states or activities."[39] We can illustrate the problem linguistically: while the psychological analogy trades on the distinction between me, myself, and I, each of these words has the exact same referent: "me" is the objective case of "I" and "myself" is a pronoun used to identify the very same thing. The failure of the analogy is evident when I say "*I* reminded *myself* to return the Uriah Heep record that Ken lent *me*." William Lane Craig and J.P. Moreland rightly conclude, "There is no more reason to think that the individual designated by 'I', 'me' and 'myself' constitutes a plurality of persons in God's case than in any human being's case."[40] At best one might conclude that rather than explain the one/three paradox, the PA seems to obscure it in another (the paradox of self-consciousness).

A Divine Cherry Pie: The Whole/Part Analogy

Legend tells us that when the good St. Patrick brought Christianity to Ireland, he explained the doctrine of the Trinity with a shamrock: just as the three leaves comprise the one clover so the three persons comprise the one God. I refer to this type of illustration as a whole/part analogy because it attempts to explain the relationship of Father, Son and Spirit to the Trinity in the terms of parts to the whole. Whole/part analogies are among the most common and simple trinitarian analogies and thus are favored by Sunday school teachers the world over: just as an egg is composed of the yolk, albumen, and shell, or a candle of wax, wick, and flame, so generations of catechumens have been informed that God is composed of the Father, Son, and Spirit. One of the great attractions of the WPA is that the model is so readily adaptable to different forms. One time after giving a lecture on the one/three problem, I was accosted by an eager undergraduate who believed he had identified the perfect analogy: the Trinity is like a cherry pie cut into three slices. (I wondered: why *cherry*?) As the student explained to me, each slice is one hundred percent cherry pie, composed of the same crust and filling, and yet added up, these slices comprise just one cherry pie! While his description of the pie was certainly appealing (especially since it was just before lunch), the illustration faced the same problem as St. Patrick's shamrock (not bad company to be in, I suppose). Each of Patrick's leaves is but one third of the whole shamrock and each of the student's slices is but one third of the cherry pie. However, scripture nowhere suggests that the Father (or Son or Spirit) is *one third* God. Thomas did not say to Jesus, "My Lord and my God-part" (cf. Jn. 20:28). And John did not write, "In the beginning was the Word, and the Word was with God, and the Word was part of God" (cf. Jn. 1:1). And Paul did not write, "yet for us there is but one God, part of which is the Father . . . and part of which is the Lord, Jesus Christ" (cf. 1 Cor. 8:6). In scripture, Father, Son, and Spirit are all referred to as God without qualification, including any hint that they are parts of a whole. Hence, it seems that the analogue we need is not three slices that equal one pie so much as three *pies* that equal . . . one pie!

Perhaps we should not be too hard on the Sunday school variants of the WPA, but for the analogy to be of use to us it will have to be made more rigorous. To this end, the analogy has been taken up recently by William Lane Craig and J.P. Moreland in their attempt to recognize the full divinity and distinction of the three persons whilst avoiding tritheism. Their WPA builds on the central premise that "while the persons of the Trinity are divine, it is *the Trinity as a whole that is properly God.*"[41] That is, in keeping with monotheism there can only be one fully divine being. But if the persons are not "properly" God, then what are they? To answer this question, Craig and Moreland introduce a secondary class of divinity—being divine without being God, that is, without exemplifying the divine nature. Hence the claim: while the Trinity alone is God (exemplifies the divine nature) each constituent part—Father, Son and Spirit—is divine but not God *per se*. (Compare: the slices are cherry pie stuff, but none is itself a whole pie.) The key challenge for Craig and Moreland is to defend the theological adequacy of a conception of the persons as divine in a secondary sense. To explain the claim, they begin with a cat illustration, arguing that there are two ways something may be called feline:

> One way of being feline is to instantiate the nature of a cat. But there are other ways to be feline as well. A cat's DNA or skeleton is feline, even if neither is a cat. Nor is this a sort of downgraded or attenuated felinity: A cat's skeleton is fully and unambiguously feline. Indeed, a cat just is a feline animal, as a cat's skeleton is a feline skeleton. Now if a cat is feline in virtue of being an instance of the cat nature, in virtue of what is a cat's DNA or skeleton feline? One plausible answer is that they are parts of a cat. This suggests that we could think of the persons of the Trinity as divine because they are parts of the Trinity, that is, parts of God.[42]

And so just as a cat is composed of feline DNA, a feline skeleton, and other feline parts and a cherry pie is composed of cherry filling and crust, so God is composed of Father, Son, and Spirit. In essence, Craig and Moreland offer a *third* interpretation of (2), one which maintains the is of identity, but applies it to the notion of derivative deity:

(2c) The Father is a part of God, the Son is a part of God, and the Spirit is a part of God.

Next, they develop this whole/part thesis by arguing that God is one soul with three minds (or sets of cognitive faculties). Since each of these minds belongs to the same soul, they argue that we do not have three gods.[43] Craig and Moreland suggest Cerberus, the three-headed dog of Greek mythology as an analogy. Just as that one dog has three mind/parts, so God has the mind/parts of Father, Son, and Spirit.

While Craig and Moreland's model provides an impressive theoretical advance over mere shamrocks and cherry pies, the adequacy of the proposal ultimately depends upon the viability of (2c) in light of scripture, the creeds, and common sense. Here we can note two difficulties beginning with the problem of diminished deity.[44] This problem arises from the claim that the Trinity alone is, properly speaking, God. While this move is necessary to prevent the model from collapsing into tritheism, denying that the Father, Son, and Spirit are actually divine is surely a radical solution since it appears to denigrate their deity. To compare, if an audience pays good money to see U2, they will not be satisfied if only Adam Clayton shows up for they don't want part of U2, but the whole group. In that respect, part of U2 is clearly inferior to the whole. Similarly, if the Father, Son and Spirit are all only a part of God, then it would seem that each is inferior to the whole, such that for a true experience of God nothing but a full "trinitophany" would suffice. And so it is very difficult to see why Craig and Moreland's relegation of the Father, Son, and Spirit to "secondary deity" does not collapse into second-class deity. Of course, as noted above, one does not get this sense in scripture: when the Jews longed for *Immanuel* they would not be satisfied with a *part* of God; their desire was for relationship with that individual who exemplifies the divine nature and nothing else. And scripture clearly assumes that Christ was indeed fully God with us.

The second problem, which concerns the danger of tritheism, can be illumined by the analogy that Craig and Moreland develop between the Trinity and Cerberus, the three-headed mythological dog. They point out that Cerberus would have three brains (and thus three points of view), and that we could name each of Cerberus' minds separately (they settle on "Rover," "Bowser" and "Spike"). And yet, according to Craig and Moreland, Cerberus has a single canine nature (he is one dog). Thus the three heads are all parts of the single dog such that "If Hercules were attempting to enter Hades and Spike snarled at him or bit his leg, he might well report 'Cerberus snarled at me' or 'Cerberus attacked me.'"[45] Similarly, the Father, Son and Spirit are three minds sharing one soul, and in virtue of that we describe them as one god. One might thus conclude that the entire analogy rests on our intuitive agreement with Craig and Moreland's assessment of Cerberus. But consider another (less mythological) analogy: conjoined twins. In this case *nobody* is inclined to say that these two individuals constitute one human person. Rather, they are two full exemplifications of the human nature sharing one body. Given that strong intuition, we should likewise conclude that Rover, Bowser and Spike are not three parts of one dog but rather three dogs sharing one body. And if the conjoined twins are two persons, and Rover, Bowser and Spike are three dogs, then it follows that the Father, Son and Spirit are three gods. And there lies the dilemma. It would seem that the WPA either leaves us with no fully divine person or too many gods!

One Happy Family: The Social Analogy

You are in the front row of a Rush concert. As you watch Geddy Lee, Alex Lifeson and Neil Peart belt out "Limelight" you reflect that Rush is a perfect group of three rock stars. In your concert reflections you would have unwittingly stumbled upon a form of the social analogy according to which God is more like a perfect community than a self-conscious divine mind.[46] Consider the fascinating passage in Genesis 18 where Moses encounters three mysterious visitors on the plains of Mamre. Augustine argued that this event is a theophany of the three persons of the Trinity.[47] If we accept his interpretation, then it would seem that the three divine persons bear a relationship analogous in significant respects to human persons (e.g. each can assume a distinct, personal bodily manifestation). Many other (less obscure!) texts reinforce this conclusion. For instance, the fact that Jesus prayed to God the Father implies that both Jesus and the Father are agents who can engage in personal relations. Cornelius Plantinga Jr. rightly concludes from such cases that the New Testament depicts "Father, Son, and Spirit as distinct centers of knowledge, will, love, and action."[48] And so, a straightforward reading of the New Testament leads to the central claim of social trinitarianism which Craig and Moreland summarize as follows: "in God there are three distinct centers of self-consciousness, each with its proper intellect and will."[49] Even Donald Macleod, a critic of the social view of God, acknowledges the legitimacy of the inference: "There can be little doubt, if we take the Scripture as our guide, that the distinctions within the godhead are analogous to those which obtain between individual human beings . . . Each is both conscious and self-conscious, and each plays a distinctive and unique role in redemption."[50]

Admittedly many theologians remain nervous about recognizing three centers of divine consciousness, believing that it will lead to tritheism.[51] The concern is a legitimate one, but we cannot let it control our reading of the New Testament. The inference to three minds can be grounded in Thomas Nagel's claim that a sufficient condition for something having conscious is whether there is something it is like to be that thing.[52] There is something it is like to be a dog, a bat, and a human being, so each of these has a mind. But there is nothing it is like to be a flower, a rock or a bacterium, and so none of these has a mind. Clearly there is also something it is like to be the Father, the Son, and the Spirit. For instance, the Son's experience of his baptism by John was surely different from the Father's and Spirit's experience of the same event. And if each had different experiences of this event and thus different points of view, then *eo ipso* each has a different mind.[53]

Since it affirms three distinct minds and agents in the Godhead, the SA endorses (2a). But this creates a serious tension for while the SA protects the distinction of the three persons (against the PA) and the divinity of the three persons (against the WPA), it struggles to explain (1). If Father, Son, and Spirit are three divine persons in the same way that Geddy, Alex and Neil are three rock stars, then why does it not follow that we have three gods? How does the SA avoid either embracing a contradiction or collapsing into rank and file tritheism?[54] Leonard Hodgson offers an intriguing solution which begins by distinguishing between two types of unity or "oneness": mathematical (numeric) and organic. Hence, there is mathematically one person in the chapel if there is only *one* instantiation of personhood in the chapel. By contrast, organic oneness is a unity of intimate relation which "consists in nothing else than the unifying activity which unifies the component elements."[55] So while there may be mathematically two people in the chapel, as a married couple they are organically one. In making this distinction Hodgson offers us *two* possible meanings for (1):

(1a) There is organically one God.
(1b) There is numerically one God.

While (1b) expresses the assumption of the PA (and, indeed the assumption of this chapter to this point), Hodgson opts for (1a). The appeal of (1a) is clear as it avoids the contradiction that follows from (1b), (2b) and (3). And thus we will avoid a contradiction by embracing (1a) and (2a). Whether we will avoid tritheism is another question.

Many social trinitarians (that is, advocates of the SA) recognize that their account depends on a plausible articulation of "organic unity." To this end, Cornelius Plantinga Jr. offers four possibilities. The first is one group or family; thus he writes "there are three divine persons, but only one divine family or monarchy or community, namely, the Holy Trinity itself."[56] Second, Plantinga suggests the organic unity of will: "Father, Son, and Spirit must be regarded as tightly enough related to each other so as to render plausible the judgment that they constitute a particular social unit."[57] Third, he suggests the unity of sharing a single divine nature: "These three are wonderfully united by their common divinity, that is, by the possession by each of the whole generic divine essence."[58] Finally, Plantinga argues that we can speak of one in terms of there being one principle of divinity: the Father.[59]

The big question is whether Plantinga's four points are adequate to save the SA from the tritheist charge. As we evaluate his points, we need to be clear that they *do not provide a cumulative case for organic unity* and as such they should be considered separately. One can thus understand Plantinga to be offering four possible interpretations of organic oneness:

(1ai)   There is one divine family.
(1aii) There is one divine will.
(1aiii) There is one divine nature.
(1aiv) There is one divine principle.

The real question is whether any of these interpretations of organic unity is adequate to avoid a collapse into tritheism. The problems with (1ai) and (1aii) are evident when we consider Brian Leftow's "Olympian Trinity" illustration. As Leftow points out, if the Greek gods Zeus, Hera and Venus were to find themselves in perfect agreement, this would not warrant the conclusion that there is one God![60] (Nor could we say that there is only one human being at the cabin in virtue of there being one group of three human beings at the cabin who had a perfectly harmonious time.) The claim of (1aiii) is, if anything, even worse, for it would then follow that we could speak of there being one human being in virtue of there being one human nature and this is obviously erroneous. Finally (1aiv) only offers a solution if it collapses into subordinationism such that the Father alone is fully God because the Father alone is the source of divinity. Unfortunately, this is simply an Arian restatement of (1b): there is numerically one God: the Father. As such, it seems that the SA still cannot offer an explanation of (1) that is coherent and orthodox.

This brings us to a second, oft overlooked problem with the SA. While it is appealing for its close fidelity to scripture, it appears to have a very unscriptural implication: the one God is impersonal. This at least seems to follow from the most common interpretation of (1a), namely that God is one as one community or family (1ai). Traditionally theologians have believed that "Trinity" refers to the one God who himself has the attributes of personhood, being omnipotent, omniscient, perfectly loving, etc. It is for this reason that Christians believe it proper to address the triune God with personal pronouns. But everything changes if the triune God is in fact a single *divine family* for then it follows that while the *persons* are omnipotent, omniscient, perfectly loving, *the Trinity as such is not*. To appreciate the problem, consider the following illustration. Imagine that you are a spy for the CIA. You go on a six month mission into the Middle East to trace the development of terror cells and are assigned to a contact at CIA headquarters named Mel. Mel guides you through the mission via a sophisticated form of text messaging; then after six months he calls you back to Washington to be debriefed. But when you enter the office you find three people sitting in the room and one man stands and says "We are Mel! I am Malcolm, this is Ellen, and that is Lanny. 'Mel' was an acronym for us."[61] Since Mel is not actually a person, Mel does not think, is not conscious, has no thoughts, etc.[62] Surely it is not adequate to say that the Trinity is simply the name of a divine group (e.g. Tri=Father; Ni=Son; Ty=Spirit) which itself has no personal characteristics. To say the least this is deeply counterintuitive.[63] One more brief point: one might argue that it is rather deceptive for God to be revealed as a personal agent when "God" is actually only a name for the group of three divine persons![64]

Conclusion

There is a delightful scene in the film *Million Dollar Baby* which begins with the hardened boxing trainer but devoted Catholic Frankie Dunn (played by Clint Eastwood) emerging from mass. As usual, he is trailing poor Father Horvak and peppering him with difficult questions, this time focused on "the same old 'one God-three God' thing." In his attempt to illumine this opaque doctrine, Dunn asks whether the Trinity might be "like snap, crackle and pop all rolled into one big box." His efforts are rebuffed by Father Horvak who is offended by the comparison of God to Rice Krispies. And yet there is a wonderfully honest spirit in Frankie's desire to understand what he is confessing every Sunday. Father Horvak shouldn't see such questions as an impious distraction, but rather as part of a desire to know the triune God ever more intimately. And yet, we must admit that in our finitude this enquiry is likely to end in failure, but it should not end in despair. Leonard Hodgson once addressed discouragement with the limitations of theology in understanding God by drawing an analogy with our limitations in understanding human beings. As he put it, after failing in our anthropological studies one "is apt to feel . . . that no such incredibly mysterious creature as a man could possibly exist. But as he lays the book down and goes out of his study, he finds no difficulty in resuming his social intercourse with his fellow creatures. Just so does the theologian continue to find pardon, peace and joy in communion with God."[65]

3

On Not Understanding the Creation

Maker of Heaven and Earth . . .

One *Family Circus* cartoon memorably captures the central dilemma with creation. In the scene as young Billy and his mother are looking out at the Grand Canyon Billy poses an interesting dilemma: "The ranger said the river dug the canyon Mommy, and you said God did it. Who's right?" It's a good question. After explaining that the Grand Canyon was formed through the Colorado River's slow erosion of the surrounding plateau, what more is added by saying that God did it? Like Billy, many Christians begin with a rather simplistic and unreflective conception of God's action in the world, one which is summarized in the simple words of that Sunday school classic "Tell Me Why":

> Tell me why the stars do shine,
> Tell me why the ivy twines,
> Tell me why the skies are blue,
> And then I'll tell you just why I love you.
>
> Because God made the stars to shine,
> Because God made the ivy twine,
> Because God made the skies so blue,
> Because God made you, that's why I love you.

But when we learn that stars shine through nuclear fusion, ivy twines due to tropism, and the sky is blue as a result of the Rayleigh effect, what then is added by saying that God creates these effects? In short, if I assume that the ranger's explanation of the canyon's origin falsifies the Hopi Native American account, then why do I assume there is still room for the Christian one?

The pain we feel as we attempt to integrate faith into our emerging scientific understanding of the world is intensified by the sharp edge of Ockham's Razor (named after William of Ockham), the principle that explanations must not multiply entities beyond necessity, or that a simpler explanation is the preferred one. In short, if a scientific account adequately explains a given phenomenon, then we have no justification to add a theological one. Practically speaking, the problem can be illustrated with American missionary Bruce Olson's attempt to improve standards of hygiene among the South American Motilone tribespeople. In an attempt to win over the witch doctor to his proposed reforms, Olson described the disinfectant with which he intended to kill germs as a "magic potion" which, he explained, would kill the "demons" plaguing the people with illness. In order to illustrate the power of his potion, Olson invited the witch doctor to a demonstration:

> I took out my microscope and put a lump of dirt under it. I had her look into the eyepiece.
>
> "Oh, yes, I can see them [the demons] dancing around," she said and began singing her chants.
>
> Then I put some disinfectant on the dirt, and told her to look again. She saw that the disinfectant had killed the germs. It shook her. She had seen that the germs didn't die when she sang her chants.[1]

Eventually Olson persuaded the witch doctor to introduce the disinfectant to ceremonies as a way of preventing disease. What the witch doctor did not realize was that in doing so she was taking the first faltering steps away from primitive animism and toward a scientific understanding of the world. For anyone who comes to understand what germs really are and how disinfectant really works, it is impossible to retain an explanatory framework of demons and potions. But here's the pinch: if the scientific worldview undermines the supernaturalism of animism, it would seem to undermine the supernaturalism of Christianity as well. Indeed this is precisely the point of the following story told by Chet Raymo:

> In the fall of 1976, the first outbreak of Ebola virus appeared at a remote hospital in Yambuk, Zaire, staffed by Belgian nuns. Within a few weeks the virus took a deadly toll, causing horrible deaths from internal hemorrhaging. The courageous nuns did what they could with their limited pharmaceuticals and scientific training, but the plague raged unabated. When the first representatives of the Centers for Disease Control (CDC) in Atlanta and the World Health Organization (WHO) arrived in Yambuku, they found the hospital pitifully cordoned off with a strip of gauze bandage, the surviving nuns reduced to prayer.
>
> The scientists set to work, taking blood and tissue samples for study in the field or for shipping to Atlanta for more detailed analysis, working out transmission patterns of the disease, and looking for the animal or animals that might be reservoirs or vectors for the virus.[2]

Raymo assumes that just as Olson's scientific approach to disease renders the witch doctor's framework otiose, so does the CDC and WHO's containment of the outbreak undermine Christian prayer. As Raymo bluntly puts it: "It was not prayer that contained this pandemic-threatening virus, but science."[3] Of course the Christian can reject this conclusion by plausibly suggesting that the arrival of the CDC and WHO was not an alternative to the nuns' prayers but rather an answer to them. Nonetheless, one may feel that the theological account has been uncomfortably tacked on to the real story found in the triumphal advance of science.

We thus find ourselves with an interesting conclusion. While one might argue that science has not *falsified* the Hopi, Motilone or Christian view of the world, relative to science each does begin to seem rather superfluous as a means to understand the world. The mood is captured in Pierre Laplace's legendary dismissal of God from his cosmology: "I have no need of that hypothesis." The dilemma is more than the superfluity of religion, however, for in addition many scientists believe that science requires a formal commitment to *methodological atheism*: that is, the assumption that there is no God active in the universe. As William Pollard explains, "From the standpoint of science every event is the product of empirically ascertainable antecedents with which it is causally related. To speak of an event as an act of God, or to say that it happened because God willed that it should, seems a violation of the whole spirit of science."[4] To test Pollard's claim one need only contemplate the effect upon science were we to begin invoking divine action to explain natural phenomena. (If God made the canyon, there's nothing left for the hydrologist to explain.) But this methodological taboo places the Christian scientist in a bind, forced to ignore all supernatural causes, and thus effectively to lock God out of the world.

The result is a sort of "John the Baptist dilemma" in which supernatural explanations seem fated to decrease even as natural explanations increase. Given the importance of this emerging dilemma, it is worthwhile clarifying it more precisely, beginning with the following widespread assumption:

(1) An explanation of a phenomenon in terms of scientific natural law renders otiose an explanation in terms of divine action.

Clearly (1) depends upon Ockham's Razor. Hence, if science successfully explains the spread of disease through a germ theory then there is no sense in appealing to demons and magic potions. The second premise modestly references the astounding success of science over the last three centuries:

(2) Science continues to explain more phenomena in terms of natural law.

And now comes the pinch, for together (1) and (2) lead to the following conclusion:

(3) Therefore, science continues to render otiose ever more explanations of phenomena in terms of divine action.

Initially, (3) might not seem that troubling, at least not in the same league as a logical or moral paradox. Nonetheless, its effect is ultimately no less devastating as it consigns theology to the steady retreat toward irrelevance immortalized in Matthew Arnold's haunting poem "Dover Beach":

> The Sea of Faith
> Was once, too, at the full, and round earth's shore
> Lay like the folds of a bright girdle furled.
> But now I only hear
> Its melancholy, long, withdrawing roar,
> Retreating, to the breath
> Of the night wind, down the vast edges drear
> And naked shingles of the world.

This retreat, already two hundred years on when Arnold wrote his poem, has continued apace over the last century. Hence, many scientists today assume that Christianity is like the ruins of Tintern Abbey: a grand relic of the past, but no longer fit for human habitation.

The theologian protests this long, withdrawing roar for science can never replace Christian theology. But how then should we construe God's action in the world? To begin with we must avoid two equal and opposite errors. At one extreme lies the error of deism which, in a drastic concession to science, denies that God acts in the world at all. At the other extreme lies the error of omnicausalism which claims that God does everything in the world. While avoiding these extremes, we must also guard against a more subtle (and particularly seductive) error lying "in the middle": interventionism. This view that God occasionally intervenes in natural events is correct to affirm divine action in the world but by construing this action as *intervention* it implies that God is typically absent from the world and so it too must be rejected.[5] In the remainder of the chapter we will focus on two models of divine action that seek to steer a path between these three errors.

Before we turn to consider our two theories of divine action, we will survey four different types of divine action in order to consider which properly characterize God's causal relations with the world:

(a) Creation: the act of bringing everything into existence.
(b) General preservation: the act of sustaining everything in existence.

    (c) Miracle: a specific act that overrides natural law.
    (d) Particular non-miraculous action: a specific act that occurs
         through natural law.

We begin with (a), the first great divine action of creation which a Christian affirms when confessing the "Maker of Heaven and Earth." Within the orthodox Christian tradition, this confession has been understood not as a fashioning out of some pre-existent stuff but rather as the absolute bringing of all creation into existence out of nothing. When the claim was first made,[6] it was an incredibly bold (if perplexing) move, placing Christians in conflict with Democritus' eminently reasonable principle "from nothing, nothing comes."[7] Based on this principle, it was widely assumed that the universe must have always existed.[8] This left Christian theologians in a defensive posture until the 1920s when scientific evidence started to mount that the universe was in a dynamic state of expansion instead of the expected steady state of equilibrium. The current consensus of Big Bang cosmology that the universe leapt into being out of nothing about fourteen billion years ago provides a surprising convergence of contemporary cosmology with traditional theology; as astrophysicist Robert Jastrow evocatively puts it: "For the scientist who has lived by his faith in the power of reason, the story ends like a bad dream. He has scaled the mountain of ignorance, he is about to conquer the highest peak; as he pulls himself over the final rock, he is greeted by a band of theologians who have been sitting there for centuries."[9] While the deist believes that (a) exhausts God's involvement with the world (he set it in motion and now has gone on to other things), scripture attests to God's ongoing concern for creation and involvement with it. As John Polkinghorne observes, "God is not like the law of gravity, totally indifferent to context and uniformly unchanging in consequence."[10] For this reason we must push beyond the initial creative act to explore the nature of God's subsequent action within creation.

    The next category of divine action, (b) affirms that God sustains the entire creation in being moment by moment. While we should not read too much metaphysical baggage into scripture, many passages would seem to affirm the divine preservation of all things (e.g. Acts 17:28; Col. 1:17; Heb. 1:3). Some theologians argue that general preservation exhausts divine action upon creation; that is, God actualizes his will through one general preserving action on the whole of creation.[11] As Willem Drees puts it, "rather than seek to understand God's action *in* the world, we might attempt to envisage the world *as* God's action."[12] Limiting divine action to (b) is appealing because it avoids the metaphysical difficulties with conceiving of God's particular action and the moral problems that attend God's specific action in evil events.[13] Nonetheless, scripture attests not only to God's general sustaining action, but also to his action in specific events including two specific events mentioned right in the Apostles' Creed: the incarnation and resurrection of Christ.

It seems then that we must expand our concept of divine action to include supernatural divine interventions, and this brings us to (c) miracles. We often speak loosely of miracles: I call it a miracle that my team made the playoffs or that your old jalopy is still running. However, the formal definition of miracle concerns God's action in the world and encompasses such biblical events as the Red Sea parting, an ax head that floats in water, and people emerging unscathed from a roaring furnace. What is more, most Christians believe that miracles, though very rare, may yet occur today.[14] Consider for instance, the case of seven year old Victoria Roberts. Back in January 2005 Victoria's parents received the devastating diagnosis that she had contracted aplastic anemia, a rare and potentially fatal disease. A year and a half later and after more than forty transfusions and emergency medical procedures, she was preparing to go into surgery for a bone marrow transplant—her last hope of survival. Victoria would have to undergo a battery of further tests, chemotherapy, and have two teeth removed, and even then survival was not guaranteed. And then, the day before the scheduled procedure, Victoria's oncologist called the child's parents into her office. While they came in expecting the worst, after they sat down the doctor informed them that new tests showed Victoria's bone marrow had inexplicably returned to normal and *she was no longer showing any sign of aplastic anemia.*[15] Although the doctor may have viewed the recovery as a medical anomaly, to Victoria's devoutly Christian parents it was nothing less than a divine answer to prayer. As Victoria's mother Jacqueline observed: "We know that God does miracles and we have had so many people praying for us and there is power in prayer."[16]

So what precisely is a miracle? In the eighteenth century David Hume offered a definition which has become enormously influential: a miracle is an event that violates a law of nature.[17] Hume's definition has been used by skeptics to reject miracles altogether based on the assumption that the laws of nature are inviolable. Based on Hume's definition even some Christians have become skeptical of miracles not because they believe that the laws of nature in themselves restrict God, but rather because God, having laid down the laws of nature, would not then proceed to violate them through miraculous interventions. As Nancey Murphy puts it, "many Christians . . . seem to suppose that God, like a U.S. senator, must obey the laws once they are 'on the books.'"[18]

Despite its influence, Hume's definition is inadequate since a violation of natural law need not be a miracle, nor need a miracle be a violation of natural law. To take the first point, Terrence Nichols observes that if a rock suddenly began to float in the air we might call it an anomaly which violated known laws of nature, but we would probably not call it a miracle.[19] But now picture that same rock beginning to levitate immediately after an anguished agnostic walking in the woods cries out to God for evidence of his existence. What might have been dismissed before as merely anomalous now appears to be miraculous. Since the event is the same, the crucial difference is found in the shift in context. There is an important lesson here: miracles are events that occur within a climate of expectation, and thus that context may be as essential as divine action for calling an event a miracle.

This brings us to our second point: given the importance of context, a miracle need not entail a violation of natural law. To illustrate, I once knew a married couple who were working with poor farmers in Mexico. In the midst of a very bad drought in their region and with a hopeless forecast of sunny skies, this couple traveled to a farm in order to pray with the farmer for rain. Incredibly as they prayed the sky clouded up and it began to rain. Shocked and delighted, they prayed more fervently which was followed by an increase in the rain's intensity. In fact, the rain soon grew so heavy that the farmer began to worry that the water might wash away precious topsoil. Hence they began to pray that the rain would taper off which it did soon after. In total, the weather patterns changed three times following their prayers. The crucial point is that even though a meteorologist could provide a complete natural account of the precipitation that day, it seems intuitively proper to conclude from the context that these natural events were miraculous.

Many biblical miracles can likewise be understood as events occurring within natural law: consider, for example, Gideon's fleece (Judg. 6:36–40). In order to discern God's will Gideon requested that the fleece be wet with dew while the surrounding ground remains dry. When this occurred the next morning, Gideon sought further assurance by requesting that the next day the ground be wet and the fleece dry. When that occurred he concluded that these two events together were sufficient to infer God's miraculous guidance.[20] And Gideon drew this conclusion even though the pattern of dew, like the pattern of rain, could have been explained through natural processes alone. To take an even more striking example, Colin Humphreys has recently provided a fascinating account of how the major Exodus miracles including the Red Sea crossing and Moses' drawing water from a stone, could have been wholly natural events.[21] Humphreys' point is not that these events were not miracles after all, but rather that God could have orchestrated the conditions for these events to occur within the constraints of natural law.[22]

But are there limits to the "naturalization" of miracles? What of the paradigm miracles in the Creed: the incarnation and resurrection? Anders S. Tune speculates that even in the latter case "in theory it is possible, even if only infinitesimally likely, that a certain set of quantum states and higher-ordered structures (such as a living human body) could change (become decaying flesh, water, and various gases) and then spontaneously return to the previous conditions (the living body)."[23] In other words, though almost inconceivably improbable, Tune believes that *in principle* a deceased body could naturally reconstitute itself, and that God could have orchestrated events so that Christ would resurrect in this way through wholly natural processes.[24] If Tune is correct then even the resurrection need not necessarily constitute a violation of natural law. Still, even if we were to grant that claim, since the incarnation is by definition the incursion of the Son of God into space time, it requires divine intervention. And so miracles cannot all be explained as natural events defined as miraculous solely by context.

So at least some miracles involve a divine intervention in which God is the sole cause. Might this subset of miracles constitute violations of the laws of nature? Even this claim is doubtful. To begin with, even if we granted that it would be inconsistent for God to institute a norm and then consistently to violate it, this point seems to be irrelevant for if miracles are violations at all, they are not *regular* violations but rather *exceptions*. Such exceptions do not undermine the norm any more than a speeding ambulance undermines the speed limit. Further, we cannot assume that God is obliged to observe his laws in the same way as created beings. (By analogy, parents are not being inconsistent when they don't observe the curfew that they place on their children.) Finally, and most basically, it is simply erroneous to think that miracles would constitute any sort of violation at all. C.S. Lewis illustrates the point by comparing divine and human action in creation:

> If I knock out my pipe I alter the position of a great many atoms: in the long run, and to an infinitesimal degree, of all the atoms there are. Nature digests or assimilates this event with perfect ease and harmonises it in a twinkling with all other events. It is one more bit of raw material for the laws to apply to, and they apply. I have simply thrown one event into the general cataract of events and it finds itself at home there and conforms to all other events. If God annihilates or creates or deflects a unit of matter He has created a new situation at that point. Immediately all Nature domiciles this new situation, makes it at home in her realm, adapts all other events to it.[25]

Lewis' analogy illustrates that both divine and human action involve "incursions" into the world of natural causes/events. Thus, if human intentional actions do not violate natural law, then neither do divine intentional actions. And with that, Hume's definition loses its last toehold: God, as it turns out, is free to act miraculously either through natural or supernatural means.

We now come to our final category: (d) particular non-miraculous divine action claims that God is in an ongoing, dynamic interaction with natural processes. Initially one may think that general preservation and occasional miraculous interaction together provide an adequate conception of the range of divine action. But while miracles are divine responses to specific events that are so unusual they even appear to violate natural law, non-miraculous divine action entails God's empowerment of the very regularities of natural law. And while preservation involves a general upholding of the whole of creation in being, non-miraculous divine action is limited to the specific empowerment of particular agents to act and interact within creation. Interestingly, the scriptures strongly suggest that God is present through the ongoing processes of creation. The psalmist observes that God waters and enriches the land while the streams provide water for grain as God has ordained (Ps. 65:9). God drenches the furrows which nourish crops (Ps. 65:10), allows water to flow by his decree (Ps. 104:7–8) and guides meteorological events: "He makes clouds rise from the ends of the earth; he sends lightning with the rain and brings out the wind from his storehouses." (Ps. 135:7; cf. Job 38ff.). God acts to create the fetus within the womb (Ps. 139:13–14) and grants life to all things (Ps. 104:29–30). While these passages are not technical descriptions of divine action, they nonetheless suggest an ongoing, personal mode of action that is neither a general preservation nor a miraculous intervention. The concept of ongoing divine action through the natural processes of creation is also important at a broader theological level, for it undermines the interventionist error that construes God as an occasional visitor to the world. As John Calvin memorably put it, "providence means not that by which God idly observes from heaven what takes place on earth, but that by which, as keeper of the keys, he governs all events. Thus it pertains no less to his hands than to his eyes."[26]

Given that preservation is metaphysically too basic to figure into scientific discussion and miracles are, by definition, highly unusual "one-offs," the greatest potential for conflict with science centers on (d), and so we will focus our development of models of divine action here. With that challenge before us, we can now turn to our two models of divine action beginning with the "Immanent Agent" (IA) model. The core assumption of the IA model is that God does not transcend the causal sequences of creation but rather acts within these sequences. So while the IA model accepts (1)–(3), it limits the explanatory scope of natural causation by stipulating that some events are caused by God alone and as such cannot be explained by science:

(4) Some phenomena can only be explained in terms of divine action.

(5) Phenomena explained in terms of divine action cannot be explained in terms of natural law.

(6) Therefore, science can never wholly eliminate explanations of phenomena in terms of divine action.

In essence, the IA model secures divine action by positing intrinsic, unbridgeable gaps in the causal structure of the world, and then proposing that God acts through those gaps to realize his will.

The second theory of divine action, the "Transcendent Agent" (TA) model, disagrees with the core premise of the IA model that God's causation of an event excludes the presence of a natural cause. On the contrary, the TA model contends that God transcends natural causes and thus can cause an event at the same time that a natural entity causes the same event. Accordingly the TA model rejects (1) as a false dichotomy: God is not like other agents such that his active realization of an event negates creaturely participation. He is not one cause among others but rather is the wholly other ground of all agents. As such, God does not have to jostle with creation in order to realize his will and there can be no opposition between divine and created agency. Given God's transcendence over natural causes, the identification of a natural cause of an event does not at all diminish God's active presence in that same event. Thus, the TA model affirms double causation, the view that both God and created entities act as causes of the same event. And this entails that a scientific explanation does not exclude a theological one. To formalize this position, we begin with the following:

(7) God transcends all natural causes and acts as a theological cause of all natural events.

(8) Therefore, all phenomena can be explained both in terms of divine action and natural law.

As such, the advance of science described in (2) is limited to natural law and so says nothing of the extent of divine action. From this follows a robust conclusion:

(9) Therefore, science cannot render otiose any explanation of a phenomenon in terms of divine action.

With these two positions on divine action before us we can now turn to consider each in more depth so as to assess their respective answers to our practical dilemma.

God as Immanent Agent

Good biographies typically do not try to smooth out the tensions that exist between differing accounts of the same individual but rather embrace them as evidence for the complexity of the biographical task. Such is the quality of Jack Miles' Pulitzer Prize winning book *God: A Biography* that he openly identifies two very different portraits of God: the immanent and the transcendent. The immanent image emerges in the creation account in Genesis 2 when the Lord God (Yahweh Elohim) physically forms the man and then, realizing that Adam needs a companion, gets back to work to create woman. The text portrays the Lord God's interaction with Adam and Eve as surprisingly mundane, occurring in "language that any human being might use when speaking to another."[27] And when the Lord God "discovers" that Adam and Eve have disobeyed he launches into a "long, emotional outburst . . . the Lord God does indeed act as the original of a human creature made of dust and passion."[28] While there are aspects of the text that are most certainly anthropomorphic,[29] many take the overall effect of the narrative to undermine the view that God is a transcendent cause. Instead, the text reveals God in the terms of the IA model as working in partnership with creation, not determining but rather cajoling and persuading as he leads creation into his providential will.

While its strengths are clear, the IA model also faces two challenges. First, theologians have traditionally understood God's control of creation in the terms of *meticulous providence*, meaning that every event that occurs is within God's providential plan. This is an extrapolation both from the divine attributes of omnipotence and omniscience as well as texts like Acts 17:28 and Ephesians 1:11. Charles Spurgeon eloquently summarizes the standard doctrine of meticulous providence as follows:

> I believe that every particle of dust that dances in the sunbeam does not move an atom more or less than God wishes—that every particle of spray that dashes against the steamboat has its orbit as well as the sun in the heavens—that the chaff from the hand of the winnower is steered as the stars in their courses. The creeping of an aphis over the rosebud is as much fixed as the march of the devastating pestilence—the fall of sere leaves from a poplar is as fully ordained as the tumbling of an avalanche.[30]

The problem for the IA model is that once we reduce God to being one agent alongside other agents acting within creation, it is difficult to see how this level of control can be maintained. To use a very simple analogy, if I could control the opinions of others, I could ensure that they would think highly of me. But if I relinquish that control, I thereby limit myself to persuading them to hold a high opinion of me, a process that is by no means guaranteed success. Similarly, it would seem that the IA model limits God to a form of persuasive providence rather than the meticulous sort that is central to the Christian theological tradition. Hence if the IA model is to defuse the worry that it undermines divine providence, it must provide an account of divine action. This involves two components: the causal joint of divine action (i.e. the place within the created chain of causes at which God acts) and the causal mechanism (i.e. the means by which God acts within the world). We will begin by considering the question of the causal mechanism.

Since the IA model seeks to understand how God acts in the world in parallel with created agencies, to understand the causal mechanism of created agencies should provide illumination for the divine causal mechanism as well. Created agencies act through the transmission of energy, and so it seems reasonable to conclude that God likewise acts within the world through the transmission of energy. Unfortunately, there is one big problem: there doesn't seem to be any place where God can input energy into the universe (i.e. there is no causal joint with room for God to act) because God as creator exists *outside* the causal continuum. Since all the energy in the universe is already locked into a causal sequence God cannot appropriate some of it for his own actions. One might reply that God creates his own energy which he adds to the universe except that this appears to be excluded by the law of conservation of energy which states that the amount of energy in the universe is fixed. David Bodanis' fascinating summary of the law's implications is worth quoting at length:

> It's as if when God created the universe, He had said, I'm going to put X amount of energy in this universe of mine. I will let stars grow and explode, and planets move in their orbits, and I will have people cre-ate great cities, and there will be battles that destroy those cities, and then I'll let the survivors create new civilizations. There will be fires and horses and oxen pulling carts; there will be coal and steam engines and factories and even mighty locomotives. Yet throughout the whole sequence, even though the types of energy that people see will change, even though sometimes the energy will appear as the heat of human or animal muscle, and sometimes it will appear as the gushing of waterfalls or the explosions of volcanoes: despite all those variations, the total amount of energy will remain the same. The amount I created at the beginning will not change. There will not be one millionth part less than what was there at the start.

> Expressed like this it sounds like the sheerest mumbo jumbo— Faraday's religious vision of a single universe, with just one single force spreading all throughout it. It's something like Obi-Wan Kenobi's description in *Star Wars*: "The Force is the energy field created by all living things; it binds the galaxy together."

> Yet it's true! When you swing closed a cupboard door, even if it's in the stillness of your home at night, energy will appear in the

gliding movement of the door, but exactly that much energy was removed from your muscles. When the cupboard door finally closes, the energy of its movement won't disappear, but will simply be relocated to the shuddering bump of the door against the cupboard, and to the heat produced by the grinding friction of the hinge. If you had to dig your feet slightly against the floor to keep from slipping when slowly closing the door, the earth will shift in its orbit and rebound upward by exactly the amount needed to balance that.[31]

As Bodanis illustrates, every event in the universe, be it a baby's sneeze or a supernova's explosion, occurs through the transfer of pre-existent energy whilst the total amount in the cosmos remains constant. This seems to close the universe off to divine intervention that is mediated by energy. If we assume that God normally acts in accord with natural processes and the universe precludes the addition of energy, then God is effectively locked out of the universe. But perhaps this is too quick. Recall that Bodanis fancifully summarizes the law of conservation of energy with God declaring: "The amount [of energy] I created at the beginning will not change." But if this is taken to mean that God *cannot* add energy then it reveals the erroneous Humean conception of miracles. In light of our discussion, one could instead characterize the original divine intention as follows: "The amount I created at the beginning will not change *except when I add to it.*" Hence, the law of conservation of energy dictates that *all things being equal* the amount of energy will remain the same. But that says nothing about whether after the fact God can add more energy to effect his will.

While this is a possible solution, nonetheless many will wince at the implication that due to divine action the total energy in the universe is constantly increasing.[32] Fortunately, there is another intriguing approach to the causal mechanism problem at hand. Some IA model advocates like John Polkinghorne have argued that there is another way of action in creation which does not require energy: action through pure information. Not surprisingly, the notion of action through input of pure information is controversial: as Nancey Murphy puts it, "to whom or what is the information contributed? How is it conveyed without any energy at all?"[33] Doesn't this proposal simply skirt around the issue since it offers no mechanism to explain the input of information without energy?[34] Murphy's objection overlooks the fact that human beings appear to act in the world through mental intentions without the production of energy. Lewis' action of knocking out his pipe was not an event dependent upon prior energic causes but rather one that was inputted *de novo* into the causal sequence as an *intentional act of free will*. What is this other than action through pure information (the information being Lewis' *intention* to knock his pipe)? Philosopher Roderick Chisholm formalizes this point by distinguishing between events that originate as a result of energy transfer (efficient cause) and those that arise from an intentional agent's purposeful action (agent cause).[35] An agent stands outside of the chain of efficient causation and has the ability to initiate its own causal series. Since human beings act *de novo* without producing new energy, surely it is not too much to propose that God does as well. Hence Keith Ward argues that human action in the world provides a powerful analogy for God's action: "if God or human beings ever really act intentionally, then there must be events occurring that laws of physics alone do not explain. It is in that sense that any responsible action entails the existence of gaps in physical causality."[36]

Even if the IA model succeeds in providing a causal mechanism, it also must account for the place of divine action, the so-called causal joint. The universe must be the *kind* of place that is open to the input of (human and divine) agent causes. The problem is that scientific advances have often assumed that the universe must be closed to such causal input. Hence, the IA model needs to establish that there are open points of indeterminacy, gaps in the causal sequence of the world, through which free agents can act. John Polkinghorne points out that "those gaps must be intrinsic and ontological in character and not just contingent ignorances of the details of bottom-up processes."[37] The central challenge is that the continual progress of science seems to leave ever fewer possible entry points for God's direct causal action. As E.O. Wilson puts it, "Today, thanks to the relentless advance of the science which Newton pioneered, God's immanence has been pushed to somewhere below the subatomic particles or beyond the farthest visible galaxy."[38] If this is true then we had better heed Polkinghorne's caution closely, especially since yet another abortive attempt to equate divine action with a gap that is later closed will only further undermine the plausibility of God's action in the world. As Thomas Tracy warns, "if we cast our theological lot with a particular interpretation, we take the risk that new developments in physics or in the philosophy of physics will significantly undercut our theological constructions."[39]

With that important caveat, we can note that quantum indeterminacy and chaos theory have been recently suggested as causal joints, though for the sake of time we shall limit our discussion to the former. It is crucial to note that even though the quantum world is indeterminate, the macroscopic world of human experience remains predictable and law-based. William G. Pollard illustrates the relation between the two spheres by contrasting the prediction of group and individual behavior:

> One could predict with reasonable certainty that at the end of five years half of the class which had started as freshman together would be married and the other half would still be single. With respect to any individual freshman, however, no prediction at all could be made other than a knowledge of the probability of marriage characteristic of the whole group.[40]

Thus while the vast groups of quantum events that comprise macroscopic objects (like trees and rocks) exhibit law-like behavior, at the level of the individual quantum indeterminacy reigns. This indeterminacy is summarized in Werner Heisenberg's uncertainty principle, formulated in 1926, which specifies that it is impossible to measure (and so predict) both the velocity and position of a subatomic particle. To illustrate, consider first the prediction of a baseball's trajectory after being hit. According to the laws of classical mechanics, if we had all the information on the moment the ball was hit and we knew all the variables (e.g. wind velocity, air density), we could project perfectly the ball's trajectory. At T_1 the ball will have position x and velocity p, at T_2 it will have position y and velocity q and so on. Such macroscopic events as a baseball's flight through the air are predictable in a way analogous to Pollard's group behavior. But as Pollard points out, that certainty disappears when we move from groups to individuals. And so, paradoxically, while we could predict the future position and velocity of the baseball, we cannot predict the future position and velocity of any of its constituent subatomic particles! In short, in terms of predictability quantum particles are more like people than baseballs and prediction of their behavior is closer to the approximations of psychology than the certainty of calculus!

When quantum indeterminacy was first encountered in the 1920s it met with sharp resistance as captured in Einstein's famous retort that "God does not play dice." Kathryn Tanner explains the theological resistance to chance: "Isn't . . . the idea that outcomes in the world are determined by statistical probabilities, by some blind mechanism or chance, incompatible with the idea that God directs the world according to purposes, for ends, of God's own devising?"[41] However, for the IA model this indeterminacy is not a *threat* to divine sovereignty, but rather the very means to secure it. The central claim is that events in the quantum world are not determined by prior physical causes, and as such the quantum world provides space for God to enter in and determine particular physical outcomes so as to guide the course of events providentially. The proposal offers a way to escape the determinism that locks God out of the world which was famously captured in the illustration of LaPlace's demon. In the early nineteenth century French scientist Pierre-Simon Laplace argued that if there were an individual that knew the exact position and momentum of every particle in the universe at one particular moment, it could use the complete laws of physics to retroject all past events and project all future events with certainty. Note that this appears to lock out the free action of both God and human beings. But Laplace's concern was not with human free will, but rather with the explanatory irrelevance of God. In order to exorcise Laplace's demon and carve out space for divine action, all we need to do is demonstrate that the behavior of quantum particles is indeterminate. Our account of *how* God might do this must be both speculative and brief. The IA model can mollify Tanner's concerns about this indeterminacy curtailing God's providential control by claiming that God set up the physical behavior of quantum particles to be undetermined, so that he might determine it.

While we must be very tentative in any attempt to explain *how* God determines events, one possibility is that it occurs by a process similar to the "observer effect" of quantum mechanics whereby a probability wave collapses upon divine observation.

Although the quantum proposal is ingenious, one might object that the scale of quantum events appears too small to ground divine providential control of the macroscopic world. Nicholas Saunders puts the huge gap between the quantum and macroscopic worlds in perspective: "imagine the difference in size between a pinhead and planet Earth. If we could shrink them both until the Earth was the size of a beach ball, the pinhead would now be the size of a large quantum object. At first sight, then, it seems truly amazing that burning bushes should be related to events on this scale."[42] Advocates of the quantum approach to divine action are aware of the problem and propose two possible ways to link quantum events with the macroscopic world. The first approach draws upon the principle of amplification highlighted in the so-called "butterfly effect." This concept from chaos theory refers to the phenomenon that minute effects in complex systems magnify over time, thereby leading to macroscopic effects. Hence, in the classic illustration, a butterfly fluttering its wings over the landscape in China today causes thunderstorms next week in California.[43] In the same way that the perturbations of a butterfly's wing beats can magnify until they lead to a super storm cell's formation, so God's observation effect of a quantum event can magnify until it results in providential, macroscopic effects. Perhaps then God's providence is manifest through an ongoing process of collapsing certain wave packets in order to actualize his will for creation. And as a result of his perfect foreknowledge and middle knowledge (i.e. his knowledge of counterfactual possibilities) God knows precisely which wave packets must be collapsed in order to achieve the desired effects. So, for instance, God would know that collapsing a particular number of wave packets would eventually culminate in the wind that parted the Red Sea (Ex. 14:21).

As an alternative to magnification, one might link the quantum and macro-worlds through the sheer number of divinely determined quantum events.[44] Just as a huge number of tiny grains of sand forms a great beach, so the vast number of quantum events that God determines meticulously guides macroscopic reality. Nancey Murphy pursues this approach to its logical terminus by arguing that God determines *all* quantum events.[45] In this case it is relatively easy to conceive of macro objects being determined by the position and velocity of subatomic particles given that the former are composed of the latter. Imagine the futility of attempting to make a picture on a computer if you could determine the color of but one lowly pixel on the monitor. Now consider if you could determine the color of all 786,432 pixels on the screen. In virtue of controlling each of these tiny pixels you could control the entire display. Similarly, if God controls every microscopic quantum event, then he maintains control over all macro events as well thereby ensuring a very robust doctrine of providence. This might sound like occasionalism,[46] but Murphy is quick to add that "every created entity, however small and ephemeral, has an existence independent of God."[47] She gives as an analogy the famous paradox of Buridan's ass in which a donkey, placed at equal distance from two identical bales of hay will be unable to choose arbitrarily to walk to one or the other bale and so will starve to death. Similarly, while God respects the created integrity of macroscopic organisms, subatomic particles by nature require a determining cause to actualize one state over another: "God's governance at the quantum level consists in activating or actualizing one or another of the quantum entity's innate powers at particular instants, and . . . these events are not possible without God's action."[48]

As we turn to evaluate the IA proposals on the causal joint, two concerns come to the fore. To begin with, as soon as one identifies God's action with a particular area within creation, one must confront the problem of the God of the gaps. While advocates of the IA model are quite confident that quantum and/or chaotic phenomena are indeed ontologically indeterminate (and thereby fitting locales of divine action), the history of physics warns against such confidence. Consider Robert P. Crease and Charles C. Mann's description of the self-confidence of physicists at the end of the nineteenth century:

> In 1894, Albert Michelson of the University of Chicago, one of the most prominent experimenters of the day and the future recipient

of a Nobel Prize, told an audience that "it seems probable that most of the grand underlying principles have been firmly established and that further advances are to be sought chiefly in the rigorous application of these principles to all phenomena which come under our notice . . . [T]he future truths of physics are to be looked for in the sixth place of decimals."[49]

Now imagine a theologian who, upon hearing Michelson's pronouncement on the secured area of physics, proceeded to build a model of divine action upon it. In just over ten years that model could have been rendered obsolete by an obscure physicist working in the Swiss patent office. How do we know that there is not an Einstein even now laying the foundations for a future scientific revolution that will render current IA proposals obsolete? Indeed the view that quantum events are ontologically indeterminate (the so-called "Copenhagen Interpretation") is underdetermined by the data as there are currently two deterministic interpretations of quantum events (the proposals of David Bohm and Hugh Everett), either one of which would undermine this open causal joint. Such is the perennial danger of all such proposals that Dietrich Bonhoeffer famously repudiated any attempt to locate God's action in "gaps" as fundamentally misguided:

> It has again brought home to me quite clearly how wrong it is to use God as a stop-gap for the incompleteness of our knowledge. If in fact the frontiers of knowledge are being pushed further and further back (and that is bound to be the case), then God is being pushed back with them, and is therefore continually in retreat. We are to find God in what we know, not in what we don't know.[50]

Though we cannot definitively dismiss all attempts to locate God's action in a particular point in the world, repeated failures in the past combined with a concern for theology's eroding credibility should make us very reticent to pursue this project.

This brings us to the difficulty that the IA model faces in accommodating both creation's autonomy and God's meticulous providence. In essence, insofar as the IA model commits itself to the incompatibility of human autonomy and divine control, it places itself in a dilemma whereby the more autonomy God

grants creation, the more control he must yield. While amplification may allow for God's action through some quantum events,
it hardly appears adequate for the comprehensive, meticulous
providence of traditional theology. As Murphy observes, "the
majority view has been that God acts in all things at all times, not
just on rare occasions."[51] Murphy's proposal provides an intriguing alternative in which God really is involved in all events. But
then a different tension arises for, given that God must act coop-
eratively with created entities, Murphy's view heightens the
delicate nature of the balancing act between divine and created
autonomy. Although Murphy states that God respects the
created nature of subatomic particles, Nicholas Saunders observes, "It is . . . difficult to understand precisely what these innate
powers actually are in scientific terms if God maintains and
determines them entirely."[52] Hence, Murphy's view still may
force us to choose between divine sovereignty and created freedom, and that is a choice few would care to make.

God as Transcendent Agent

While the Lord God of the Genesis 2 – 3 narrative is strikingly
anthropomorphic, as Miles illustrates, the picture is quite different in the first account of creation in Genesis 1. In this case God
(*Elohim*) creates with sovereign ease by speaking the world into
existence without the intimate methods of the Lord God. While
the Lord God interacts intimately with man and woman, the transcendent God of Genesis 1 remains at a distance, creating not so
much to have a partner in fellowship as an *image* to act as a regent
of his rule within creation.[53] The divine sovereignty of Genesis 1
is on display in many other passages as well (e.g. Ps. 65; 104; Job
38; Isa. 40). And while the IA model portrays God as interacting
personally with human beings and seeking to persuade them of
his will, the TA model focuses upon texts that demonstrate God's
determinative influence over free human choice. Thus, strange
though it may seem to us, scripture sees no tension between
Pharaoh hardening his own heart (Ex. 8:15,32; 9:34) and God
hardening Pharaoh's heart (Ex. 9:12; 10:1,20,27; 11:10; 14:8).
Similarly, Luke claims that "all who were appointed for eternal

life believed" (Acts 13:48) as if God sovereignly determines *our* response to the gospel. And for those who don't respond to the gospel Paul states unapologetically that God hardens whomever he chooses (Rom. 9:18) just like a potter forms the clay (Rom. 9:21). When we draw these texts together we see a powerful portrait of a God who utterly transcends the cause-effect relations of created being. And one then reinterprets the personal portraits of God in light of these conclusions. In John Calvin's words, the anthropomorphic (IA) descriptions of God in scripture are like a caregiver's baby-talk babble to an infant child.[54]

The TA model boasts a proud theological lineage in the Augustinian, Thomist and Reformed theological traditions including recent defenders like Austin Farrer and Kathryn Tanner.[55] The first principle of the TA model is that God, as transcendent cause of all, is utterly different from all created beings. This has important implications for divine action since it removes God from the binary opposition that is central to the IA model which says that the more a created entity is involved in an event, the less God is involved. As Tanner puts it, "If God is not a kind of thing, then the one God can be directly and intimately involved with the production of the world in all its aspects, without threatening to compromise or dilute either God's divinity or the natures of any of the things in the world."[56] On this basis, the TA model argues in (6) that all created events, just like human free actions, manifest the double causation of both divine and natural explanations. Since God acts at a different level from creation, we don't have to find a *space* for him to act. As William Stoeger observes, this allows us to say that "At the level of the sciences there are no 'gaps,' except the ontological gap between absolutely nothing and something."[57] That is, "There are no gaps is [sic] the secondary causal chain . . . the whole chain demands a primary cause to support and sustain it."[58] Thomas Aquinas explained that God is the primary cause of all events by sustaining (preservation) the whole of creation and concurring with all events within creation.[59] Tanner explains the nature of God's double causation/concurrence: "God does not need to replace the activities of creatures with God's own in order to achieve God's ends. God can instead give rise to the very powers and acts of creatures that further those ends."[60]

The TA model has scriptural and historical support and maintains a sovereign conception of God's nature while avoiding the God of the gaps. Nonetheless, it encounters some significant difficulties of which we will note three. First, the TA model faces the objection that if God is the primary determining cause of all events then there is no room for created freedom and human beings are reduced to being mere puppets jostled about on the cosmic stage by the divine puppeteer. But while the TA model affirms that God determines human actions, it counters that such determination is compatible with free will.[61] Hence, created beings can act as free causes even if God determines our causal agency. Ultimately then, one's response to the TA model will depend on whether one finds the compatibilist view of freedom compelling. But if one agrees with Immanuel Kant that the notion of being "freely determined" is a "wretched subterfuge"[62] one will have to reject it.

Second, since the TA model views God as determining all events and some of those events are evil, it appears to implicate God in evil events. But how can a good God determine free agents to carry out evil acts such as murder and rape? Defenders of the TA model typically respond by denying that God is culpable for the evil choices of creatures because his will in such events is only "permissive" rather than "active." As Francis Turretin put it, "Sin (which is repugnant to the divine will) cannot be produced by the providence of God effectively; but nothing hinders it from being ordained by his providence permissively and directed efficaciously without any blame upon divine providence."[63] But if God is the primary active determining cause of all things, is it not inconsistent then to stipulate that he only *permits* evil events to occur? Either God is the cause of all events or not. Frankly this move appears to be another wretched subterfuge, a last ditch effort to indemnify God from culpability in evil by sheer stipulation.

Finally, the TA model is uninformative since it offers no insight into the actual nature of divine action, treating it instead as an impenetrable mystery. This problem is central because our willingness to accept the TA model's view of human freedom, providence and evil really depends on the adequacy of the model for illuminating the nature of divine action. And it must be said that apart from ensuring the meticulous reach of providence, that payoff is rather sparse. Indeed, Polkinghorne warns that it is "a strategy of absolutely last resort"[64] and "a fideistic evasion of the problem."[65] The problem is that by definition the TA model places God's causal action securely beyond human understanding, treating it as a black box and thereby evading the problem rather than answering it. Polkinghorne thus observes, "It is not clear to me what is gained by so apophatic an account of God's action. In the end, the answer seems to be 'God only knows.'"[66] Moreover, one might worry that universalizing God's action loses the particular action at the heart of (d), thereby collapsing either into *de facto* deism or omnicausality. As Philip Clayton puts it, "it might . . . seem that the God who does everything is a God who does nothing."[67]

Conclusion

So what precisely is our answer to Billy's simple question? Did God dig the Grand Canyon or did the Colorado River do it? The IA model responds that there is a complex partnership at work with God aiding in the actualization of the geologic and hydrologic processes that formed the canyon. While potentially informative, this approach is also fraught with difficulties. For that reason the TA model is appealing in its simplicity as it places God *above* the causal processes rather than in their midst. But on the downside it appears uninformative and is fraught with its own tensions. And so, there seems to be no non-controversial answer to Billy's question. That is, there is no clear way to fit God's action into the world. The basic problem is summarized in an illustration I first heard in graduate school. As the story goes, two theistic scientists were just about to conduct an experiment when one suggested to the other that they should pray for the experiment to go well. The other objected, pointing out that if God intervened in response to their prayers then his action would skew the results, thereby negating the validity of the experiment. Hence, while we desire to affirm God's action in the world, we seek to affirm it without upsetting or overriding the natural processes of creation. Tragically, we are left with a creator that seems estranged from his creation.

4

On Not Understanding the
Incarnation

And in Jesus Christ his only (begotten) Son our
Lord; who was conceived by the Holy Ghost, born
of the Virgin Mary . . .

In her delightful children's classic *The Best Christmas Pageant Ever*
Barbara Robinson tells the story of how the infamous six Herdman
children ("absolutely the worst kids in the history of the world"[1])
first encounter the Christmas story. Through a series of events they
begin going to Sunday school where they are confronted by the per-
functory preparations for the stale Christmas pageant. Year after
year it is the same affair and the church has grown hardened to it.
But the Herdmans have never heard the Christmas story before and
are fascinated. Shorn of the baggage of over-familiarity, they hear the
story with fresh ears which allows them to ask embarrassing questions and facilitate novel insights. So intrigued do the Herdmans
become that they scheme until they have co-opted all the main roles
in the play, at which point they proceed in delightful fashion to leave
their indelible stamp upon each one. For instance, Imogene portrays
Mary with a gritty reality since she "didn't know that Mary was supposed to be acted out in one certain way—sort of quiet and dreamy
and out of this world."[2] Imogene's interaction with the baby Jesus is
characteristic of the many felicitous impieties that unfold:

> Imogene had the baby doll but she wasn't carrying it the way she
> was supposed to, cradled in her arms. She had it slung up over her

shoulder, and before she put it in the manger she thumped it twice on the back.

I heard Alice gasp and she poked me. "I don't think it's very nice to burp the baby Jesus," she whispered, "as if he had colic." Then she poked me again. "Do you suppose he could have had colic?"

I said, "I don't know why not," and I didn't. He *could* have had colic, or been fussy, or hungry like any other baby. After all, that was the whole point of Jesus—that he didn't come down on a cloud like something out of "Amazing Comics," but that he was born and lived . . . a real person.[3]

Amazingly, while the pageant that results lacks refinement and polish, it is powerfully moving as the audience (and reader) are brought to wrestle anew with the gospel story. Ironically, absolutely the worst kids in the history of the world have challenged the church to rediscover the awesome mystery that lies at the heart of Christmas.

In Robinson's book, the church's problem is not simply that the story of Christmas is too familiar. Indeed, as with our general problem with the Apostles' Creed, the problem is actually the opposite: the gospel is not familiar enough. We subtly think of Jesus as less than fully human, expecting Mary to be "quiet and dreamy" and assuming that the baby never needed to be burped: "Little Lord Jesus, no crying he makes" rather than "Jesus, stop crying for goodness sake!" In short, Robinson's real target may be the tendency to view Jesus as a less than fully human, airbrushed icon. If this is correct, then our problem is not actually over-familiarity, but rather lack of familiarity with the implications of *God becoming man*. This tendency to elevate Christ's divinity at the expense of his humanity is deeply rooted in the Christian tradition and continues to flourish among evangelicals.[4] But we should also note that since the Enlightenment the opposite tendency has risen to prominence such that humanity is often elevated at the expense of divinity. Thus while the church has often stressed the divine uniqueness of Christ, many modern thinkers have instead emphasized his human ordinariness.[5]

This tendency to emphasize either divinity or humanity is *ultimately* rooted in the logical tension between the two confessions.

As John Hick evocatively put it, "to say, without explanation, that the historical Jesus of Nazareth was also God is as devoid of meaning as to say that this circle drawn with a pencil on paper is also a square."[6] If Hick is correct then the central message of the good news is literally *nonsense* and so the Christmas story is little more than a sentimental load of balderdash. But is it really the case that the confession of divine incarnation is tantamount to a square circle? If we are to deal adequately with this logical challenge to the incarnation, we will first have to specify precisely what the ground of the objection is. Since there are multiple points of potential conflict between the two natures, we will focus on that which arises between the omniscience of God and the finite knowledge of Jesus. If God is essentially omniscient, then it would seem that Christ was essentially omniscient, but this claim appears to contradict the scriptural witness to Christ's human mind. After outlining the nature of this problem at more length we will identify and evaluate two different models of the incarnation that aim to remove the conflict: the Word/flesh (WF) model and the Word/person (WP) model.

The Logical Problem(s) of the Incarnation

When I was a university student, my roommate and I invited some Mormon missionaries over to our humble one bedroom flat with the intent of engaging them in a debate. Unaware of our intentions, the missionaries promptly launched into their evangelistic presentation about Joseph Smith's new revelation of Jesus Christ while pausing at key points to probe our feelings in response to their message. At the culmination of the presentation, they shared with us the promise in Moroni 10:4–5 that if we prayed about the message, then the Holy Spirit would reveal its truth to us by a burning in our chests: now the ball was in our court. But rather than obligingly pray the prayer, I replied that feelings can mislead. How then could I know that the burning is the work of the Holy Spirit and not wishful thinking . . . or even heartburn? I then added that we had some serious intellectual reservations remaining, and with that I launched into our planned apologetic assault with the following dilemma. While the Book of Mormon proclaims that God is eternal and unchanging, Mormons believe that God was once a man who became divine. But surely this is contradictory, for if God is eternally unchanging then he cannot *become* God. The poor missionaries were completely caught off-guard and could provide no response. But to their credit they at least admitted that there was a serious problem. Without further explanation, it is simply incoherent to say that God is both immutable and changing.

As the Mormons left I was satisfied that we had dealt a critical blow to their faith. But all the while I never realized the degree to which a very similar problem attends the Christian doctrine of the incarnation. Consider first the Chalcedonian Definition, the centerpiece of the venerable Chalcedonian Creed (451):

> To confess . . . one and the same Christ, Son, Lord, Only-begotten, to be acknowledged in two natures, *inconfusedly, unchangeably, indivisibly, inseparably*; the distinction of natures being by no means taken away by the union, but rather the property of each nature being preserved, and concurring in one Person and one Subsistence . . . one and the same Son, and only begotten, God the Word, the Lord Jesus Christ.[7]

This definition provides a clear, if somewhat unwieldy summary of the guidelines for proper Christology: we must confess Christ as existing in both divine and human natures while ensuring that we do not confuse, change, divide or separate those natures. That is, Christ is always and fully both divine and human, from which it follows that he has both the omniscience of God and the limited knowledge of a human being. Many theologians have responded to dilemmas like ours by reiterating the Chalcedonian guidelines thereby treating them as an *answer*. But a moment's reflection should make clear that far from being an explanation of the claims of orthodoxy, this definition establishes the paradox. After all, by this definition we affirm that God is eternal and unchanging and that God the Son became a man. Nor is that the only apparent conflict. For instance, while most classical Christian theists have denied that God can suffer,[8] Christians confess that Christ suffered. And Christians typically believe that although God is atemporally eternal (existing outside time)

Christ existed in time. Moreover, many argue that while God is impeccable (unable to sin), Christ's temptations only make sense if he could have sinned. Finally, while God is omnipotent, omnipresent, and omniscient, it seems that Christ was not. Nowhere does Chalcedon hint at a resolution to these conflicts. And thus, John Hick rightly observes, "The Chalcedonian formula . . . merely reiterated that Jesus was both God and man, but made no attempt to interpret the formula."[9]

It is important to understand that Christians don't believe that God simply *happens* to be immutable, impassible, atemporal, impeccable, omnipotent, omnipresent, and omniscient. Rather, each of these attributes is *essential* to the divine nature. An essential property is one that, if no longer exemplified, would mean the entity as such no longer exists. For example, being unmarried is an essential property for being a bachelor. Consider Hank who when at work describes himself as a bachelor. However, on the weekend his coworkers see Hank out for dinner with his wife and five children. No doubt they will be unimpressed with his Monday morning explanation that he is a *married* bachelor. The reason is obvious: by definition Hank's rebuttal is nonsense and his original statement was a lie, for in virtue of being married he cannot be a bachelor. But then if even one of the seven properties listed above is both essential to divinity and incompatible with humanity, then "divine man" is as meaningless as "married bachelor." And so we appear to have at least seven pairs of incompatible attributes: immutability/mutability; impassibility/passibility; atemporality/temporality; impeccability/peccability; omnipotence/finite power; omnipresence/finite presence; omniscience/finite knowledge. Philosophers refer to these as incompossible pairs, meaning that these attributes are contradictory and so cannot possibly be exemplified simultaneously in the same individual. In the same way that no shape can be both square and circular, it seems that no person can be both divine and human.

A full treatment of this problem would have to analyze each of our allegedly incompossible paired terms, assessing whether each attribute is essential for its respective nature[10] and if so, then whether our understanding of them can be revised in some other way to remove the apparent conflict. Unfortunately such a

comprehensive treatment is far beyond what we can hope
to accomplish in this short chapter, and thus we shall limit
ourselves to a consideration of the final paired terms: omnis-
cience/finite knowledge.[11] Although the definition of omniscience is controversial,[12] for our purposes the following will
suffice: omniscience entails knowing all truths and believing no
falsehoods. So defined, the Christian theological tradition has
overwhelmingly understood God as omniscient.[13] While it must
be admitted that there is no precise analytical definition of God's
perfect knowledge in scripture, it is at least implied in passages
like Psalm 147:5 and Romans 11:33 and 16:26. This conclusion is
reinforced by deep intuitions that God is necessarily omniscient,[14]
leading to the consensus theological opinion of the Westminster
Confession that "In his sight all things are open and manifest; his
knowledge is infinite, infallible, and independent upon the creature; so as nothing is to him contingent or uncertain."[15]

It hardly bears pointing out that human beings are not omniscient, either essentially or contingently. We can know this simply
by observing that the human brain, amazing though it is, is still
finite and thus could not possibly hold an infinite number of true
beliefs. Only a brain of infinite size and complexity could be truly
omniscient, and Jesus did not have an infinitely large brain. On the
contrary, the evidence is that Jesus learned, for he was gradually
"filled with wisdom" (Lk. 2:40; cf. 2:52). Obviously an individual
cannot *increase* in wisdom if he already has it all! Moreover, while
Jesus demonstrated great insight into the thoughts and intentions
of others, he was also unaware who touched his clothing with the
intent of being healed (Mk. 5:30), and he professed not to know the
time of his second coming (Mt. 24:36). More controversially, there
is evidence that Jesus had some false beliefs and made false statements. For instance, Jesus asserted that David entered God's house
and ate the loaves when Abiathar was high priest (Mk. 2:26) when
in fact the high priest was Ahimelech (1 Sam. 21:2–7). Moreover, in
Matthew 23:35 Jesus appears to confuse Zechariah son of Berach-
iah with Zechariah son of Jehoiada.[16] So while Jesus undoubtedly
demonstrated incredible wisdom and knowledge, the evidence
clearly implies that he was not omniscient.

At this point we can turn to summarize the resulting logical
dilemma with respect to omniscience:

(1) Jesus is God.
(2) God knows all true propositions.
(3) Jesus did not know all true propositions.

Though these propositions are contradictory, Christian theologians have unapologetically embraced all three. For instance, Athanasius commented: "If they still want to argue because Christ asked questions, let them hear that there is no ignorance in the deity but that not knowing is, as has been said, proper to the flesh."[17] That is, while Athanasius concedes that Christ asked questions in order to *learn* what he did not *know*, in his divinity he remained omniscient. Similarly, the Reformed theologian Riissen asserts, "while we acknowledge that Christ as God was omniscient, yet as a man we confess that he was endued with knowledge great above all others, but yet finite and created, to which something could be added and truly was added."[18] But these statements merely heighten the mystery: how is it that the divine one who has no ignorance asked real questions? How is it possible that the omniscient one *learned*? At least the Mormon missionaries acknowledged the paradoxical nature of their beliefs while Athanasius and Riissen seem oblivious to the problem with theirs.

Honesty bids that we follow the lead of our Mormon missionaries by admitting that our theology appears to have a contradiction. And so we must consider how to address the conflict between omniscience and finite knowledge, a task that shall occupy the remainder of the chapter as we survey the WF and WP models. We can begin with a brief summary of the two models by noting the particular emphasis of each regarding the four key Chalcedonian terms on the two natures of Christ: *inconfusedly, unchangeably, indivisibly, inseparably.* The first two criteria, which emphasize the importance of distinguishing these natures in the one individual, are central to the WP model of the incarnation. The second two criteria, which emphasize the unity of the one individual in which these two natures are exemplified, represent the central emphasis of the WF approach. As such, while each model seeks to uphold the Chalcedonian Definition, each does so with a different starting point and emphasis. With that framework in place we will now consider whether either model offers a viable means to demonstrate the compossibility of omniscience and finite knowledge in the person of Christ.

And the Word Became Flesh . . .

A few years ago I tested the adequacy of a computer translating program by translating the Greek text of John 1 into English. The result was serviceable, if rather unremarkable . . . until I got to verse 14 when these words leapt off the screen: "The Word became *meat* and lived among us." My first reaction was a mixture of amusement and nervousness, as if the program had carelessly blundered into a heresy. (Can a translating program *blaspheme?*) And then it occurred to me that all in all that was a serviceable, if inelegant, translation; after all the relevant Greek word *sarks* means flesh or meat. I felt like a pious child shocked at one of the Herdmans in Sunday school asking incredulously: "You mean God became *meat?*" While this pivotal verse powerfully captures the mystery and offense of the incarnation, it is also central to the WF model which emphasizes the unity of Christ's natures without division or separation. This brings us to the core commitment of the WF model which is succinctly summarized by Robert Jenson: "When you talk of Christ, be prepared to attribute to him anything and everything the scriptures attribute to the triune God, and anything and everything the scriptures attribute to Jesus as one of the human community."[19] Jesus Christ is the same identical person as the Son of God, and this means that anything true of the former is true of the latter as well. Traditionally WF theologians have sought to understand the incarnation of this single subject through the body/soul model: that is, the relation of the divine Christ to his human body is analogous to a human soul to its body: just as I am a soul "incarnate" in my body, so is the Word incarnated in his body.

Simple and appealing though this body/soul analogy may be, it conceals a serious tension which becomes evident in the theology of its great fourth-century exponent Apollinaris. Though a close associate of orthodox champion Athanasius and a vociferous opponent of the Arian heresy, Apollinaris was ultimately branded a heretic due to the perceived inadequacy of his WF model. Apollinaris proposed that the divine Word became incarnate by taking the place of the human soul in his union with a human body.[20] Though intending to provide a rational and orthodox account of the incarnation, Apollinaris was judged a heretic at the Council of Constantinople (381) based on the charge that he didn't provide for a full incarnation in virtue of his denial that Christ had a human spirit. And there is little doubt that Apollinaris' theology betrays a devaluation of Christ's human mind and psychology; after all, he explained that while Christ took on flesh, "yet . . . he is not a human being; and though he is preached as human by the same apostle, yet he calls the whole Christ invisible God transformed by a visible body, uncreated God made manifest in a created garment."[21] Apollinaris' language of God donning a "created garment" reminds me of a Christmas message I heard at a church where the pastor described Jesus as the perfect Christmas gift: God wrapped up in human skin. While I knew the pastor had no intention of preaching Apollinarianism, had he offered the illustration in late fourth-century Constantinople he would likely have been hauled before the local bishop to answer charges of heresy. Jesus is not simply God "wrapped in human skin," nor is the incarnation merely the donning of a "created garment." God the Son actually *became* a man and thus, as Thomas Oden observes, "Jesus had a human *psyche*, the full range of affective experience, and fully human emotions."[22] Apollinaris' devaluation of the humanity of Christ thus leaves us, as Augustus Strong colorfully put it, with "a Christ of great head and dwarfed body."[23]

Subsequent WF theologians have often been charged with deemphasizing the humanity of Christ, if not with the overt Apollinarian heresy, then with the more subtle error of *monophysitism*, the teaching that Christ had only a divine nature. Martin Luther's critics launched the monophysite charge against him, charging that his problems began with his use of the *communicatio idiomatum*, that is, the communication of natures. By this principle, which was intended to stress the unity of natures in Christ, Luther argued that we can qualify divine properties of the human nature and *vice versa*. To take what is probably his most striking example, Luther defended the statement that *God died* on the cross because the human Jesus died on the cross and whatever is true of the human Jesus is true of the divine Son as well.[24] Thus since there is a single incarnate subject, we can predicate the human qualities of Christ's divine nature, and the divine qualities of his human nature.[25] Though Luther's insistence on the unity of the incarnation is surely admirable, it clearly heightens the paradoxical tension for God did not really die, certainly not in the sense that human beings do. Consequently, Luther's critics rejected his application of the *communicatio*,[26] alleging that it confused the natures thereby violating Chalcedon. Critics of Luther and his epigones have commonly charged that the victim is the human nature. As William Lane Craig and J.P. Moreland observe, "it is very difficult to see how a human nature can really share all the attributes of deity without actually being deity."[27]

While Apollinaris and Luther were both accused of losing the humanity of Christ, other WF models have sought unity at the expense of the divinity. This tendency emerges in the kenotic incarnational theory pioneered in the nineteenth century by the Lutheran theologian Gottfried Thomasius,[28] and has attracted a number of proponents since.[29] While the starting point of traditional WF models is Christ's divinity, kenoticism begins with the humanity. As such, the kenoticist argues that the incarnation is a guide to assess our modal intuitions regarding which attributes are truly essential for divinity. Hence, if a divine attribute is incompatible with humanity then Christ must have ceased to exemplify that attribute while incarnate. Philosopher Stephen Davis tersely summarizes this methodology with respect to Christ's knowledge: "the fact that I believe both that Jesus Christ was God and that Jesus Christ was non-omniscient leads me to deny that omniscience is essential to God."[30] Davis then goes on to explain how, as a kenoticist, he would go about revising his intuitions on the property of omniscience based on the incarnation:

> What would be claimed . . . is that it is not precisely *omniscience* which is a requisite of deity. It is rather a distinct property, the property of being omniscient-unless-freely-and-temporarily-choosing-to-be-otherwise, which is a logically necessary condition of deity . . . It will be this compound property rather than omniscience *simpliciter* which will be said to be an essential property of any individual who is God.[31]

So Davis claims that the incarnation requires us to revise our intuitions regarding omniscience by construing it as a complex property that includes the ability to become temporarily non-omniscient. However, this revised view of omniscience presents a problem for it allows the possibility that all three persons could simultaneously divest themselves of omniscience. And so Feenstra rightly points out that there must always be at least one divine person who maintains actual omniscience. He thus adds to Davis' understanding of omniscience the stipulation that *at most two* divine persons could divest themselves of actual omniscience at any given time.[32]

While kenoticists like Davis and Feenstra attempt to reinterpret the nature of deity such that Christ can remain divine while incarnate, David Brown takes a more radical view by suggesting that in the incarnation Christ divested himself not of certain non-essential divine attributes, but rather of his very deity. This has an incredible implication: though God the Son is divine, he is not essentially so! Brown then summarizes the implications this has for the incarnation: "divine attributes apply exclusively before the Incarnation, human attributes exclusively to the period of the Incarnation, and divine attributes again exclusively to the post-Incarnation period."[33] This view allows us to retain our intuitively compelling, unqualified definition of divine omniscience, but it requires us to adopt the non-intuitive claim that divinity is not essential to God's (or at least Christ's) being. Brown's kenotic view of the incarnation has other radical implications. For instance, he admits that "on this model one must speak of God's death simpliciter, i.e. admit that there was a time when God the Son was not . . . ."[34] In other words, Christ became truly mortal at the incarnation such that when he died *he ceased to exist*, an event that temporarily reduced the Trinity to a binity!

Kenoticism undoubtedly has many virtues: it defends the unity of the incarnation and integrity of Christ's human nature while offering an account of the incarnation that is logical and comprehensible. Unfortunately, it also faces significant drawbacks. Of the two recent approaches considered, Brown's is certainly the more extreme, for he abandons Chalcedon's teaching on the two natures of Christ.[35] As such, he believes that Christ ceased to exemplify the divine nature at the incarnation such that throughout his span on earth he was *only a man*. What is more, his view of the incompossibility of natures forces Brown to affirm that when Christ regains his deity he ceases to be human. But as we will note in chapter six, this view of the incarnation as a temporary interlude in the divine life of God the Son is not orthodox. Instead, the church has always confessed the *eternal* nature of the incarnation. For these reasons it seems to me that the Davis/Feenstra proposal is more promising since it seeks to maintain the two natures of Christ while redefining them in accord with the demands of a fully human incarnation. The central problem with this version of kenoticism relates to its *ad hoc* construal of the divine attributes. As Craig and Moreland put it:

> In answer to the question "How can God remain God if he gives up omniscience?" we are told that it is because he retains the essential property of being-omniscient-unless-he-gives–up-omniscience! Imagine a case in which a human being is said to have abandoned all properties incompatible with becoming an ant and yet to have remained a human being. If we objected that rationality is essential to being human and that therefore he had ceased to be human, would it be a satisfactory answer to be told that only rationality-except-when-kenotically-an-ant is essential to being human and that he retains this property?[36]

In essence, the "complex properties" of the Davis/Feenstra proposal look suspiciously like contrived "statements masquerading as attributes."[37] We are not at liberty to "cook" our definition of divinity to suit our interests. As such, the position is explanatorily vacuous, for it offers no real explanation of the incarnation. What is more, we must keep in mind the strength of the intuitions that God's essential property of omniscience is not qualified and conditional, but rather unqualified and unconditional. God knows all things—that's just part of what it *means* to be God. We must thus think of the incarnation in light of this basic intuition rather than the other way around.

The Spirit of the Lord is On Me . . .

It must have been an incredible moment. Everyone at the synagogue waited with baited breath as the intriguing carpenter from

Nazareth opened the Isaiah scroll and read: "The Spirit of the Lord is on me, because he has anointed me to proclaim good news to the poor" (Lk. 4:18). The Spirit was indeed upon Christ. Just a few weeks before he had been baptized by John in the Jordan, an incredible event that had culminated in the descent of the Spirit upon him and the words of the Father from heaven declaring Christ his beloved Son (Lk. 3:22). This image of Christ as chosen by God as evidenced in the Spirit's presence provided the basis for the adoptionist Christology that flourished in Rome around AD 200 according to which Jesus was a man uniquely chosen by God. While adoptionism was rejected by the church, it found a brilliant new exponent in the towering third century theologian Origen. However, Origen's Christology was far more sophisticated than the crude adoptionism of his predecessors. Instead he sought to explain the incarnation in the terms of an intimate and wholly unique union between the Word and Jesus Christ that existed from the first moment of Christ's existence. While Origen's Christology would also be judged inadequate, it is perhaps the first great example of the WP model. While the WF model focuses upon the indivisibility and inseparability of the natures, the WP model seeks to guarantee that these natures remained unconfused and unchanged, that is, completely distinct. Otherwise, you will no longer have the two natures of the Chalcedonian definition. As a result, while the WP model does not deny a single incarnate subject, it rejects the WF model's emphasis on a single incarnate subject *of predication*, fearing it will lead to a confusion of the natures.

As we saw, the WF model drew upon Plato's view of the human person as a soul united to a body. By contrast, many early advocates of the WP model depended heavily upon Aristotle's anthropology. Aristotle believed that Plato's view was fundamentally misguided: contrary to Plato, we are necessarily embodied beings, and so the body is not ancillary to our being, but rather is part of our essential identity. To capture this hypothesis, he proposed that the human being is a "hylomorphic compound" of soul and body. Since both parts are *essential* the person is not a soul connected to a body but rather an embodied soul or ensouled body. As Aristotle explained it, the soul serves as the form of the body, as that which makes the body a *human* body.

From this it follows that were the soul not present, the body would no longer be a human body. If one holds these assumptions, then the WF model must be rejected for with no human soul the Son ends up uniting with a nonhuman body, and thus there cannot be a full incarnation. Since the soul and body cannot be prised apart on this anthropology, the only possible incarnation is one in which the Son unites with a soul/body unity. Only in this way can we ensure that every aspect of humanity has been assumed by Christ such that it can then be redeemed by him. As the Reformed Belgic Confession states, Christ "did not only assume human nature as to the body, but also a true human soul, that he might be a real man. For since the soul was lost as well as the body, it was necessary that he should take both upon him, to save both."[38]

While the WF model tends to emphasize one of the natures, the WP model has the tendency of so separating the natures that the incarnation becomes a union of two people: the Word and the Christ. The danger of a collapse back into adoptionism is evident in one of the WP model's great early defenders, the brilliant fifth-century theologian Theodore of Mopsuestia. Though Theodore shared with Apollinaris the indignity of being declared a heretic, at least for him the condemnation occurred posthumously.[39] To see the ground of the council's discomfiture, consider Theodore's description of the incarnation:

> so also the Lord, although at a later stage he had the Logos of God working within him and throughout him in a perfect way, so as to be inseparable from the Logos in his every motion, even before this had as much as was needed for accomplishing in himself the mighty things required. Before his crucifixion, because it was needful, he was permitted to fulfill by his own purposes a righteousness which was for our sake, and even in this undertaking he was urged on by the Logos and strengthened for the perfect fulfillment of what was fitting, for he had union with the Logos straightway from the beginning when he was formed in his mother's womb.[40]

As one reads this passage Theodore seems to refer to two different individuals, "the Lord" (i.e. Jesus Christ) and "The Logos" (i.e. the Word). Thus, while Theodore can speak of the incarnation as consisting of the Word perfectly working "within" and "throughout" the Lord, he will never say what the WF advocate confesses: namely, that the Word *became* the Lord.

At first blush it appears that Theodore is offering a heterodox translation of John 1:14 along the lines of "the Word united inseparably with the Lord who dwelt among us." As a result, his WP model looks rather like a crude strain of adoptionism in which God the Son "adopted" the man Jesus, thereby uniting with him in a particularly intimate way.[41] But an intimate union is not really an incarnation at all. As such, Athanasius, who approached Christology within a WF framework, had little patience for this approach. J.N.D. Kelly thus summarizes Athanasius' dismissal of the WP model as follows: "How can they be called Christians . . . who say that the Word entered into a holy man, just as He entered into the prophets, and not that He became man, taking His body from Mary, and who dare to assert that Christ is 'one' and the divine Logos 'another'?"[42] While Theodore's Christology is not an instance of "rank and file" adoptionism, it nonetheless does appear to be liable to the Nestorian species of adoptionism according to which the Word united with the man Jesus.[43] Ironically then, while the WF advocates tend to undermine the fullness of the incarnation by losing either the full humanity or the full divinity, the WP model is in danger of undermining the incarnation by reducing it to an intimate moral union between the Word and the man Jesus.

While Luther championed the WF model of the incarnation, John Calvin and his epigones defended the WP approach. And so while Luther stressed the full communication of attributes between the natures, Calvin's focus was to maintain carefully the distinction of the natures. As a result, he denounced as "impudence" Luther's claim that Christ dwelt solely in a physical body, "the narrow prison of an earthly body," combined with the perplexing claim that this physical body was omnipresent.[44] Denouncing this as mere confusion, Calvin countered that Christ has always been both omnipresent in his divinity and concretely located and limited in his humanity:

> For even if the Word in his immeasurable essence united with the nature of man into one person, we do not imagine that he was

confined therein. Here is something marvelous: the Son of God descended from heaven in such a way that, without leaving heaven, he willed to be borne in the virgin's womb, to go about the earth, and to hang upon the cross; yet he continuously filled the world even as he had done from the beginning![45]

Hence, according to Calvin the incarnation does not exhaust the Word, for he remains omnipresent throughout the universe even while incarnate as Christ. William Stacy Johnson and John H. Leith summarize Calvin's position as follows: "the '*Logos*' in its union with the human nature of Jesus did not exhaust itself but maintained an 'extra' or transcendent dimension throughout Jesus' earthly life."[46]

Lutherans responded by disparaging what they came to call "Calvin's extra," as if Christ became fully incarnate *except* for all the "extra" divine parts that couldn't quite be crammed into a human body! Nonetheless, Calvin's distinction of a divine extra makes it possible to distinguish between Christ's omnipresence *qua* his divinity and spatial limitation *qua* his humanity. This formula of "reduplicative predication" allows for a qualified communication of attributes to counter Luther's *communicatio idiomatum* in the sense that all divine and human properties belong to a single subject and can be predicated of that subject, *so long as the predications are appropriately qualified with respect either to the divine or human nature.* WP theologians thus seek a via media between the WF confession that God died and the Nestorian confession that only Jesus died.[47] To that end they employ reduplicative predication to claim that "God died *qua* Christ's humanity" or (even better), "Christ died *qua* his humanity, but not *qua* his divinity." As Thomas Oden puts it, "the subject of the humiliation is the human nature, unconfusedly united with the divine nature, which 'neither died nor was crucified.'"[48] As for the attribute of omniscience, Donald Macleod observes: "if we take seriously the deity of Christ we have no option but to believe that as the eternal *Logos* he knew all things, including the hour of the *parousia*. It is difficult to formulate any concept of incarnation which could eclipse such omniscience without involving a renunciation of deity."[49] Hence, one can argue that Christ was omniscient *qua* divinity but not *qua* humanity. Advocates of the WP model thus consider reduplicative predication to be an essential tool for uniting the natures without confusion, thereby avoiding the twin dangers of monophysitism and kenoticism.

Critics retort that reduplicative predication is less an *explanation* of our central dilemma than a complex *relabeling* of it. What precisely does it mean to predicate properties of Christ with respect either to his human or divine nature? One early approach, encapsulated in the writings of Pope Leo the Great, suggests that Christ did some things as divine and other things as human. Hence, in his "Letter to Flavian" Leo wrote:

> it is a human thing to hunger and thirst and get tired and sleep. But to satisfy five thousand men with bread and to bestow on a Samaritan woman living water whose consumption enables its drinker to thirst no more, to walk on the surface of the sea without sinking and to moderate "the swellings of the waves" when a storm has come up—that is a divine thing without question.[50]

Unfortunately, this picture of Christ acting human here and divine there results in a disintegrated individual as if the incarnation could be turned on and off depending on when the divinity is required.

While Leo's "oscillating" incarnational model is unworkable, WP accounts that affirm the coextensive actuality of the natures have their own tensions. Consider for instance how Wayne Grudem explains Christ's impeccability: "His divine nature could not be tempted with evil, but his human nature could be tempted and was clearly tempted."[51] If the human nature is peccable as Grudem states, then Jesus could have sinned. That is, during his fast Jesus could have caved in and transformed a lump of granite into a steaming loaf of fresh baked ciabatta (with garlic butter). But Grudem rejects this consequence given that, as he puts it, "the moral strength of his divine nature was there as a sort of 'backstop'."[52] Grudem seems to be saying that had Jesus begun to contemplate sinning, his divine nature would have stepped in! But surely Grudem is confused, for a *nature* is not an agent that acts but rather a set of kind-essential properties. For instance, in order for an animal to be a dog it must exemplify the set of kind-essential properties necessary to be a dog, that is, the dog nature. And so it is simply confused to think that the *nature* of the dog acts upon the dog to guide its behavior! But then it is likewise confused to think that Christ's divine nature could act upon him to prevent a fall into sin. Be that as it may, if the divine nature ensures that the incarnate Christ will not sin in any possible world where he exists, then there is no world where Christ could sin and thus it is *he* (rather than one of his natures) that is impeccable.

One of the most powerful defenses of the WP model is found in philosopher Thomas Morris' recent book *The Logic of God Incarnate* and the follow-up essay "The Metaphysics of God Incarnate."[53] Morris' proposal centers on a model in which Jesus has two minds or centers of consciousness and is especially helpful both for its perspicacity and Morris' application of it to the attribute of omniscience. Morris identifies the two minds as "the eternal mind of God the Son" and "the distinctly earthly mind with its consciousness that came into existence and developed with the human birth and growth of Christ's earthly form of existence."[54] Together they include the full range of Christ's divine and human awareness. As Donald Macleod puts it, "He is aware of the Father, of himself, of the universe and of other men as God; and he is equally aware of them as man. This latter includes the fact that he has a human consciousness of being the Son of God. It also includes the fact that his human consciousness is (not merely was) a developing one."[55] Morris argues that these two minds are related by way of an "asymmetric accessing relation" extending from the divine to the human such that "the human mind was contained by but did not itself contain the divine mind."[56] As a result, "everything present to the human mind of Christ was thereby present to the divine mind as well, but not vice versa."[57] In the incarnation Jesus has a human consciousness which gradually developed over time, even while the mind of the Word maintained the omniscience essential to his divine nature.

Given the importance of this asymmetric accessing relation to the model's success, Morris then explores different illustrations which might illumine the concept. He suggests for instance, the case of a lucid dream where one finds oneself both a character within a dream, even as one is "transcendently" aware of dreaming.[58] Another illustration is found in cases of multiple personality

disorder (in current nomenclature: "dissociative identity disorder") in which "the unconscious mind stands to the conscious
mind in much the same relation that the two-minds view sees
between the divine and human minds in the case of Christ."[59] Since
we have some conception of multiple minds in single individuals
we have a workable model to think about the incarnation. The next
question concerns which mind ultimately takes precedence:

> Did Christ have erroneous beliefs, such as would have been
> acquired through the natural functioning of his human mind in
> the social and intellectual environment in which he lived? Did he
> have a geocentric picture of the cosmos? Did he really not know
> who touched the hem of his garment? He had a limited human
> mind and a divine mind, so what is the answer, yes or no?[60]

When faced with such pointed questions, Morris ultimately
retreats to Christ's divine omniscience: to know what Jesus really
believed we look to his divine mind.[61] And so the last word comes
from the divine Word.

Morris' model clearly identifies both the promise and problem
with WP christologies. On the one hand, the two minds conception offers a powerful means to defend the omniscience and cognitive finitude of Christ simultaneously. But on the other hand,
all WP christologies struggle to ensure sufficient emphasis upon
the single subject of incarnation. As Robert Jenson puts it, "it
must be the one *hypostasis* (person) to which we attribute the
story of salvation" such that it is "by Christ—and by him alone—
divine things are done humanly and human things divinely."[62] As
such, we must be careful not to predicate actions and/or properties of one or another of the natures, for the sole actor in the incarnation is Christ. Unfortunately, reliance upon reduplicative
predication is an unstable compromise, for as Peter Geach argues,
it tends to collapse into Nestorianism. Geach first points out that
reduplicative predication effectively sunders the incarnate Christ
into two subjects: "subject A" (Christ as human) is "temporal,
non-omniscient, etc" while subject B (Christ as divine) is "eternal,
omniscient, etc." This division arises from the logical form of the
reduplicative formula which can be summarized as "A as P is Q"
(e.g. Christ as divine is omniscient). Geach then argues that this

logical form is mistaken, and that the correct analysis is instead "'A' subject, 'is as P, Q' predicate—so that we have not a complex subject-term, but a complex predicate-term."[63] The point is that the statement that "Christ as divine is omniscient" is not predicating "omniscience" of a complex subject (Christ as divine); rather, it predicates a complex property "as divine is omniscient" of the simple subject Christ. Geach then draws out the implications:

> This niggling point of logic has in fact some theological importance. When theologians are talking about Christ as God and Christ as Man, they may take the two phrases to be two logical subjects of predication, if they have failed to see the Aristotelian point; and then they are likely to think or half think that Christ as God is one entity or *Gegenstand* and Christ as Man is another. I am sure some theologians have yielded to this temptation, which puts them on a straight road to the Nestorian heresy.[64]

In other words, the reduplicative formula leads the theologian to think (erroneously) that there are two subjects of predication: Christ as man and Christ as God. But if they really believe this, then they have collapsed into Nestorianism.

It seems to me that this Nestorian danger clearly lurks behind Morris' two-minds model. What is more, the model is in danger of collapsing into a degree Christology.[65] We need to understand first that orthodox Christology has always been predicated on a kind Christology meaning that the incarnate Christ is different in kind from all other human persons. This is clearly the assumption of the New Testament writers who believe that Jesus is the unique, incarnate Son of God. Since the Enlightenment, however, many Christians of a rationalist persuasion have been attracted to a degree Christology according to which Jesus is different from other human beings not in *kind* but only in degree. Arguably the first great degree Christology of the modern era is that offered by Friedrich Schleiermacher. Convinced that the two-natures doctrine (and associated kind Christology) was hopeless,[66] Schleiermacher instead proposed that Christ was different from other people only in the degree of his sense of absolute dependence on God. Appealing though this proposal has been for many

Christians of a liberal persuasion, by orthodox standards it evis-
cerates the content of the New Testament and the creeds. So if
Morris' proposal ends up construing Christ as different only by
degree then it must be rejected. And that brings us to the problem: the omniscient Word has a unilateral accessing relation with
every mind (as does the Father and Spirit).[67] As such, what is it
about Jesus that permits us to say he is the uniquely incarnate
one? Morris fails to provide an answer that identifies the Word
uniquely with Christ,[68] but he argues that this failure is not fatal
because metaphysicians do not agree on a general criterion of
identity for persons. And if philosophers don't agree on the basis
by which we say that the star of *Hercules in New York* is the same
person as the thirty-eighth governor of California, then surely we
can forgive Morris's failure to provide similar criteria to identify
the Word and the Christ.[69] This strategy elicits two replies. First,
while we may lack a general criterion of personal identity
through time that hardly justifies the additional difficulties of the
WP model. Similarly, if I were to claim that Tom was identical
with Tim even though Tom was born on a different day than Tim,
it would hardly be a defense of my claim to invoke the controversies in theories of personal identity! Second, since theology
abhors a vacuum, this Christology is liable to collapse into a
straightforward degree formulation: e.g. that Christ was "incarnate" in virtue of being uniquely open to the Word's accessing
relation. And this demonstrates the vulnerability of Morris'
model to adoptionism. On that score, Morris' model provides a
negligible improvement over the unstable early WP Christology
of Theodore of Mopsuestia.

The tendency of Morris' view to collapse into degree
Christology can be demonstrated by considering its counterintuitive implications for the possibility of multiple incarnations.
While Morris believes that there has only been one incarnation,
he admits that his theory leaves room for the possibility that the
Word *could* be incarnate in/as more than one individual *simultaneously*. Indeed, apparently there is no upper limit to the number
of possible incarnations: "there seems to be no good reason to
think that this accessing relation could not hold severally
between any number of finite, created minds, or ranges of consciousness, and the properly divine mind of God the Son. And if

this is possible, multiple divine incarnations are possible in any number."[70] As such, the Word could presently be incarnate as hundreds or thousands of people! This possibility has been recently taken up by John Hick as a means to justify religious pluralism. Hick argues that the notion of multiple incarnations makes good sense, for "given that the historical influence of Christ, as the visible expression of divine love, is of benefit to humanity, would it not have been much more beneficial if the Logos had also become incarnate in the other great centers of human civilization?"[71] Based on this possibility we can now ask whether "such epoch-making spiritual leaders as Moses, Gautama, Confucius, Zoroaster, Socrates, Mohammed, Nanak may not in fact have been divine incarnations."[72]

While Morris rejects Hick's pluralist trajectory, the very fact that his model allows for the possibility speaks to its inadequacy.[73] To make this point clear, we can return to the law of the transitivity of identity considered in the discussion on the Trinity in chapter two (if A is identical to B and B is identical to C then, necessarily, A is identical to C). So for instance, based on the statements that "the morning star is the evening star" and "the evening star is Venus" we can conclude that "the morning star is Venus." Further, according to the law of the indiscernibility of identicals, if A is identical with C, then anything true of A is also true of C. Hence, if Venus is the second planet from the sun, then it follows that the morning star is the second planet from the Sun. Now as we keep in mind the WF claim that there is one subject in the incarnation, let us consider the implications of multiple incarnations. On Morris' view it is logically possible that the Word who "incarnated" as Jesus Christ also "incarnated" as Bono. But if "the Word is Christ" and "the Word is Bono" then by the law of the transitivity of identity it follows that "Christ is Bono." But how could this be *possible* in light of the indiscernibility of identicals? To take one example, Christ was ruling at the right hand of the Father in 1987 at the same time that Bono was climbing the charts with "I still haven't found what I'm looking for." But then it follows that Bono cannot be identical with Jesus. As Brian Hebblethwaite puts it, "If Jesus was the same person as God the Son, so would other incarnations be. They would all have to be the same person. That makes no sense, least of all if they exist simultaneously in the eschaton."[74] Hebblethwaite's final point on the eschaton brings the problem out in sharp relief. At the second coming we expect the Son of Man to come on the clouds, and we don't expect Bono or anyone else to be with him.[75] Frankly, we can make no sense of this claim, unless we retreat to a non-ortho-dox reinterpretation of the incarnation in terms of degree Christology. But then if the WP model collapses into an adop-tionist degree or Nestorian Christology then we have strong grounds to reject it.

Conclusion

"The mystery of the umbilical cord"[76] that unfolded on that first Christmas so long ago stands as one of the preeminent mysteries of Christian faith. But is it, as Hick intimated, as devoid of mean-ing as calling a circle a square? Frankly, this charge seems to me overreaching, for even if both the WF and WP models have come up short, each appears to offer further avenues of exploration that are not open to such a baldly contradictory claim as a square circle. That said, we must admit that both models have failed as yet to provide an account of the incarnation that is logical, fully orthodox, and plausible.[77] And thus, each balances on an unstable perch over the various abysses of egregious theological error. The truth of the incarnation remains as yet a mountain that we cannot ascend, though we can see its apex far above. But if this doctrine remains a mystery, I submit that it is one that invites neither skep-ticism nor dull acceptance, but rather the simple fascination of the Herdman children. As we continue to struggle in our ascent of this mystery, it invites us too back to the incredible moment of that first Christmas long ago in order to hear the magical pro-nouncement anew. To quote the proclamation of the angel Gladys Herdmann: "Hey! Unto you a child is born!"[78]

5

On Not Understanding the Atonement

suffered under Pontius Pilate, was crucified, dead, and buried; he descended into hell; the third day he rose from the dead . . .

In 2004 Mel Gibson's *The Passion of the Christ* ignited a firestorm of protest. In contrast to previous cinematic treatments of the passion which had offered a relatively restrained portrayal of Christ's suffering and death, Gibson fixed his camera steadfastly upon the saviour to record every crushing blow and splatter of blood. The vitriolic reaction among critics, while predictable, was surprising in its intensity. While many reviewers made legitimate stylistic and artistic points, as well as raising concerns about allegedly anti-Semitic undertones, the deepest objections were squarely directed at the film's two hours of non-stop, brutal violence. Time and again the critical reviews evinced a level of moral indignation surprising in the jaded world of film criticism. For instance, Jonathan Rosenbaum of the *Chicago Reader* protested the film's sickening misanthropy:

> The charges of anti-Semitism and homophobia being hurled at the movie seem too narrow; its general disgust for humanity is so unrelenting that the military-sounding drums at the end seem to be welcoming the apocalypse . . . If I were a Christian, I'd be appalled to have this primitive and pornographic bloodbath presume to speak for me.[1]

Along similar lines, David Edelstein (*Slate*) acerbically dismissed Gibson's efforts as "The Jesus Chainsaw Massacre"[2] while Jami Bernard (*New York Daily News*) railed against the film's "compendium of tortures that would horrify the regulars at an S&M club." Along with her strong moral indignation, Bernard admitted a more fundamental perplexity about the motivation behind Gibson's effort: "'The Passion of the Christ' is a brutal, nasty film that demonizes Jews at an unfortunate time in history. Whatever happened to the idea that the centerpiece of every major religion is love?"[3] Indeed, this same puzzlement was evident in a number of critics who could barely conceal their bewilderment at the film's melding of divine love with gross violence. Echoing the thoughts of many, Rick Groen (*Globe and Mail*) caustically observed: "Looking to heaven, Mel Gibson has made a movie about the God of Love, and produced two hours of non-stop violence. We can only pray that next time, looking to Mars, he'll make a movie about the God of Violence, and produce two hours of non-stop love."[4]

In all these cases I would submit that the deepest source of indignation and bewilderment derives not from Gibson's cinematic effort per se, but rather from its forceful and uncompromising depiction of the central event of Christianity. As it would turn out, the real scandal is not Gibson's *Passion* but rather *Christ's* passion. If that is correct then the critics are rather like people going to a boxing match and then complaining to the promoter about the violence. It isn't the promoter's fault if you find the violence of boxing appalling! He was just delivering the goods! Nor is it Gibson's fault if the film critics find the violence of his film appalling, for he was just depicting the Christ event. And so when Rosenbaum indignantly snorts, "If I were a Christian, I'd be appalled to have this primitive and pornographic bloodbath presume to speak for me," he apparently is unaware that Christians do allow this event to speak for them.[5] One can only imagine how the critics might react were they to sit in on congregational singing on a Sunday morning:

> What can wash away my sin?
> Nothing but the blood of Jesus;
> What can make me whole again?
> Nothing but the blood of Jesus.

Oh! precious is the flow
That makes me white as snow;
No other fount I know,
Nothing but the blood of Jesus!

One can picture the horrified faces of our secular critics nestled in the back pew as they witness the shocking display of seemingly decent people singing devotionally about bathing in a fount of blood! And if that wasn't enough to clear the skeptics' pew, a rousing rendition of "There is Power in the Blood" followed by a meditative "O Sacred Head Now Wounded" would surely send the last few critics packing in horror.

Of course, Christians are not mere sadomasochists who take perverse pleasure in the violent suffering and death of Christ. Countless Christians found the viewing of Gibson's *Passion* to be a wrenching affair, indeed that much more so given their devotion to Christ. They do not glory in this horrific event out of sheer perversity, but rather because they believe that it "washes away our sin" and so offers the one hope of reconciliation to God. This may seem to offer the Christians a brief reprieve from the charge of perversity, but if so, it is only at the cost of saddling them with a claim that strikes many as incredible at best and morally reprehensible at the worst. How could *any* event, let alone one so horrific as the crucifixion, offer an *answer* to the endless catalogue of evils that comprise human history? And since it is too easy to abstract evil let us keep in mind the depth of the problem with a brief list of a few of the haunting evils of the Holocaust compiled by Robert Nozick:

> It is difficult enough even to chronicle what occurred—knowledge of much of the suffering and bestial cruelty has disappeared along with its victims—and simply reading the details staggers and numbs the mind: the wanton cruelty of the German perpetrators in continual beatings, the forcible herding of people into synagogues then set on fire to burn them alive there, dousing gasoline on men in prayer shawls and then burning them, dashing children's brains against walls while their parents were forced to watch, so-called 'medical experiments', machine-gunning people into graves they were forced to dig themselves, ripping beards off

old men, mocking people while inflicting horrors on them, the inexorable and unrelenting organized process that sought to destroy each and every Jew and to degrade them completely in this process, the lies about resettlement in the east in order to maintain some hope and partial cooperation, calling the street from the Treblinka railroad station to the gas chambers through which the Jews were forced to walk naked *Himmelfahrstrasse*, the street to heaven—the list is endless, and it is impossible to find one particular event or a few to encapsulate and symbolize all that happened.[6]

One stands dumbfounded before this grisly catalogue of horrors. What can possibly be said to make sense of any of this, let alone to justify it? Indeed, the evil of even one of these events might seem sufficient to engulf the most ambitious theodicy as readily as the Red Sea swallowed the Egyptian army. While Christians believe that the death of Christ provides an *answer* to these horrors, Nozick dismisses it as utterly incapable of bearing this incredible weight:

> Whatever changed situation or possibility the crucifixion and resurrection were supposed to bring about has now ended; the Holocaust has shut the door that Christ opened . . . It might be thought that what Christ accomplished according to Christian theology, he accomplished forever, once and for all. He died for all our sins, past and future, small and large. But not for *that* one, I think.[7]

Not only does the cross seem utterly unable to alleviate the weight of evil, but in fact it adds to the sum total of evil. Invoking the cross as the means to address evil appears to make about as much sense as prescribing a series of rapid shots to the head in order to address a headache: far from addressing the problem, the "treatment" will only *exacerbate it*. But things are worse still for not only is the atonement evil but it appears likely to increase the evil of the world: Jesus' call for us to take up *our* crosses in christic emulation (Lk. 9:23) adds to the amount of evil by encouraging complicity to patterns of oppression. (*My husband beat me again. Well I guess that's just my cross to bear . . .*)[8] As such, it should not surprise us that many consider the cross to be not the great answer to human suffering, but rather another great problem. Indeed, as Gerald O'Collins notes, atheists frequently view the cross of Christ as a disproof of God's existence, "as the place where God is absent and any belief in an all-powerful, all-loving God should decently end."[9]

These serious charges go to the very heart of Christianity. Our response shall focus on the three main atonement theories—ransom/victory, satisfaction/substitution, and example/influence.[10] Each seeks to explain how the atonement is not simply another inexplicable evil, but rather the one hope for deliverance from all evil. While I will argue that each approach fails as a comprehensive theory, I will explore the possibility of reinterpreting these traditions as mutually enriching metaphors or models of a fundamentally mysterious reality. While that avenue shows promise, in the final section I will argue that even the chastened metaphorical approach to the atonement cannot avoid the problematic moral implications of satisfaction and substitution.

One final note is in order. Though I will tend to treat the words "atonement" and "cross/crucifixion" as roughly synonymous, in my view the fullest sense of the atonement is found in both the death and life of Christ, or what Reformed theologians refer to as his passive and active righteousness.[11] While our discussion here is concerned with the death (passive righteousness) of Christ, controversies also surround the alleged imputation of Christ's active righteousness to the Christian.[12]

Come, Thou Precious Ransom, Come . . .

It is an oft-noted peculiarity of theological history that, while the patristic era saw an orthodox consensus emerge on the Trinity, incarnation, and other key doctrines, thinking on the atonement was dominated by a range of images with little systematic attempt to bring them into a cohesive picture.[13] To the extent that a theoretical framework emerges in these early centuries, it encompasses two interrelated themes: the atonement as ransom from slavery and military conquest or victory. While this ransom/victory approach to the cross was influential for centuries, the second millennium saw it in significant retreat in favor of our second and third theories. The theory regained popularity with Gustav Aulén's influential endorsement in *Christus Victor* (1931),[14] and this interest has been sustained with the recent rediscovery of the Pauline theme of liberation from sin,[15] as well as broader postmodern trends away from theory and toward narrative.

The ransom/victory theory is drawn from two sets of texts. To begin with, there are biblical passages that illumine the work of the atonement in the terms of liberation by a military ruler. For instance, Paul writes that God "has rescued us from the dominion of darkness and brought us into the kingdom of the Son he loves" (Col. 1:13). What is more, "having disarmed the powers and authorities, he made a public spectacle of them, triumphing over them by the cross" (Col. 2:15; cf. 1 Cor. 15:24–28). Within this context of "military conquest" we find the second group of texts that speak of the salvation of human beings as a form of liberation from slavery to sin which comes through Christ's life, given "as a ransom for many" (Mk. 10:45). Paul echoes the slave market by saying that we were bought at a price (Rom. 3:24; 1 Cor. 6:20, 7:23; Titus 2:14; cf. 1 Pet. 1:18).

So how do we bring these varied texts together into a coherent, explanatory whole? Wherein lies the *theory*? The ransom theory is predicated upon the war between God and the devil in which God saved us for we *could not* save ourselves. The beginning point is the recognition of the slavery of human beings to sin, and specifically to the devil, the prince of this world. But Jesus defeated the demonic minions on the cross, thereby triumphantly ransoming us out of slavery. When we seek to understand *how* Jesus ransomed us back from the devil things get interesting. The economic transfer explanation is simplest:

(1) The devil maintains full rights of ownership over human beings.
(2) Full rights of ownership must be surrendered if one accepts payment for that which is owned.
(3) The devil accepted payment for his ownership of human beings in the life of Christ.
(4) Therefore, the devil must surrender his full rights of ownership over human beings.

On its own this is a comprehensible argument, readily appreciable through the economy of the slave market, or (to update the image a little) a used car lot. If I provide the $300 price for a 1978 Ford Pinto and sign the proper documents, the dealer surrenders his ownership of the vehicle and I am free to drive the car away. Still one might contend with (3), for what evidence do we have that the devil accepted the life of Christ for the life of human beings? More to the point, *why* would the devil do this, thereby surrendering his ownership of humanity? At this point, some of the patristics took a rather controversial step by appealing to a divinely orchestrated deception of the devil. With this emendation, the ransom becomes more like a covert rescue operation than a straightforward economic exchange. Gregory of Nyssa famously articulated this deception with the image of the devil "swallowing" Christ as a fish swallows a fishhook (Christ is the bait and the cross is the fishhook). The same image was taken up by Rufinus of Aquileia:

> the divine virtue of the Son of God might be like a kind of hook hidden beneath the form of human flesh . . . to lure on the prince of this world to a contest; that the Son might offer him his human flesh as a bait and that the divinity which lay underneath might catch him and hold him fast with its hook . . . Then, just as a fish when it seizes a baited hook not only fails to draw off the bait but is itself dragged out of the water to serve as food for others; so he that had the power of death seized the body of Jesus in death, unaware of the hook of divinity which lay hidden inside. Having swallowed it, he was immediately caught. The gates of hell were broken, and he was, as it were, drawn up from the pit, to become food for others.[16]

While the vivid imagery would have captivated the Herdmans (see chapter four) the reasoning is not as clear as one might hope. We can modify the economic transfer explanation as follows:

(1) The devil maintains full rights of ownership over human beings.

(2') Full rights of ownership must be surrendered if one attempts to exercise them improperly.

(3') The devil exercised his full rights of ownership over human beings improperly by torturing and crucifying Christ.

(4) Therefore, the devil must surrender his full rights of ownership over human beings.

On this revised construction the images of ransom and victory are drawn more intimately together: as Christ defeats the devil he wins our ransom. On either form of the argument—as straightforward exchange or covert operation—we have a rational picture of Christ's liberation wrought through the cross. In addition, the picture is vivid and rooted in human experience. All told, this is an admirable example of rational theological reflection.

There is no doubt that the ransom/victory theory is enormously appealing, for it is simple, logical, and visceral. As well, we have seen that it boasts some suggestive biblical precedents. Even so, the model has also encountered its share of criticisms. To begin with, many have charged that the conception of redemption construed in the terms of warfare with and liberation from demonic oppression is no longer plausible. While the objection is not often articulated explicitly, the basic assumption seems to be that demons and angels belong to the same defunct pre-modern world as dragons, sprites, and fairies. To use William James' expression, they are no longer live options of belief. But to play the devil's advocate (quite *literally* in this case), it should be noted that those who reject the existence of such beings typically offer no *argument*. Instead, they appeal vaguely to the sensibilities of "modern man" as in Rudolf Bultmann's memorable words: "We cannot use electric lights and radios and, in the event of illness, avail ourselves of modern medical and clinical means and at the same time believe in the spirit and wonder world of the New Testament."[17] Unfortunately, Bultmann never addresses the phenomenon of highly educated Christians who use electric lights, radios, and even *laptops and iphones*, and *still* believe in evil spirits.[18]

Even if one did follow Bultmann in "demythologizing" all non-divine spirit agencies, this would not undermine the ransom/victory model. One need simply reinterpret these agencies as personifications of the various dimensions of individual and corporate human depravity as expressed through complex social and economic structures. As O'Collins puts it, "uncontrollable greed, exploitation, institutionalized injustice, the arms race, revenge attacks and violence of all kinds. Anxiety and impotence in the face of evil forces 'out there' have not disappeared; they have simply relocated."[19] It seems to me that corporate, systemic evils provide a formidable adversary from which we require liberation.[20]

A more pointed criticism has frequently been raised, however. For the ransom/victory account to succeed as a model it must explain *to whom the ransom is paid*. The traditional explanation in which the ransom is paid to the devil raises two difficulties. First, in order to explain the devil's actions the model requires an element of divine deception *via* the cruciform equivalent of a "fish-hook." Not only does this arguably amount to a form of divinely orchestrated entrapment, but at a more visceral level the notion of God being reduced to a scheme to outwit the devil just does not comport with biblical conceptions of divine sovereignty. In *this* sense we might legitimately discount the theory as mythology. In addition, Anselm made an important criticism when he trenchantly pointed out that God owes the devil nothing but a good ass whooping (not Anselm's words).[21] As such, God is under no constraint whatsoever to "bargain" with or "trick" the devil in order to win us back. The devil is a squatter in the house and is owed nothing but a summary eviction notice. But if the devil has no rights over us then the ransom/victory theory suddenly loses one element that is crucial for its theoretical integrity and we no longer have a clear explanation of the atonement.

One can maintain the liberation while abandoning the dubious picture of bargaining with the devil, but insofar as one does so, the rational picture is critically weakened. While we could defuse the worries about divine honesty and sovereignty by reconfiguring the payment as God's ransom to himself, this revision sacrifices explanatory coherence in order to safeguard the divine nature.[22] At this point the theory veers close either to the satisfaction/substitution model (God satisfies himself through the penal suffering of his Son) or to a subset of the example/influence model. Either way, ransom/victory does not appear to hold together if pushed to yield a fully coherent theoretical account of atonement. Not all proponents see this as a problem however. Indeed, Gustav Aulén charged that criticisms are misguided because ransom is not really a *theory* at all.[23] Further, since Aulén was critical of rational argumentation in fundamental matters of faith, he viewed the non-theoretical framework of ransom as a *virtue*. While it may indeed be that, insofar as we have been seeking a rational, theoretical explanation of the atonement, it looks like we shall not find it here.

He Paid the Debt I Could Not Pay . . .

Many evangelicals do not realize how mysterious the atonement is, not because they have not thought about its logic, but rather because they uncritically assume the logic of the satisfaction/ substitution theory. I recall a young Christian coming up to me excitedly one evening and exclaiming belatedly: "At last, I *understand why Jesus had to die!*" While I shared his enthusiasm, inside I thought "I wish *I* understood why Jesus had to die." It was not that I was unfamiliar with the explanation that this individual had encountered, but rather that I felt the answer to be so singularly inadequate. Nicky Gumbel offers a familiar rendition of the argument in the popular Alpha Course where he asks us to imagine two friends who grow apart over time.[24] As one eventually becomes a judge, the other spirals into a life of crime. When the criminal is brought into the courtroom of his former friend, Gumbel observes that *justice* requires that the man be sentenced appropriately for his crime and so the judge assigns the just penalty. However, in love the judge takes off his robes, steps down off the bench, and writes out a check to pay the fine. And this is precisely what Christ did for us.

There are two concepts that emerge as central to this explanation: satisfaction and substitution. The first is not explicit in Gumbel's illustration because the judge is not the originator of the law but only the enforcer of it. (By contrast God is the source of the law by which he judges us.) However, the picture implies the concept of satisfaction, namely that the law is satisfied through the judge's actions. Scripture points to this notion in Romans 3:25: "God presented Christ as a sacrifice of atonement, through the shedding of his blood—to be received by faith." The Greek word for "sacrifice of atonement" (*hilasterion*) is frequently translated "propitiation," a word which carries the connotation that God has been satisfied through this sacrificial act. Along with this, the passage also implies *substitution* for it is Christ who (somehow) takes our place. The concept of substitution is explicit in Galatians 3:13: "Christ redeemed us from the curse of the law by becoming a curse for us, for it is written: 'Cursed is everyone who is hung on a pole.'" But the most explicit summary of substitution is found in Paul's incredible observation that "God made him who had no sin to be sin for us, so that in him we might become the righteousness of God." (2 Cor. 5:21)

So how are these concepts of satisfaction and substitution to be drawn into a coherent picture? While the concept of *satisfaction* was first applied to the atonement by the third century theologian Cyprian,[25] it is not until Anselm, Archbishop of Canterbury (1033–1109) that this notion was drawn into a systematic theory in one of the most influential books in theological history, the elegant *Cur Deus Homo*? (*Why the God Man*?). Anselm sets out to provide a rational theory for the *necessity* of the incarnation through a dialogue between Anselm and his interlocutor Boso. When Boso asks why it was necessary that God become a man (1.2) Anselm proceeds with dazzling scholastic confidence to explain the cross in the terms of necessary "economic" relationships between God's honor and human sin. Anselm defines sin as the debt we incur when we fail to grant proper honor to God (1.11). When we incur this debt, compensation commensurate to the offense must be paid back so God's honor may be restored (1.19). But this creates a terrible dilemma for while only humans can properly atone for the offense to God's infinite honor, only God is able to do so. Rather than leave human beings in this hopeless situation, God becomes a man (so that he may properly pay) while remaining divine (so that he is able to pay) (2.6).

Through the centuries Anselm's argument has exercised great influence such that, while most evangelicals have never read Anselm, his explanation—retold countless times in popular hymnody and lively evangelistic illustrations—runs in their blood. Consider the words of "My Jesus I Love Thee": "I love thee because thou hast first loved me, and purchased my pardon on Calvary's tree." (While the language of Christ's "purchase" might invoke the slave market image, the reference to pardon rather than freedom suggests that the satisfaction of God is in view.) This language is part of Christianese—that familiar language that Christians speak at church meetings and Bible studies: "Jesus washed my sins away." "Jesus paid the debt I owed but could never repay."

While Anselm's conceptual framework has deeply influenced evangelicalism (and Protestantism more generally), the Reformation did introduce one significant innovation upon Anselm's theory: the categorial shift from the economic to the punitive, specifically the biblical category of *penal substitution*. The reformers did not so much disagree with Anselm as seek to supplement his explanation with a richer biblical basis rooted in passages like 2 Corinthians 5:21 and Hebrews 8 – 10. Since those texts depict Christ fulfilling the temple sacrificial system, the image is not so much one of economic transfer as it is penal substitution. We can bring together these themes and summarize the theory of satisfaction/substitution as follows:

(5) *Qua* his justice, God demands that human sin be punished.
(6) *Qua* his love, God desires relationship with human beings.
(7) Only God is able to provide recompense for sin against God's infinite majesty.
(8) Only a human being may rightly provide recompense for a human sin against God's infinite majesty.
(9) Therefore, the divine person Jesus Christ becomes human and so is both able to provide recompense for sin (as divine) and may rightly provide recompense for sin (as human).

While the satisfaction/penal substitution fortress appears solid, we shall test its structural integrity by lobbing four incendiary objections. To begin with, it has frequently been objected that it reduces the cross to an impersonal economic exchange. While that is a legitimate objection against some articulations of the theory, it is not a necessity of the approach, particularly in the Protestant emphasis upon penal substitution.[26] More serious is the charge that these theories assume a reductionistic, individualistic, and atomistic framework which obscures the corporate and social dimensions of sin.[27] Corporate, social evils are more than the sins committed by a select group of individuals for the sin and evil is *greater* than the sum total that was carried out by specific individuals, and thus there must also be corporate sin and evil. Take for instance the corporate guilt of IBM's collaboration with the Nazis[28] or the sins of the allied nations captured in the haunting documentary *The Long Way Home*. How are these corporate sins—irreducible to any single individual and greater than the sum of the sins of all individuals—atoned for on the cross?

Important though that objection is, we shall concentrate on the third and fourth problems which bring us to the heart of the critique. The third problem is that the explanatory power of the theory is illusory. If we reconsider the illustration offered by Nicky Gumbel we will find that it is sharply disanalogous at two points so critical that they undermine the entire analogy. To begin with, while debt may be transferable, it would seem that punishment (let alone a sentence of torture and execution) is not. Ingersoll put the point well:

> A man has committed murder, has been tried, convicted, and condemned to death. Another man goes to the governor, and says that he is willing to die in place of the murderer. The governor says: "All right, I accept your offer; a murder has been committed, somebody must be hung, and your death will satisfy the law."
>
> But that is not the law. The law says, not that somebody shall be hanged, but that the murderer shall suffer death.[29]

To pursue Ingersoll's point, imagine the Alpha audience's perplexity if Gumbel's illustration depicted the judge subjecting himself to capital punishment so that his friend may go free. Far from *explaining* the atonement, if anything that would highlight the injustice, or at least inscrutability, of the event! As such, we simply cannot sustain the analogy between economic substitution (i.e. paying another's fine) and punitive substitution (i.e. dying for another).

The second disanalogy concerns the contrasting relationship that the judge and God have to the law.[30] Initially the difference may not be evident since theologians have often depicted the law as a reality external to God which he must observe. Luther provides a classic example:

> to wit, that our most merciful Father, seeing us to be oppressed and overwhelmed with the curse of the law . . . Here now cometh the law and saith : I find him a sinner, and that such a one as hath taken upon him the sins of all men, and I see no sins else but in him; therefore let him die upon the cross. And so he setteth upon him and killeth him.[31]

This language of the law roving about for somebody to punish until it settles upon Christ could easily lead one to think that the law is a force external to God. But, in fact, the law is simply an expression of God's holy nature. And this leads to a most extraordinary claim: while God demands punishment, it is God who then absorbs the prescribed punishment. To say the *least* this appears perplexing. Why does God not eliminate the role for the "middle man" (the suffering Christ) and simply forgive? John Stott replies to this query that "God must 'satisfy himself'" and that "This internal necessity is our fixed starting-point."[32] However, David Edwards responds to Stott: "I find the idea of God sacrificing himself to himself not only inexplicable but also incomprehensible."[33] Stott then replies to Edwards that God's action is not simply a self-sacrifice but rather "divine self-satisfaction through divine self-substitution."[34] But one might be forgiven for wondering what difference Stott's clarification makes.[35]

We can illustrate the problem through Theodor S. Giesel's classic children's book *The Cat in the Hat Comes Back!*[36] The book tells the story of Sally and her brother (the narrator) who have been left to shovel the snow on the walk to their house while their mother shops in town (clearly the book is set in the time before child welfare laws). Suddenly the Cat in the Hat appears, enters their home uninvited, and in no time has left a horrid pink ring in the family's bathtub. When the children implore the cat to clean it up, he promptly does so . . . by transferring the ring to one of mother's new dresses! Next the Cat transfers the spot to the wall, and then wipes it onto Dad's "$10 shoes," and on it goes. As things spiral out of control, the Cat successively releases a series of cats hidden under his hat to clean up the spot (each identified with a letter of the alphabet). However, each cat only worsens the problem until all the snow surrounding the house is stained pink! At this point the Cat finally reveals the final lettered cat under his hat:

> "Z is too small to see.
> So don't try. You can not.
> But Z is the cat
> Who will clean up that spot.
> "Now here is the Z
> You can't see," said the Cat.
> "And I bet you can't guess
> What he has in HIS hat!
> "He has something called VOOM.
> VOOM is so hard to get,
> You never saw anything
> Like it, I bet.
> Why Voom cleans up anything
> Clean as can be!"[37]

At this point cat Z produces the mysterious Voom that promptly cleans up all the snow. Now the inquisitive child may rightly ask why the Cat in the Hat didn't simply produce cat Z at the beginning. Why go through the whole process of transferring the spot with the other cats? Or better yet, why didn't the Cat in the Hat just keep Voom under his hat? The answer of course, is that we would have a greatly truncated and consequently weakened children's story. But when we apply the dilemma to atonement theology, the same question is not so easily answered: why does God demand repentance *plus* satisfaction *plus* substitution as the path to reconciliation? Why doesn't he simply forgive the penitent?[38]

Finally, we can turn to our fourth objection which notes that in addition to being inexplicable penal substitution is also deeply morally problematic. As David Edwards puts it: "All the eloquence of the Song of the Suffering Servant, and of some Christian theories of atonement, cannot obscure the simple and elementary fact that it is immoral to punish anyone who is not guilty."[39] As a result, countless critics of satisfaction/substitution have charged that this theory savages the biblical conception of the loving God. There is no doubt that popular evangelistic preaching has provided ample fodder for such charges. Shirley Guthrie provides the example of a preacher holding up a dirty glass symbolizing a sinful human being. He then lifted up a hammer (the wrath of God against sin) and swung it toward the glass (God's rage unleashed on sin). Then at the last moment, he placed a pan in the path of the hammer which crumpled under its impact. The preacher then informed the terrified crowd that this is what Jesus did by stepping in to absorb the Father's rage against our sin.[40]

It should hardly be surprising that many have rejected the satisfaction/substitution framework as implying a picture of God as a vengeful, bloodthirsty deity. Rudolf Bultmann voiced this moral protest when he asked incredulously:

> How can my guilt be atoned for by the death of someone guiltless (assuming one may even speak of such)? What primitive concepts of guilt and righteousness lie behind any such notion? And what primitive concepts of God? If what is said about Christ's atoning death is to be understood in terms of the idea of sacrifice, what kind of primitive mythology is it according to which a divine being who has become man atones with his blood for the sins of humanity?[41]

While Bultmann was a well known critic of conservative Christianity, today one finds the same sort of criticisms being raised by self-confessed evangelical theologians and pastors. Steve Chalke's comment is representative: "God says love your enemies but then doesn't love his until he's got blood—how can God run on a different ethic to the way he's asked his people to live?"[42] Similarly, the character Kerry in Brian McLaren's *The Story We Find Ourselves In* observes: "That just sounds like one more injustice in the cosmic equation. It sounds like divine child abuse. You know?"[43]

The defender of penal substitution rejects the charge of divine child abuse as a distortion of the doctrine. Hence, Sinclair Ferguson rejects this characterization of the atonement as "it suggests that God the Father is not truly revealed in Jesus Christ.

Behind the Savior stands—it is feared—an ogre God, who is other than love."[44] The difference between God and the pagan deities is that if they are propitiated at all, it is by the offerings of terrified sinners, whilst God secures his own propitiation by sending his Son. And as Stott points out, he does it all out of love: "It cannot be emphasized too strongly that God's love is the source, not the consequence, of the atonement. As P.T. Forsyth expressed it, 'the atonement did not procure grace, it flowed from grace.' God does not love us because Christ died for us; Christ died for us because God loves us."[45] Since the Son goes willingly, it is deeply misleading to view him as "victim" of the Father: "God is not primarily a judge who exacts a compensating penalty from Jesus as a man. Jesus as the God-man freely offers his life to the Father."[46] Jesus is not *persuading* the Father to love us but rather is *proving* the Father's love for us.

This fourth objection extends beyond concerns of satisfaction/substitution to the worry that the doctrine will legitimize abuse and thus perpetuate evil. If we rightly reject the popular conceptions of the vindictive Father demanding the hapless Son's sacrifice in favor of a self-satisfaction motivated out of divine love, the picture becomes even more perplexing. Edwards comments:

> Self-punishment of this sort by a mentally healthy person is inconceivable. Of course God's sense of justice must be both stronger and more justified than any human judge's or parent's. But precisely because God's justice is the justice of holy love, it seems all the more difficult to think that he could do something which would be condemned if done by a good judge or a good parent.[47]

The problem extends back to the doctrine of God and the notion of self-sacrifice. The essence of these objections focuses on the tension between the God who demands sacrifice and the merciful God revealed in the parable of the prodigal son. Some years ago liberal Protestant Paul Wernle wrote: "How miserably all those finely constructed theories of sacrifice and vicarious atonement crumble to pieces before this faith in the love of God our Father, who so gladly pardons! The one parable of the Prodigal

Son wipes them all off the slate."[48] Robin Collins has made the point memorably by retelling this parable as a tale of penal substitution:

> There was a man who had two sons. The younger said to his father, "Father, give me my share of the estate." So the father divided his property between them. Not long after that, the younger son went off to a distant country, squandered all he had in wild living, and ended up feeding pigs in order to survive. Eventually he returned to his father, saying, "Father, I have sinned against heaven and you. I am no longer worthy to be called your son. Make me one of your hired servants." But his father responded: "I cannot simply forgive you for what you have done, not even so much as to make you one of my hired men. You have insulted my honor by your wild living. Simply to forgive you would be to trivialize sin; it would be against the moral order of the entire universe. For nothing is less tolerable in the order of things than for a son to take away the honor due to his father and not make recompense for what he takes away. Such is the severity of my justice that reconciliation will not be made unless the penalty is utterly paid. My wrath--my avenging justice--must be placated." "But father, please..." the son began to plead. "No," the father said, "either you must be punished or you must pay back, through hard labor for as long as you shall live, the honor you stole from me." Then the elder brother spoke up. "Father, I will pay the debt that he owes and endure your just punishment for him. Let me work extra in the field on his behalf and thereby placate your wrath." And it came to pass that the elder brother took on the garb of a servant and labored hard year after year, often long into the night, on behalf of his younger brother. And finally, when the elder brother died of exhaustion, the father's wrath was placated against his younger son and they lived happily for the remainder of their days.[49]

Even if Collins' paraphrase draws upon some of the caricatures of penal substitution that have already been challenged, his primary point retains its force: why cannot God simply forgive? Why does he embark upon this whole scenario of self-punishment and self-satisfaction?

Jesus, I My Cross Have Taken . . .

The last point—why not just forgive?—is a common refrain among critics of penal substitution. After all, isn't God more inter-ested in changed lives than spilt blood (cf. 1 Sam. 15:22)? So what good is another sacrifice when God really desires repentance and change? As Ingersoll put it, "A man steals, and then sacrifices a dove, or gives a lamb to a priest. His crime remains the same. He need not kill something. Let him give back the thing stolen, and in the future live an honest life."[50] This emphasis on personal moral change brings us to the third explanation of the atonement which arose at the same time as that of Anselm and has continued for a thousand years as the primary alternative to it. Developed by Peter Abelard, the moral exemplar (or example/influence) theory takes a sharp detour from a key assumption of the ransom/vic-tory and satisfaction/substitution theories. While these other theories are objective (that is, they see the primary force of the atonement in the objective work achieved by God in Christ), the example/influence theory is subjective insofar as it sees the pri-mary work of the atonement in the effect it has upon individuals (revealing the love of God to us) and the response it invokes in them (motivating us to be like Christ).

As with our other theories, example/influence depends upon certain key biblical texts. To begin with, we are called to emulate the cross through lives of discipleship (Lk. 9:23; Rom. 12:1; 1 Pet. 2:21; 1 Jn. 2:6). This sentiment is expressed in Isaac Watts' classic hymn "When I Survey the Wondrous Cross": "Love so amazing, so divine, Demands my soul, my life, my all." When we contem-plate the incredible love of God, we are drawn to follow Christ in a life of self-sacrifice. Abelard argued that the cross reveals the love of God for human beings as captured in Jesus' words: "Greater love has no one than this: to lay down one's life for one's friends" (Jn. 15:13). Abelard thus wrote:

> our hearts should be set on fire by such a gift of divine grace, and true love should not hold back from suffering anything for his sake . . . Therefore, our redemption through the suffering of Christ is that deeper love within us which not only frees us from slavery to sin, but also secures for us the true liberty of the children of

God, in order that we might do all things out of love rather than out of fear—love for him who has shown us such grace that no greater can be found.[51]

As such, the primary rationale behind the atonement is epistemological (informing us of God's love and the weight of sin) and volitional (motivating us to respond). These two themes can readily be combined into a single theory of the atonement.

(10) In order for human beings to be saved they must be made aware of their condition of sin and provided with adequate motivation to respond to it.
(11) Christ's atonement provides awareness of the human condition of sin and adequate motivation to respond to it (motivating us to ask forgiveness and follow Christ).
(12) Therefore, human beings can be saved through Christ's atonement.

This account is both admirably simple and ethically appealing as it replaces the unsettling specter of divine violence with a God whose arms are open wide to his prodigal children. As such, it is hardly surprising that the history of theology has seen a long line of defenders of the example/influence theory from Abelard and Socinius up to René Girard.[52] One also sees the growing influence of this approach among those within (or emerging from) evangelicalism. For instance, "post-evangelical" Dave Tomlinson writes: "The Atonement is not about God's changing attitude toward us; instead, the Atonement is about how our attitude toward God changes as we see forgiveness acted out before us."[53]

Despite its virtues, the example/influence view faces its own problems. The first great problem is whether (10) is an adequate articulation of the human problem. For one thing, this view seems to lead to the Platonic/Greek theory that evil and suffering arise from ignorance. However, Plato's view is erroneous for we can *know what is right* and still *choose what is wrong*: "This is the verdict: Light has come into the world, but people loved darkness instead of light because their deeds were evil" (Jn. 3:19). Since our fallen condition is due to more than a litany of bad examples, more is required to break the cycle than the influence of a subjectively compelling act of love.[54] Our very choice of role models requires radical reformation. (The role models I held as a sixteen year old—mainly lead guitarists from heavy metal bands—are rather different from the role models I have today.) It is thus hardly surprising that for the most part advocates of the example/influence theory simply elide more objective references to the fallen human condition and the determinative divine action required to correct it.

The second objection reveals the incapacity of the example/influence theory to address the offense of atonement violence. In short, the central stumbling block is not a particular interpretation of how God used the violence of the cross, but rather the prospect that God used violence at all. So Leanne Van Dyk observes, "At the core of all the criticisms is the problem of violence—specifically, the presumed link between the violence of the cross and the saving effects for the world."[55] While the critics of Gibson's film would have been offended by an explanation of the cross in terms of divine self-substitution, I suspect they would have been equally offended by an explanation of it as divine loving inspiration. And so as Boersma trenchantly observes, "we can only exclude all violence from moral-influence theories if we categorically exclude any divine involvement in the crucifixion."[56] Hence the dilemma: insofar as a theory seeks to remove direct divine involvement in the act in order to guard divine goodness, the very meaning of the event as a *divine* action is undermined.

This leads to the third point: ironically, the subjective example/influence view falls under the related concerns that it will make human beings complicit in further violence. So Boersma: "If Christ voluntarily suffered and sacrificed himself to the point of death, does this not lead to human self-sacrifice?"[57] Hence, moral influence theories ironically face the same objection as satisfaction/substitution: why did God choose so violent a means of reconciliation?[58]

Metaphors of Atonement

Thus far each of our three purported theories of the atonement has failed to provide an explanation for the cross. Perhaps then we should shift our tactic and view them not as mutually exclusive theories, but rather as partial, metaphorical descriptions of a reality that transcends any single theory. Once we take that view a number of factors fall into place. Yes, Jesus *did* liberate us from bondage to the devil and our own sinful nature. And in so doing, Jesus satisfied God's holy nature which visits divine wrath upon sin. And through this revelation of God's holiness and love we are drawn to take up our crosses in lives of self-sacrifice. Hence, the fullest and most correct understanding of the atonement draws us simultaneously to the defeat of sin and the devil, the self-substitution of God, and our response of loving devotion. This approach promises to retain the strength of each purported theory while warning against the error of taking any one part for the whole. Though appealing, this step is also radical, as it amounts to a concession that we have failed in our theoretical-explanatory aspirations. Hence, the critic might view it as tantamount to silencing the calls of the creditors by a declaration of bankruptcy. Even so, it is not altogether clear that this declaration of explanatory bankruptcy can definitively silence the calls of the creditors if the metaphors themselves prove susceptible to moral objections. In this section we will continue our focus on the most contentious concepts in atonement theology—satisfaction and substitution—and I will argue that construing these twin concepts as metaphors does not address the coherence and immorality objections.

If satisfaction and substitution are metaphors, we can begin with the question of whether they might be replaced altogether. The classic scenario is the missionary who, when faced with a people that has no conception of sacrificial lambs but much familiarity with sacrificial pigs, translates John 1:29 as "Behold, the pig of God!" While at first blush such a translation will strike many as misguided if not blasphemous, it is more difficult to prise apart the theological objections from the cultural ones. There is a reasonable case to be made for the cultural relativity and thus permissibility of such a translation. But what about the more radical case of a people that has no conception of blood sacrifice at all? As Leanne Van Dyk puts it:

> what if the consciences of twenty-first-century Christians are not comforted by these images of punishment and sacrifice? Are the

resources of our theological traditions flexible and resilient enough to discover other biblically rooted images, ones that comfort contemporary people and arouse their hearts to gratitude for God's boundless mercy?[59]

Van Dyk is not proposing that we *reject* satisfaction and substitution outright, but rather that these metaphors no longer communicate the reality of God's salvific action in our culture; as such, we might better focus on alternate biblical metaphors such as victory/ransom or example/influence.

The standard objection to such proposals is that metaphors are irreducible and thus *not* interchangeable. Garrett Green thus argues: "The notion that metaphors are substitutable . . . runs afoul of recent theories of metaphor which stress the unique ability of metaphorical language to say what cannot be said in any other way."[60] Green adds that insofar as we *do* substitute revealed metaphors we are in danger of losing the revelation itself: "The danger thus is that to replace the fundamental metaphors by which we respond to/understand God is to replace the gospel with idolatry."[61] In short, an atonement doctrine without the metaphors of satisfaction and substitution is no longer a *Christian* atonement doctrine.

Green makes an important point. We are certainly not at liberty to mix and match metaphors to our own taste. As Boersma warns, "We cannot simply ignore biblical metaphors because we feel that they don't really reflect the way things are or should be."[62] However, Van Dyk is not suggesting that we replace satisfaction/substitution with anything to our liking, but rather with other "biblically rooted images." Further, one might argue that the strangeness of satisfaction/substitution to modern people may *necessitate* a substitution. The essence of a metaphor is found in its novel illumination of a given subject matter (seeing *this* as *that*) which includes an irreducible participatory sense. Given the extent to which this is woven into the forms of life of different languages, it is hardly surprising that metaphors, like jokes, are very difficult to translate fully. For instance, the Korean metaphor "cold rice" (*chan bap*) refers to a person or thing that is unpopular (after all, everybody likes *warm* rice). Even though that metaphor can readily be explained to a westerner, it will not "speak" to those who do not have rice as a staple in their diet. Through this cultural background the metaphor incarnates the concept, allowing it to be *experienced* in a novel way. The irreducibility of the metaphor includes this experiential sense that transcends the words and concepts. Do modern westerners understand what the sacrificial system of ancient Israel was, how it was woven into the social order, and how Christ both shattered and fulfilled it? If not, then we may no longer be at the point of deciding *whether* to communicate the metaphors of punishment and sacrifice. Perhaps sacrificial metaphors are *no longer comprehensible* in a society that purchases its meat shrink-wrapped at the supermarket, and which considers it a sacrifice to drive in a car without air-conditioning.

While there is some plausibility in the claim that we no longer grasp the biblical metaphor of sacrifice in the way the Hebrews did, it appears overreaching to claim that it is so inaccessible that we have no choice but to abandon it. Though the metaphor of cold rice may not speak to a westerner, "cold French fries" would be an excellent equivalent given that it has a very similar lack of culinary appeal and for a similar reason. The lesson (to invoke another metaphor) seems to be that we can wade into the waters of a novel metaphor even if we are not fully immersed. Surely the same is true in the metaphors of satisfaction and substitution. Indeed, I suspect it is the degree to which we *do* grasp the metaphors that we become unsettled by them. Perhaps our failure is not in understanding the metaphors' function per se, but rather in understanding *how they could be appropriate*.

Another avenue remains however: one might seek to neutralize the more uncomfortable dimensions of substitution and satisfaction by seeing them as derivative of a more fundamental, inoffensive "root metaphor."[63] For instance, perhaps we could subsume the image of the propitiating God to the God who forgives the prodigal such that all images must be understood in light of the God who stands before us, arms extended in love. Might this approach render innocuous the objections to satisfaction and substitution?

There are two important responses to this proposal. The first is to recognize that many defenders of satisfaction/substitution have developed persuasive arguments that penal substitution is the root metaphor for understanding all others, including the loving God of the prodigal.[64] Note that Jesus, standing against the backdrop of the Old Testament sacrificial system, understood his own mission as an atoning work (Mk. 8:31) and spoke of his blood as being poured out for the forgiveness of sins (Mt. 26:28). If we are faithful to scripture, we must recognize the central place of sacrifice and substitution within Christ's work. As Gruenler observes:

> Jesus' sense of eschatological completion, like the flower of humble and simple beginnings, that contains in seed form the whole genomic pattern of redemption and courses its way upward in stages of growth through the growing stem until finally it breaks forth into the glorious blossom intended all along by divine design. Jesus' view of atonement needs to be seen through such an image of organic unfolding in redemptive history.[65]

As we noted above, this theme is present in Hebrews, 1 Peter, and the writings of Paul and John. As such, we have strong grounds to view satisfaction/substitution as the root atonement metaphor. And so the attempt to explain the atonement through the replacement or subordination of satisfaction/substitution must be judged a failure.

There is a deeper problem as well: even as metaphors satisfaction and substitution are still logically and morally problematic.[66] As such, it is only if these concepts are finally *rejected* in favor of a God who simply forgives in love that the offense is removed. And this amounts to rejecting the satisfaction/substitution metaphor itself which, as we have seen, cannot be done. Let us begin with the substitution concept. The problem here is that it is a basic truth that one ought not punish those who are not guilty. As such, we would call both immoral and confused a judge's choice to be executed so that his old friend could go free. And yet we are told that in the case of Christ *it is* proper for one person to suffer for the sins of another. So we have no means to understand the concept of substitutionary punishment.[67] Recognizing the metaphorical framework through which the concept comes to us does nothing to soften the radical blow to our native sense of justice when we read passages like 2 Corinthians 5:21 and 1 Peter 2:24.

The issue is more complex with the companion concept of satisfaction for here we must first identify which concept is at issue: is it (as has traditionally been believed) the more problematic concept of propitiation or appeasement of divine wrath or is it the less problematic concept of the expiation of sin? When we examined this issue above in the section on substitution/satisfaction we observed a number of texts which teach or imply that God's wrath is visited upon human sin, and averted through Christ's substitution, resulting in God's propitiation or favorable disposition (e.g. Rom. 3:25; 5:9; Heb. 2:17; 1 Jn. 2:2). C.H. Dodd however argued that this interpretation is a vestige of paganism and that the text is really concerned only with expiation.[68] According to Dodd, "divine wrath" consists of a purely passive recognition of the destructive consequences of sin.

While Dodd's proposal initially attracted some interest, it was devastated by the critiques of Roger Nicole and Leon Morris,[69] so that it is now recognized that the appeasement of divine wrath is an essential aspect of texts like Romans 3:25. Expiation is the result of God propitiating his own personal wrath against sin, and so propitiation and expiation are *two sides of the same coin*. That said, we have already noted an uncomfortable vein of pagan thinking in the evangelistic preaching that sees Jesus' sacrifice as the placation of a raging Father. Rather, as we have seen, Christ is a gift arising out of the Father's love. As John put it, "This is love: not that we loved God, but that he loved us and sent his Son as an atoning sacrifice for our sins." (1 Jn. 4:10; cf. Jn. 3:16). But divine wrath must remain and with it God's satisfaction and thus propitiation in light of the sacrifice of Christ.

The problem with the concept of divine satisfaction is twofold. First, it appears inconceivable that a perfect moral being should need to have his wrath placated by a sacrifice since rage or anger appears to belong to inferior moral beings. One could counter that this simply evinces a failure to appreciate the disanalogies between imperfect human anger and holy divine anger. Unfortunately, the second problem is more intractable: why does God satisfy himself through sacrificial suffering? As Steve Chalke asked incredulously, why does God tell us to forgive and then demand blood?

Conclusion

In this chapter we have surveyed a range of theoretical explanations of the Christian doctrine of the atonement. While each of the
purported theories—ransom/victory, satisfaction/substitution,
example/influence—captures a biblical dimension of the work of
Christ, none of them presents a complete and coherent explanation of why Jesus died. What we do know is that he *did* die and,
according to scripture, that he did so to reconcile us to the Father.
This incredible truth is communicated to us through a variety of
rich, bewildering and unsettling images which all point back to
the justice, love and mercy of God. At the very least, to recognize
that God's anger at sin is placated through his own subsitution-
ary act liberates God from the comfortable bourgeois Christianity
that is endemic in western culture: our God is anything but familiar, safe or readily comprehensible. But what do we say to the
critics aghast in the back pew? Perhaps the best we can do is
present the atonement faithfully and allow each individual to be
confronted by its raw, inexplicable power. In this regard at least
one film critic seems to have appreciated Gibson's *Passion* on its
own terms. Though raised a Catholic, Roger Ebert never understood the cost of the atonement until viewing the film:

> For we altar boys, [mass] was not necessarily a deep spiritual
> experience. Christ suffered, Christ died, Christ rose again, we
> were redeemed, and let's hope we can get home in time to watch
> the Illinois basketball game on TV. What Gibson has provided for
> me, for the first time in my life, is a visceral idea of what the
> Passion consisted of . . . This is not a sermon or a homily, but a
> visualization of the central event in the Christian religion. Take it
> or leave it.[70]

6

On Not Understanding the Ascension

he ascended into heaven;
and sitteth at the right hand of God the Father
Almighty;
from thence he shall come to judge the quick and
the dead . . .

Even one hundred years ago nobody could have conceived of the unprecedented size and antiquity of the universe as we now know it. First the solar system was swallowed up inside a massive galaxy with *billions* of suns just like our own while we were demoted to the unimpressive suburbs of one of its spiral arms. And then this galaxy was reduced to being but one member of a local group. We now know that this group is part of the Virgo Supercluster which itself is little more than a faint smudge on the sprawling canvas of the known universe. The existential impact of these discoveries has been striking. As John G. Williams observes, "As we probe into the terrifying reaches of space, we are confronted in a way that nobody can evade or ignore by the new vastness and emptiness which makes those homely old pictures look trivial and ridiculous."[1] Apparently in the minds of many scientists and philosophers the most notable casualty of this view of the universe is the notion that human beings are somehow *special*. Bertrand Russell captures the mood in his story of a theologian's nightmare which opens with a character named Dr. Thaddeus dying and going to heaven where he expects to receive a warm welcome from his creator. After pounding on the gates for awhile, he is finally admitted by a puzzled janitor who knows nothing of men. Since the janitor cannot decide what to do with the strange creature, he takes Dr. Thaddeus to the librarian with the comment "This . . . says that it is a member of a species called 'man,' which lives in a place called 'Earth.' It has some odd notion that the Creator takes a special interest in this place and this species. I thought perhaps you could enlighten it."[2] As it happens, the galactic sub-librarian spends *years* searching through old records in order to identify this obscure planet and its lowly inhabitants.[3] But when his report finally arrives it is, to say the least, anti-climactic:

> I am quite at a loss to imagine why [the sun] has aroused any special interest. It closely resembles a great many other stars in the same galaxy. It is of average size and temperature, and is surrounded by very much smaller bodies called "planets." After minute investigation, I discovered that some, at least, of these planets have parasites, and I think that this thing which has been making inquiries must be one of them.[4]

With the final realization of his own cosmic insignificance in a vast, indifferent universe, Dr. Thaddeus is sent into a fit of despair, an understandable reaction given his demotion from image of God to parasite!

Russell's parable illustrates the widespread assumption that the size and antiquity of the universe reveal it to be meaningless.[5] Not surprisingly, if one accepts that assumption then the claims of the Apostles' Creed will appear childish if not absurd. Consider for instance the personal return of Christ: how could anybody believe that the return of one individual to an obscure planet in an average galaxy would have cataclysmic implications for the entire universe?[6] When put in those terms, the claim boggles the mind! As strong as these intuitions regarding the implausibility of Christian faith may be, they depend upon the dubious premises that a universe of a certain size and age cannot be purposeful and that organisms as small as human beings cannot be intrinsically valuable. But why believe that? Frankly this seems to be more an emotional reaction than a reasoned argument.[7] If we can get beyond the *assumption* that the universe must be small and young for it (and us) to have meaning, then we simply have no reason to accept Russell's skeptical conclusions. This brings us to a second point: recent work in cosmology provides support for the meaningfulness of the universe and our place within it in the extraordinary fine-tuning for life in the initial conditions of the universe right up to the formation of planet earth.[8]

While this may be enough to guarantee the continued plausibility of theism *simpliciter*, numerous plausibility problems attend the specific cosmic claims of various religions. Take Mormonism for instance. The Mormon "Book of Abraham" provides God's celestial address: "And I saw the stars, that they were very great, and that one of them was nearest unto the throne of God; and there were many great ones which were near unto it; And the Lord said unto me: these are the governing ones; and the name of the great one is Kolob, because it is near unto me, for I am the Lord thy God"(3:2–3).[9] Thus, according to Abraham's vision, God has a literal, physical throne somewhere out in space, apparently in close proximity to a star named Kolob![10] The implications are astounding: if we could identify the correct coordinates of Kolob, then NASA could launch a space probe which would eventually arrive at the doorstep of God!![11] (Now *that's* a mission worth some federal funding!) But seriously, how could intelligent people living in the twenty-first century believe this stuff? I mean *really*, God lives up in the stars? However, before I devote too much effort toward mocking Mormon doctrine it should be noted that science presents a challenge no less significant to key articles of the Apostles' Creed including the confession of Christ's ascension into heaven. I mean just *think* about it for a moment! Jesus floated up to heaven, and sat at the right hand of God, from where he shall return in the future? How can intelligent people living in the twenty-first century believe this stuff?

Christians have always confessed the ascension, session,[12] and second coming of Christ, and for centuries they understood these doctrines within the confines of the so-called "three-storied" universe of the Hebrews. That framework is summarized (albeit rather uncharitably) by Robert Ingersoll:

> In the dear old religious days the earth was flat—a little dishing, if anything—and just above it was Jehovah's house, and just below

it was where the Devil lived. God and his angels inhabited the third storey, the Devil and his imps the basement, and the human race the second floor.

Then they knew where heaven was. They could almost hear the harps and hallelujahs. They knew where hell was, and they could almost hear the groans and smell the sulphurous fumes.[13]

Admittedly not all scholars would agree that this three-tiered picture accurately represents the Hebrew worldview. Indeed, Bernard Ramm warns that this "approach to the cosmology of the Bible is so wooden, artificial, and literal that the Bible writers would not recognize such a cosmology if it were handed them all written out on a piece of paper."[14] Could it be then that Ingersoll has presented us with a strawman? The problem with that response is that even if we discard the details of the reconstruction, the three-tiered framework of hell (and/or *sheol*) *below* the earth and the heavens *above* is so basic as to be ineradicable. This is simply the way that Hebrews and Greeks construed the relationship of the human sphere to the spiritual. What is more, it conditioned the thinking of early Christian Hellenists (from Luke and Paul onwards) as much as ancient Hebrews. (Although Hellenists widely believed the world to be a sphere rather than a flat disc, they still assumed the directionality of heaven above and hell below.) As such, Christians understood the ascension, session and second coming within a broad cosmological framework that we now understand to be utterly erroneous.

The beginning of the end for the three-tiered cosmology came in the sixteenth century when Nicolaus Copernicus' heliocentric theory kicked the earth off its pedestal and sent it rotating around the sun. By the time Galileo wrote eighty years later, the fate of the geocentric universe was written on the wall. Looking back from the nineteenth century, John Henry Newman reflected on the earthshaking implications this had for all earlier Christian thinking:

had I been brought up in the belief of the immobility of the earth as though a dogma of Revelation, and had associated it in my mind with the incommunicable dignity of man among created beings, with the destinies of the human race, with the locality of purgatory and hell, and other Christian doctrines, and then for the first time had heard of Galileo's thesis. . . . I should have been at once indignant at its presumption and frightened at its speciousness, as I can never be, at any parallel novelties in other human sciences bearing on religion.[15]

Quite clearly the doctrine of the ascension just could not remain the same. As Robert Jenson explains, prior to Copernicus, "It was . . . perfectly rational to suppose that the outermost and least earthly of these domains [the Ptolemaic spheres] was that made and reserved by God for his own place within his creation, that it was the 'heaven' of Scripture. And it was equally rational to suppose that this is where Christ's risen body is at home, having 'ascended' there."[16] But with the advent of heliocentrism, theologians lost a home for the ascended Christ:

The Copernican universe is homogeneous; no part of it can be more suited for God's dwelling than any other. It can map no topologically delineated heaven. There is in a Copernican universe no plausible accommodation for the risen Christ's body; and, indeed, within any modern cosmology, the assertion that the body is up there someplace must rightly provoke mocking proposals to search for it with more powerful telescopes, or suggestions that perhaps it is hiding on the "other side" of a black hole. But if there is no *place* for Jesus' risen body, how is it a body at all? For John Calvin was surely right: " . . . this is the eternal truth of any body, that it is contained in its place."[17]

Thus as Jenson notes, the Copernican shift left Christ's humanity without any suitable abode. And if the idea of a localized heaven has passed by the wayside, then so too it would seem, has a real ascension from terrestrial Palestine.

Interestingly, it appears that even today many Christians have not yet digested the revolution initiated by Copernicus, and instead seem to hold, at least at some tacit level, to some sort of three-tiered cosmology. Consider for instance the way that Soviet state propaganda lighted upon cosmonaut Yuri Gagarin's quip after circling the earth in 1961 that he "didn't see God up there."[18]

Apparently many babushkas reacted to Gagarin's report with the anger of one Russian diplomat's aunt: "She was very upset, and when I asked her why, she said, 'What would *you* say if someone came into *your* house without so much as ringing the bell or asking your leave? . . . But here's this Gagarin going up into God's house like that and then coming down again without being punished in any way."[19] Well okay, perhaps mid-twentieth-century Russians were rather naive, but surely western Christians today are more enlightened. While that is no doubt true, on the whole we are probably not as enlightened as we think. In 1989 a major American Christian television network reported the discovery of hell in the Soviet Kola Peninsula, reporting that the Soviets abandoned a drilling project when the temperature rose to two thousand degrees Fahrenheit and their audio equipment began picking up the screams of the damned.[20] Amazingly, many Christians took this silly story seriously, some even considering it startling new evidence to convert recalcitrant atheists![21]

This incident clearly evinces the lamentable failure of Christians to think systematically about theology, science, and the relation between the two. This makes them easy targets for Robert Ingersoll's mockery of the ascension:

> Which way did he go? Of course, that depends upon the time of day he left. If he left in the evening, he went exactly the opposite way from that he would have gone had he ascended in the morning. What did he do with his body? How high did he go? In what way did he overcome the intense cold? The nearest station is the moon, 240,000 miles away. Again I ask, Where did he go? He must have had a natural body, for it was the same body that died. His body must have been material, otherwise he would not, as he rose, have circled with the earth, and he would have passed from the sight of his apostles at the rate of more than a thousand miles per hour.[22]

One can readily add a number of further queries to Ingersoll's list. Did Jesus need a space suit? How high did he go before he got to heaven? And for that matter, what about his anticipated return? How long will it take? Might NASA begin to track his approach from beyond the moon? And as he descends upon Israel, will he have to avoid the flight paths of El Al Airlines? Such questions remind us that even if Christianity can be reconciled to the size and age of the universe, we still founder on the plausibility and even coherence of the doctrines of the ascension, session, and second coming of Christ in a heliocentric universe. Roy Clements captures the problems in the incredulity of a "doubting Thomas": "Where is this Father's house, Jesus? The third street on the right past Mars? And how do you plan to get there? Rocket ship—or will you beam up, like Captain Kirk of the starship *Enterprise*? No, all these metaphysics are too airy-fairy for me."[23] The challenge then is to bring these metaphysics back to earth. One thing is clear: we can ill-afford the kind of cognitive dissonance that confesses the Apostles' Creed as if Copernicus never existed.

As we turn to reflect on the heliocentric challenge to the ascension (and by implication the session and second coming), it is clear that the first casualty is the three-tiered cosmology itself. Thus if our understanding of doctrine once depended upon it, we must recognize that it can no longer. As Mark Harris puts it, "As long as the ascension is in any way related to upward movement (like an elevator going to the clouds), I am and will continue to be unmoved."[24] But how much beyond this concession do we need to go? In his influential essay "New Testament and Mythology" Rudolf Bultmann admonishes the abandonment of all doctrines that assume the three-storied universe since "it is impossible to repristinate a past world picture by sheer resolve, especially a *mythical* world picture, now that all of our thinking is irrevocably formed by science."[25] To illustrate Bultmann's point, imagine a young man named Pepé who was raised in an indigenous people group where he was taught the following cosmogonic story: "There was an egg laid by the great white stork which broke into pieces. The broken shell shards formed the great land, the albumen created the seas, and the yolk became all life." Now imagine that Pepé leaves his native land in order to pursue a Ph.D. in cosmology at Oxford University. If Pepé were to continue to grant religious authority to that cosmogonic myth, we may not agree with his decision, but we could at least understand it. However, we would consider it ridiculous if he poured effort into proving that the myth was really congruent with science (for instance, arguing that the shell shards provided a startling anticipation of plate tectonics). Bultmann wants to keep Christians from falling into a similar absurdity of coating their religious beliefs with a veneer of scientific respectability, for such a program is no more viable for Christians than for Pepé. C.S. Lewis recognized the point when he admitted that it strikes non-Christians as absurd to learn that Christians believe that God has a son who descended from heaven "just as if God had a palace in the sky from which He had sent down his 'Son' like a parachutist," only to ascend later to his Father "as if by a balloon."[26] While the Creed appears as embarrassingly mythical as Pepé's cosmogony, Christians seem to confess it with the same sobriety that they read the newspaper.

To many, the ascension will appear just as theologically crude and scientifically absurd as the Mormon's belief in God living near Kolob. Bultmann is thus emphatic that we must recognize the deep and pervasive mythological framework of the Christian narrative. As he bluntly puts it, "the stories of Christ's descent and ascent are finished, and so is the expectation of the Son of Man's coming on the clouds of heaven and of the faithful's being caught up to meet him in the air (1 Thes. 4:15ff.)."[27] If nothing else, Bultmann is admirably consistent in his program of demythologizing the New Testament Christ-narrative from the resurrection to second coming. But that very consistency creates a dilemma, for while the ascension may appear to be a mythological vestige, no evangelical can surrender the resurrection or second coming, and so we seem to be stuck between the rock of Christ and the hard facts of modern cosmology.

Although Bultmann is right to warn against arbitrarily cherry-picking which doctrines to keep,[28] he may be guilty of doing just this. After all, the same "modern man" that rejects heaven, hell, angels and devils also rejects the very existence of God, and thus consistency would oblige Bultmann to embrace atheism.[29] But if Bultmann rejects atheism, why does he accept a naturalism elsewhere that rejects miracles (including the preeminent miracle of the resurrection)? Rather than revise doctrine based on the subjective whims of "modern man" we ought to do so based on the securest deliverances of the scientific consensus, and heliocentrism is surely one of the most fundamental and secure of those deliverances. And while science per se does not present a significant challenge to the resurrection, it does seem to challenge the ascension, session and second coming. Not only does the ascension's placing of Christ "above" us in heaven seem to be scientifically erroneous, but one might argue that it is theologically erroneous as well. The error here is as basic as the Mormon's locating God near "Kolob": that is confusing the literal with the symbolic. God is not a physical being such that he can be located near a star, or anywhere else in (or above) the physical universe.

However, if there is a theological reason to question the ascension, there is another powerful theological reason to retain it: Christ was made *eternally* man,[30] and as man we must locate him *somewhere*. In the remainder of this chapter we will thus seek a viable explanation of Christ's ascension. To that end we shall proceed in three steps, beginning in the next section by noting the biblical support for the ascension and its fuller theological meaning. Then in the second and third sections we will consider two very different models of the ascension which I call the "changing places" (CP) model and the "changing states" (CS) model that are commonly associated with Calvinism and Lutheranism respectively. The CP model maintains the physicality of the body of Christ and thus conceives of the ascension as a literal transportation of Christ's body from one physical locale to another. In contrast, the CS model draws on the claim that Jesus was transformed at the ascension such that his body came to transcend physical presence. Charles Hodge provided a helpful description of both positions, commenting that on the Reformed view (CP) the ascension constitutes "a transfer from one place to another, from the earth, as one sphere of the universe, to heaven, another, and equally definite locality" while "the Lutherans made it a mere change of state, of which change the human nature of Christ was the subject."[31] We will now set the stage for a deeper exploration of the issue beginning with a look at the biblical credentials for the ascension doctrine.

The Biblical Problem of the Ascension

Confess in your average evangelical Bible study that you have your doubts about the virgin birth or resurrection and you will likely hear an audible gasp and feel a noticeable drop in room temperature. But express similar doubts about the ascension and you will likely see little more than puzzlement on the faces of your peers. Indeed, many are only vaguely aware that it is something we are supposed to *believe* at all. Nor are evangelicals alone in this ambivalence. And it is not hard to understand why, for (with the exception of the clause "he descended into hell") no article in this creed of essentials appears to be so, well, *non-essential*. Yet even though the ascension does not initially appear to be of the same dogmatic import as the virgin birth or resurrection, the creed includes it as a central part of the confession, and a look at the scriptures shows why: the ascension is an important—even if overlooked—part of the Christ narrative. One finds a number of references to the doctrine in the epistles, arguably including the early kerygma received by Paul in Philippians 2:5–11, as well as the end of the hymnic formula in 1 Timothy 3:16 which proclaims Christ "taken up in glory." One finds additional references in Ephesians 4:8–10 and 1 Peter 3:18–22 which ends with Christ's ascension to the Father's right hand in heaven.[32] Meanwhile Hebrews refers both to the ascension (4:14; 9:24) and session (1:3) of Christ as our high priest to the Father. The ascension also figures into the gospel narratives including the longer ending of Mark (16:19) and, by implication in John 3:13, 6:62 and 14:2–3. However, the most important passages are found in Luke–Acts where the ascension forms an axis uniting the two books:[33]

> Luke 24:50–1: "When he had led them out to the vicinity of Bethany, he lifted up his hands and blessed them. While he was blessing them, he left them and was taken up into heaven."
>
> Acts 1:9: "After he said this, he was taken up before their very eyes, and a cloud hid him from their sight."[34]

This testimony leads to an important question: why does the ascension figure so prominently in the New Testament? What is the significance of this event? Consider for a moment how much easier it would have been for the biblical writers to wrap things up with post-resurrection appearances culminating perhaps in a mysterious disappearance like Christ's departure from the Emmaus disciples: "their eyes were opened and they recognized him, and he disappeared from their sight." (Lk. 24:31) But instead of just disappearing, Jesus concludes his ministry with a very visible ascension, an event which was deemed important enough to be included in the Apostles' Creed.[35] In order to appreciate the nuances of the doctrine we should understand something of its central theological significance which will equip us to appreciate why the doctrine is worth protecting from demythologization. We can start by clarifying the meaning of the ascension beginning with the significance of the cloud that envelops Christ (Acts 1:9). Whether or not we believe that Christ was *literally* enveloped in a cloud, we should not think that the primary *point* was to provide a meteorological report. In scripture clouds symbolize the presence and mystery of God (e.g. Ex. 19:3,20,24; 24:1–2) and thus a cloud here represents Christ's assumption of divine glory[36] even as it anticipates his return on the clouds (Dan. 7:13–14; Rev. 1:7). The same basic observation applies to the elevation of Christ's body: the main point is not going *up* but rather being *exalted*. Augustine argued that God and heaven are to be thought of as above not literally but rather "by virtue of their excellence."[37] If Augustine is correct, then the primary focus of the ascension is not to demonstrate that Christ physically ascended, but rather that he was exalted to a superior place.[38] Indeed, the ascension is not simply an isolated event in which Christ is exalted, but rather is part of a process of exaltation that stretches from the resurrection to second coming.[39] Given the close relationship between these doctrines, and the historical nature of the resurrection, there is a strong drive to understand the subsequent events in literal terms. And yet, this creates a deep tension for we cannot understand the session of Christ at the Father's right hand *literally*. As John of Damascus observed, "We do not hold that the right hand of the Father is an actual place. For how could He that is uncircumscribed have a right hand limited by place?"[40] The special challenge of the ascension is thus found as we seek to understand it between the literal nature of the resurrection and the metaphorical nature of the session.

Clearly the ascension is important, but what precisely is its theological significance? To begin with, the ascension protects the continued humanity of Christ. Jesus did not discard the human body at his exaltation but rather even now continues his role as mediator, the eternal God/man. As John Jansen observes, "the Incarnation was no passing concern or diversion of God, no temporary foray of God into human existence only to withdraw again into remoteness. No, God is forever the God of the Incarnation."[41] Jesus did not simply assume humanity for a time, but has eternally identified with us, changing forever to be like us so that we might forever be like him. Third, note the angel's words immediately after the ascension: "'Men of Galilee,' they said, 'why do you stand here looking into the sky? This same Jesus, who has been taken from you into heaven, will come back in the same way you have seen him go into heaven'" (Acts 1:11). Here we see that the ascension anticipates the personal second coming: just as Christ left personally, so will he one day return. Finally, the fact that Christ has physically left us entails that there is now a *real absence* and this provides the space for a healthy pneumatology. Though Christ is gone, we are not forgotten, for in his place he has sent a comforter, the promised Holy Spirit (Jn. 14:26). And lest we pine for the good old days of Galilee, Jesus even said that it was *for our benefit* that he was leaving, such was the importance of the Spirit's promised ministry (Jn. 16:7).[42]

As we proceed it should be noted that the question of the ascension and session arose during the Reformation in a surprising place: debates over the presence of Christ in the Eucharist. Martin Luther argued that Christ's body became omnipresent in the exaltation, thereby allowing it to be spiritually present within the Eucharist. But Ulrich Zwingli and John Calvin objected that Christ could not be spiritually present in the bread since they denied that his physical body was exalted to omnipresence and thus concluded that he is concretely located in heaven. This Eucharistic debate has immediate implications for our current concern regarding the place of Christ in the ascension. The CS model seeks to explain Christ's presence based on Lutheran assumptions while the CP model does so relative to the Reformed perspective. Intriguing though each explanation is as a means to restore the plausibility of the Christian confession of the ascension, as we shall see each also exacts a significant cost.

Ascension as Changing Places

The changing places model takes the Lukan ascension narrative at face value: Jesus really did ascend through space in order to arrive at heaven. Though this interpretation certainly takes the text seriously, it appears to do so by ignoring the last few centuries of scientific advance. Simply put, if the CP model is to survive, it must explain this bodily transferral in a way that is congruent with heliocentrism. But prior to developing a possible explanation we first need to be clear on the core assumptions of the CP model, beginning with the following premise:

(1) All physical substances are extended in space.

Premise (1) is an *analytic* statement, meaning that its predicate "extended in space" is simply an articulation of the *meaning* of "physical substance;" it is an analysis of the concept. As such, (1) is necessarily true: by definition, there can be no physical substance which is not extended in space. Next, we add:

(2) Jesus' body is a physical substance.

Note the form of the claim: Jesus' body is *now* a physical substance, a claim that follows from his status as eternally incarnate. From this it follows:

(3) Therefore, Jesus' body is extended in space.

This final premise requires little comment, for it follows of logical necessity from (1) and (2). Nonetheless, it raises a rather obvious question: in *which* space is Jesus presently located? To put it simply, *where is Jesus*? Scripture provides the following answer:

(4) Jesus' body is in heaven.

And there we find an answer to our question as well as a rather striking conclusion about the nature of heaven:

(5) Therefore, heaven is a spatial location.

If Jesus exists *in* heaven, and Jesus' body is physical, then it follows that heaven is a place with spatial dimensions. As Augustus Strong put it, "Heaven would seem to be a place, because Christ's body is there."[43] So the CP model commits us to the view that there are two physical spaces—earth[44] and heaven—with the ascension being the event through which Christ transitions from the one to the other. And so Wayne Grudem observes, "The fact that Jesus had a resurrection body that was subject to spatial limitations (it could be at only one place at one time) means that Jesus went *somewhere* when he ascended into heaven."[45] And Louis Berkhof refers to the ascension as "a local transition, a going from place to place" which "implies, of course, that heaven is a place as well as earth."[46] Likewise, Charles Hodge asserts that the ascension "was a local transfer of his person from one place to another; from earth to heaven. Heaven is therefore a place."[47] While this position comports with a straightforward reading of the Luke–Acts ascension narrative, it still appears completely implausible. Hence, it is critical that the CP model proffer a suitable explana-tory framework.

Though Reformed theologians have typically agreed that "the right hand of the Father" is a reference to God's rule rather than a place,[48] they have argued based on Christ's physical body that heaven is a place.[49] Indeed, many in the past explicitly endorsed the notion that heaven is somehow elevated over the earth, thereby securing the meaning of the ascension in the most literal sense. Hence, Heinrich Heppe asserts that "the ascension in the strictest sense of the word is to be thought of as a spatial bodily event, as the *raising of the God-man from a lower to a higher place*, so that from the ascension of the Lord onward until his return to earth Christ's humanity is no longer present."[50] As such, Heppe seems to distance himself from Augustine's claim that the directionality of the ascension is wholly a reference to ontological perfection, arguing instead that Christ ascended to "the highest and loftiest glory of God, which (above the air-layer enveloping the earth, as well as above the sphere of the heavenly world-bodies) is the dwelling-place of the blessed spirits, the highest (third) heaven."[51] This strikingly concrete description of Christ moving *above* "the air-layer enveloping the earth" is complemented by the seventeenth century Reformed theologian Heidegger who provides a veritable roadmap of Christ's journey: "He crossed the heavens; the first, in which the air is, and the second in which the stars, sun and planets are . . . And this highest heaven is the place and dwelling of Christ and the blessed."[52] Since the three-storied universe is unsalvageable the CP model must explain Christ's bodily transfer without any dependence upon it. Although I make no claim to exhaust the viable options, I will consider here two different possibilities which I will call the non-overlapping heaven view and overlapping heaven view. Each construes the heaven/earth relationship in a particular way and then in that light purports to offer a scientifically plausible account of how Christ moved from earth to heaven.

The non-overlapping view understands heaven and earth to be non-overlapping spheres. Nonetheless, the ascension demonstrates that it is possible to travel from one to the other (think of a literal Jacob's ladder or stairway to heaven). Incredible though that claim may seem on first blush, the CP model views it as a demand given that Jesus eternally has a physical body. In short, if the physical body of Christ passed from earth to heaven, then it would seem that there must be a physical path through which he traveled.[53] Otherwise he never would have arrived at heaven. But what kind of thing might this portal to heaven be? On this question theoretical physics offers us an intriguing possibility: the wormhole. This exotic entity is a tunnel connecting two points in space/time which theoretically would allow a person to pass from one point to another without traversing the intervening points. To illustrate, think of a sheet of paper with two points at opposite ends. In conventional wisdom the quickest way to get from point A to point B is by making a beeline between them. But if one folded the paper so that the points overlapped one another then one would no longer need to traverse the entire distance of the sheet in order to get to point B since it would be immediately proximate to A. This shortcut between the two points is analogous to a wormhole in space. (The main difference is that the sheet is two-dimensional while the universe is three dimensional.) The theory of wormholes is based on the notion that three-dimensional space is thus curved like that two dimensional piece of paper such that certain points in space can be "folded over" one another and connected like the two points on the paper. A traversable wormhole is one that is sufficiently large and stable to allow a human being to pass through it, thereby enabling travel to a distant part of the universe. Physicists speculate that wormholes might even connect two separate universes, thereby allowing travel between them.

If one could, in principle, travel through a wormhole to a separate galaxy or even universe, could one then travel through a wormhole to heaven? If we accept the spatial definition of heaven, then this seems to be a legitimate possibility. Of course, since the wormhole could theoretically open up at any point in space/time, strictly speaking the ascension is not necessary. Jesus could just as well have entered a wormhole after dinner with the disciples on the road to Emmaus. But the fact is that he did elevate through space (probably as an accommodation to first-century science as well as a symbolic representation of his exaltation). As such, we can surmise that the wormhole opened up at the apogee of Christ's ascent.[54]

While this non-overlapping theory has appeal, it also raises formidable concerns. To begin with, there is the rather obvious problem that in hitching one's wagon to a controversial concept like the wormhole, one is subject to the vagaries of scientific consensus. Hence, if physicists establish in the future that traversable wormholes are physically impossible then one would lose their means of transfer (or at least a plausible non-miraculous basis for it).[55] More basically, the account will strike many as a fanciful exercise in science fiction which adds little plausibility to the ascension.

The basis for the overlapping understanding of heaven is captured by Millard Erickson's suggestion that "God is in a different dimension of reality, and the transition from here to there requires not merely a change of place, but of state. So, at some point, Jesus' ascension was not merely a physical and spatial change, but qualitative-spiritual as well. At that time Jesus underwent the remainder of the metamorphosis begun with the resurrection body."[56] Based on these remarks, I suspect that Erickson would find the notion that heaven is just another spatial realm that can be accessed through the correct portal as lacking in theological nuance. His alternative proposal can be understood as a way to transcendentalize heaven as the spiritual dimension of this universe which would imply that Christ's journey to heaven ought to be understood more in terms of an ontological change than a geographical one. Heaven is not above the earth or a separate reality accessed through a portal, but rather is the spiritual dimension of our world. A helpful analogy of this notion of heaven is found in Alejandro Amenábar's film *The Others* in which Grace Stewart (Nicole Kidman) and her two children live in an old house that appears to be haunted. At the end of the film (warning: spoiler ahead!) we discover that in fact Grace and her children are the ghosts while their encounters with the dead were in fact glimpses of the living. This image of an overlapping spiritual reality reminds one of the key references to spiritual activity in 2 Kings 6:15–17 and Daniel 10:10–20. In building on such cryptic texts, a number of Reformed theologians appear to view heaven overlapping the world in analogous terms to this picture of the paranormal world overlapping (and interacting with) the physical world. Thus, Wayne Grudem observes that "we cannot now see where Jesus is, but that is not because he passed into some ethereal 'state of being' that has no location at all in the space-time universe, but rather because our eyes are unable to see the unseen spiritual world that exists all around us."[57] Similarly, J. Oliver Buswell writes: "I do not think that heaven is any great distance away. If it were the will of God, we could see the face of our Lord Jesus Christ at any moment."[58] And thus the ascension does not consist of Jesus moving to a spatially distinct part of the universe (let alone another universe) but rather of entering into a higher spiritual reality in our midst.

The overlapping view appears to offer a degree of theological nuance missing from the non-overlapping approach, for it qualifies that Christ's physical body and heaven's spatial reality are qualitatively different from mundane physical reality. But can we explain the relationship between the two spheres with greater precision than an analogy with ghostly hauntings? Buswell struggles to forge a more concrete analogy by appealing to the reception of radio waves: although the radio broadcast is all around us, we cannot detect it unless we are properly attuned to it. Heaven is thus a spiritual reality which exists in our midst but which we are presently unable to experience because we are not attuned to it.[59] Unfortunately this analogy breaks down at the critical point because heaven is not simply like a broadcast that can be heard but rather according to (5), is itself a concrete realm into which one can enter. Fortunately, we find a point of illumination in another controversial scientific notion: that of hyperspace or extra-dimensionality. This concept originates in string theory and posits that there are *seven* spatial dimensions that we do not experience in addition to width, length and height.[60] Astronomer and Christian apologist Hugh Ross has applied this theory to a range of theological issues including the ability of the resurrected Jesus to disappear suddenly (Lk. 24:31) and apparently to pass through solid doors (Lk. 24:36).[61] Ross argues that Christ accomplished these feats by "rotating" his body out of the three mundane spatial dimensions and into higher spatial dimensions.[62] If this is a valid explanation then it provides a fascinating possibility for the ascension as well. Perhaps heaven just is the realm of some (or all) of these extra spatial dimensions. This would seem to allow us to have a heaven that truly is a higher realm in our midst and yet one that, like the wave lengths of a radio broadcast, remains undetectable to us. As for the ascension, following Ross's account we could argue that Jesus "rotated" his physical body into the relevant hyper-dimensions (perhaps right at the moment when he disappeared in the cloud).

While the extra-dimensionality account of an overlapping heaven is certainly intriguing it faces at least two serious objections. First, while string theory has garnered much attention in the last twenty years, it remains controversial;[63] as such we should be very careful about building too much theologically on such an insecure foundation. Second, even if its scientific credentials were thoroughly established, extra-dimensionality would not achieve its aim for as William Lane Craig points out, if these higher dimensions exist then they do not constitute a separate realm from the three basic spatial dimensions; rather, the higher dimensions are *inclusive* of the lower.[64] As such, if Christ entered into higher spatial dimensions, he would still have height, width and length, and thus we would still have to account for the whereabouts of his body.

Ascension as Changing States

Perhaps the problem with the overlapping extra-dimensional account of heaven is that it does not go far enough in emphasizing the ontological difference between the incarnate Christ on earth and the ascended Christ in heaven. A more radical approach along this trajectory is found in a Lutheran Sunday school curriculum which, as Douglas Farrow summarizes, explains that at the ascension "Jesus stopped being present in one place at a time" so that "he could start being present everywhere at once."[65] The curriculum then provides an illustration for the claim: dissolve a water soluble tablet in a glass of water and explain that just as the tablet becomes ubiquitous in the water, so in the ascension Christ became ubiquitous in creation. The position offers a radical advance over the overlapping view of heaven which remains committed to the fact that Christ is concretely embodied in a specific place. By contrast, according to the CS model Christ changed states such that his humanity came to be omnipresent like his divinity from which it follows that the body of Christ, like the dissolved tablet, is to be found both *everywhere* and *nowhere*.

Not surprisingly, the CS model makes much of the point that the right hand of the Father is not a *place* but rather the omnipresent *rule* of God. Similarly, heaven is to be understood not as a concrete space, but rather the transcendent presence of God. As such, the CS model replaces (5) with

(6) Heaven transcends space.

At the same time the CS model agrees with the scriptural teaching that Jesus is in heaven (4) but in light of (6) the meaning of this is redefined:

(7) Jesus' body is in heaven.
(8) Therefore, Jesus' body transcends space.

To say that Jesus' body transcends space is to say at minimum that his body is not located at a specific point *within* space:

(9) Therefore, Jesus' body is not extended in space.

As we said above, this means that Jesus is both everywhere and nowhere, omnipresent in his humanity and his divinity. As a result, it is misguided to ask where Jesus is, for he is in no particular place. As Bruce Demarest and Gordon Lewis observe, "it is impossible to locate the Father or the Son at a particular place in space and time, such as some nova far out in space. Hence it has become commonplace to say that the ascension involved not a change of place but a change of state."[66] As we saw in chapter four, Martin Luther described this exaltation in terms of the *communicatio idiomatum*, that is, the communication of the divine and human natures such that we predicate human properties of the divine nature and, at the exaltation, divine properties of the human nature. As such, on this view at the exaltation Jesus became omnipresent in the human nature: like the Father and Spirit Jesus too is now everywhere.[67]

Although the CS model maintains the continued humanity of Christ in principle, we must ask what sense is left of the humanity of Christ once we claim that his human body is omnipresent? If the CP model is liable to the charge of having too low a view of the humanity of Christ, the CS model is surely liable to the charge of losing the humanity altogether. Robert Jenson, himself a Lutheran, is well aware of this tension, noting the danger in which we "envision the risen Christ as *not* embodied, as a pure 'spirit,' or perhaps as embodied in a a [sic] very thinned-out fashion, as—not to be too fine about it—a spook. A body requires its place, and we find it hard to think of any place for this one."[68] If every body has its concrete place then for Christ's human body no longer to have place is for that body no longer to exist. And since embodiment is central to realized human personhood, it becomes doubtful that Christ is a human being any longer. In short, the CS model appears to collapse into monophysitism.

If this charge is to have weight, we should be clear on the biblical, historical and theological reasons for the confession of Christ's eternal humanity. Note first that while scripture clearly states that Christ *became* incarnate (Jn. 1:14; Phil. 2:6) it *never* states that Christ later *divested* himself of his humanity, and so we have no right to conclude this. What is more, indirect evidence supports the continued humanity of Christ. For instance, Paul argues that our future resurrection bodies will be like Christ's (1 Cor. 15) and if ours are to be eternal, surely it is assumed that Christ's body is as well. Further, Paul describes the session as involving the continual mediation of the *man* Jesus (1 Tim. 2:5),[69] and Jesus' second coming is understood as the coming of the *Son of Man*.[70] This evidence that Jesus *remained* a man at the resurrection and ascension is reinforced by subsequent creedal testimony. The Nicene Creed simply states that Christ became a man while never stating that his humanity ceased, while the Chalcedonian Definition and Athanasian Creed both teach that Christ presently exists both in divine and human natures.[71] Given the strength of the biblical and historical testimony to the continued humanity of Christ, we should be very critical of any position that requires us to reject it.

Of course, the CS model does not explicitly reject Christ's eternal humanity, but it does seem to imply it. So in what sense can the CS model secure the physical, concretely located body of Christ? One possibility, explored by Martin Luther, is that the spiritually ubiquitous Christ becomes spiritually present in the concrete, physical elements of bread and wine at communion. Although Luther rejected the notion that the Eucharist *physically* becomes Christ's body, he did argue that it *spiritually* becomes his body. But as Jansen points out, this is surely perplexing: "Developed to safeguard the real presence of Christ in the Supper, [physical ubiquity] becomes a speculative dogmatism about the nature of Christ's heavenly body."[72] Luther recognized the perplexities of his Eucharistic doctrine: "How can a body be seated so high in glory and at the same time be here below, allowing itself to be profaned and taken by hands, mouth, and belly, as if it were a fried sausage?"[73] Here Luther faces a dilemma. Insofar as he admits that Christ's body is physical, he faces the absurdity of eating Christ like "a fried sausage." But if he responds by retreating to the spiritual presence of Christ, we seem left with a nebulous concept that again loses the concrete humanity of Christ. At this point Luther wryly invoked the mystery card by telling of an intrepid theologian who climbs stealthily up to heaven "just at midnight, when God was most soundly asleep" in order to discover the secret, but who can discover "no power that can enable a body to be at the same time in heaven and in the Supper."[74] But surely this retreat to divine mystery is wholly unsatisfactory and, in light of the viability of alternative theories, is likely to strike one as special pleading. For instance, one might find more plausibility to Zwingli's straightforward argument that if Christ has a physical body and that body is in heaven, then it cannot be present in the earthly sacrament.[75]

Even if the CS model could offer a coherent explanation of the omnipresence of Christ's human body, it would then face a dilemma regarding how to ground the *real absence* of Christ. The Heidelberg Catechism states the consequences of the ascension with simple precision: "Christ is true Man and true God: according to his human nature, he is now not upon the earth; but according to his Godhead, majesty, grace, and Spirit, he is at no time absent from us."[76] This statement represents an attempt to balance the natures: while Christ is spiritually omnipresent in his divinity, his human body has left earth and now resides in heaven. This notion of Christ's (human) absence is an important part of his own teaching at the Last Supper that prepared the way for another comforter (the Holy Spirit) who would take his place. If one affirms that Christ is omnipresent both in his divinity and humanity, then one seems to have undermined Christ's real absence and thereby rendered the Spirit's coming redundant.

Before leaving the CS model behind, we might note a distinct danger of this position. As we noted above, the key events of Christ's life and work—resurrection, ascension, session and second coming—are all intimately related such that "demythologizing" one places us on the trajectory to demythologizing others as well. Thus, insofar as the CS approach spirtualizes the ascension it places the theologian on a natural trajectory toward spiritualizing the second coming and (in the case of Bultmann) even the resurrection. For instance, if Christ's ascension involved his becoming spiritually omnipresent in his humanity, we would seem to lose any basis to conceive of the second coming in personal terms.

Conclusion

What if, as Jesus was rising off the ground, impetuous Peter had leapt up and grabbed the Lord's legs while shouting "Never, Lord! I will never let you leave us!" Then as Jesus rose up above the landscape he attempted to kick off the apostle while snapping: "Let go of me Peter! You do not have in mind the concerns of

God!" Well what if Peter *didn't* let go? What would have happened then? Where would Peter have gone? Could he have hitched a ride to heaven like riding Elijah's chariot? Or would Jesus have dissipated into the air, leaving Peter to tumble to his death on the Palestinian landscape far below? Our absolute inability to answer this very basic question suggests that we still have a very limited understanding of the ascension. We just cannot see how it *fits* into the modern world. And this leads us to a sober observation that our efforts toward making the doctrine more plausible could actually be counterproductive, with our best efforts at reconciliation coming across sounding more like a curious amalgam of naïve piety and creative science fiction than a serious doctrine from one of the world's great religions.

7

On Not Understanding Final Judgment

I believe in the Holy Ghost; the holy catholic Church; the communion of saints; the forgiveness of sins; the resurrection of the body; and the life everlasting.

At one point in the film *Talledega Nights* race car driver Ricky Bobby (Will Ferrell) sits down to eat dinner with his family. As he prays for the meal, his wife interrupts him, irritated that he keeps referring to "Baby Jesus," for as she points out, *Jesus did grow up.* Ricky is undeterred: "Well look, I like the Christmas Jesus best and I'm sayin' grace. When you say grace you can say it to grown up Jesus or teenage Jesus or bearded Jesus or whoever you want." Behind the slapstick comedy of the scene lies the human tendency to create God in our own image, a practice that is especially visible with Jesus. Among the most popular Jesuses today is the wise sage who uttered pithy aphorisms on love and forgiveness. Not surprisingly, the Jesus who demanded self-denial and warned of impending judgment has largely been forgotten. But not by everybody it would seem. Indeed, Bertrand Russell repudiated Christ precisely for his teaching on hell,[1] a teaching which the great philosopher deemed morally repugnant:

> There is one very serious defect to my mind in Christ's moral character, and that is that He believed in hell. I do not myself feel that any person who is really profoundly humane can believe in

everlasting punishment. Christ certainly as depicted in the Gospels did believe in everlasting punishment, and one does find repeatedly a vindictive fury against those people who would not listen to His preaching . . . [. . .] I really do not think that a person with a proper degree of kindliness in his nature would have put fears and terrors of that sort into the world . . . I must say that I think all this doctrine, that hell-fire is a punishment for sin, is a doctrine of cruelty.[2]

Russell's objection to the vindictive injustice of hell cuts to the heart of the traditional doctrine, but it is not the only problem with final judgment. Ironically, an equally egregious moral objection is directed at the promised bliss of heaven. The charge is articulated by Robert Ingersoll in an exchange he had with a young Presbyterian who unwittingly approached the great skeptic with an evangelistic tract, an offer of salvation, and a testimony that he was "perfectly happy." This was too much for Ingersoll who subjected the poor fellow to a stinging Socratic enquiry:

"Do you think a great many people are going to hell?"
"Oh yes."
"And you are perfectly happy?" . . . "Would you not be happier if they were all going to heaven?"
"Oh, yes."
"Well, then, you are not perfectly happy?"
No, he did not think he was.
"When you get to heaven, then you will be perfectly happy?"
"Oh, yes."
"Now, when we are only going to hell, you are not quite happy; but when we are in hell, and you are in heaven, then you will be perfectly happy? You will not be as decent when you get to be an angel as you are now, will you?"
"Well," he said, "that was not exactly it."
Said I: "Suppose your mother were in hell, would you be happy in heaven then?"
"Well," he says, "I suppose God would know the best place for mother."
And I thought to myself, then, if I was a woman, I would like to have five or six boys like that.[3]

Ingersoll presents a fair question: how can we reconcile the anticipated joys of heaven with the unimaginable horrors of hell? Isn't
this claim fundamentally incoherent, grossly immoral or both?
The contrast of a heavenly state with one of damned agony thus
compounds the moral dilemma with the traditional doctrine of
eternal punishment. Of course there would be no problem if
Christians admitted to worshipping a cruel, rapacious deity like,
say Moloch. But instead they claim that God is Supreme Love
(1 Jn. 4:8), one who, desiring to save all (1 Tim. 2:4), even sent his
Son to die for the sins of the whole world (Jn. 3:16; 1 Jn. 2:2, 4:10).
How can this claim be reconciled with the teaching of everlasting
punishment? If God is really so loving and merciful, then how
could he inflict a punishment of infinite duration and inconceivable intensity, even if the objects of punishment were wholly
debased and recalcitrant? And even if the suffering of hell were
justified, how could a heaven of infinite delights exist in its
amber glow?

Given these kinds of difficulties, it should hardly be surprising
that hell has fallen on hard times. As Clark Pinnock observes,
"The doctrine once in full flower is drooping."[4] Today reactions
to the doctrine range from vociferous denunciation to benign
neglect. It is this neglect which allows for the distorted picture of
"gentle Jesus, meek and mild." But as Dorothy Sayers reminds
us, hell is not a minor, dispensable theme in scripture:

> It confronts us in the oldest and least "edited" of the gospels: it is
> explicit in many of the most familiar parables and implicit in many
> more: it bulks far larger in the teaching than one realises, until one
> reads the Evangelists through instead of picking out the most
> comfortable texts: one cannot get rid of it without tearing the New
> Testament to tatters. We cannot repudiate Hell without altogether
> repudiating Christ.[5]

A cursory reading of the New Testament confirms Sayers' claim.
Jesus taught two parallel eternal destinies: the righteous will
enter into the fullness of God's presence, but the unrighteous will
face the "eternal punishment" (Mt. 25:46) of "eternal fire prepared for the devil and his angels" (Mt. 25:41). The horror of everlasting torment in this and other passages stands behind Jesus'

warning to be spiritually ready so as to avoid the judgment that will see one cast into the darkness (Mt. 8:12; 22:13) and fiery furnace (Mt. 13:42, 50) where there will be weeping and gnashing of teeth (Lk. 13:28). This gripping teaching was carried on faithfully by the earliest disciples. Hence, Paul warned of "everlasting destruction" (2 Thess. 1:9), Peter of "blackest darkness" (2 Pet. 2:17) and Jude of "the punishment of eternal fire" (Jude 7). But perhaps most shocking of all are the images in the Apocalypse where John describes the nature of the eternal punishment with a vividness that would empty the pews of many a seeker sensitive congregation:

> If anyone worships the beast and his image and receives his mark on the forehead or on the hand, he, too, will drink of the wine of God's fury, which has been poured full strength into the cup of his wrath. He will be tormented with burning sulfur in the presence of the holy angels and of the Lamb. And the smoke of their torment rises for ever and ever. There is no rest day or night for those who worship the beast and his image, or for anyone who receives the mark of his name. (Rev. 14:9–11; cf. Rev. 20:10,15)

While a few theologians (and many laypeople) read these varied images of darkness, gnashing teeth, a roaring furnace and a lake of crackling flames literally,[6] doing so multiplies the practical implausibilities to the doctrine.[7] Instead, it is best to interpret these different images as symbols or metaphors.[8] Even so, a metaphorical understanding of hell hardly defuses Russell and Ingersoll's objections. To illustrate, we would hardly be mollified if, after we condemned a father for promising to "beat the tar" out of his toddler, he replied that he was only speaking *metaphorically*! The moral objection does not depend on whether the father was speaking literally, but rather in his expressed intent to abuse his child. So it is with the problem of hell. Russell and Ingersoll's objections are not directed at the particular *way* individuals suffer eternally (as if combusting flesh is especially offensive), but simply *that they suffer eternally*. Indeed, if anything the problem of hell is *worse* on a metaphorical interpretation since theologians commonly warn that the *reality* of hell will be unimaginably *worse* than these metaphors can convey.[9]

We thus face a severe dilemma: how can we understand the apparent cruelty of God and callousness of the redeemed saints implied by the traditional doctrine? In formulating a response, we shall begin by tackling Russell's charge of cruelty. The crucial response that we shall consider is the free-will argument that hell is a self-imposed state that results from human free choice. After critically evaluating this response, I shall turn squarely to face Ingersoll's charge by surveying the options to relate heaven and hell. Here I will argue that the most logical means to relate the two leads to the most unthinkable consequence: that the saints shall *delight* in the suffering of the damned (an even *worse* problem than Ingersoll recognized!). Unfortunately, this seems to leave the most promising avenues of theological reflection beyond the bounds of historic orthodoxy.

Before we begin one important qualification should be made. While I will be employing the term "heaven" when referring to the final state (and place) of the redeemed, this should be understood as shorthand for the complete biblical picture of *a new heaven and new earth*. The point is an important one, for I do not believe that we are saved *out of* the material world to an ethereal heaven, but rather that our future redeemed state will include *this* creation (Rom. 8:19–21).

The Inconceivable Choice

At one point in C.S. Lewis' dreamlike fantasy *The Great Divorce* the narrator witnesses a female resident of heaven attempting to draw to repentance her earthly husband who resides in purgatory/hell.[10] When she ultimately fails, one might expect her to be grief-stricken since her beloved husband has finally chosen the way of eternal destruction. However, the husband's rejection does nothing to undermine her serene joy. When the narrator interprets this as evidence of a flawed moral character, the guide, fantasy novelist George MacDonald,[11] gently chastises him by pointing out that denying the regenerate happiness until the damned repent gives the damned power to "blackmail the universe: that till they consent to be happy (on their own terms) no one else shall taste joy: that theirs' should be the final power; that

Hell should be able to *veto* Heaven."[12] In other words, to deny the wife happiness until her husband repents is to put her under his power eternally. Are we really willing to grant the unregenerate this power? Mustn't there come a point when the redeemed are freed from the inscrutable choices of the damned? To explain this terminal rebellion Lewis invokes the inexplicable mystery of free will. That is, God so loves and values us that he will not force us to love him. Alas, this freedom results in the tragic reality of some rejecting God eternally . . . and creating hell as a result.

This free will response to Russell's objection can be applied to three alleged misconceptions of hell: namely, that God *sends* people to hell, *keeps* people in hell, and tortures people in hell. The view of the Christian God as a cruel dungeon master is a tragic, but all too common distortion. Unfortunately much of the blame must be laid at the feet of overzealous Christian teachers like the infamous fundamentalist pamphleteer Jack Chick. For decades Chick has made cartoon tracts that target everyone from evolutionists and feminists to Muslims and Catholics. One of his tracts, entitled "Somebody Goofed!" unwittingly portrays the worst misunderstandings of hell. The story opens with a wayward young man who forgoes an evangelistic offer, choosing instead to follow the bad advice of a friend. Soon thereafter the young man and his friend are killed in a train wreck only to awaken in hell. Upon realizing that he has been damned on bad advice, the young man points a shaking finger at his friend and tells him "You were wrong! You goofed!" At that moment his "friend" is revealed to be a demon who had assumed a human disguise in order to trick the young man into hell. The demon then snarls back at the horrified young man: "No little buddy. I wasn't wrong. *You were wrong.* You didn't accept Jesus Christ as your own Lord and personal savior!"[13] Surely this story represents some of the worst distortions of Christian doctrine. Especially grotesque is the image of people essentially being tricked into hell after making a few relatively trivial mistakes. And then there is the erroneous depiction of the damned young man being immediately stricken by remorse upon realization of his mistake. Once we accept this distortion of an individual being tricked into hell, it is hardly surprising that God begins to look like a sadistic torturer.

The central claim of the free-will defense is that God does not send people to hell: *they send themselves*. This claim has strong scriptural warrant, as in John 3:19: "This is the verdict: Light has come into the world, but people loved darkness instead of light because their deeds were evil." Simply put, while *God so loved the world*, many in the world did not love God in return, and thus have brought judgment upon themselves. Such is God's love that it motivated that mysterious great exchange on the cross made available to all who will choose it. C.S. Lewis stated the point well by arguing that Christianity presents us with "a God so full of mercy that He becomes man and dies by torture to avert that final ruin from His creatures, and who yet, where that heroic remedy fails, seems unwilling, or even unable, to arrest the ruin by an act of mere power."[14] Surely then God is not responsible for the impliable wills of human beings?!

A similar response is offered to the corresponding claim that God *keeps* people in hell. On the contrary, as Lewis puts it, "I willingly believe that the damned are, in one sense, successful, rebels to the end; that the gates of hell are locked on the *inside*."[15] We find biblical support for Lewis' claim in Jesus' description of "weeping and gnashing of teeth" (Mt. 8:12; 13:42,50; 22:13; 24:51; 25:30; Lk. 13:28). While it has often been assumed that this phrase reflects regret over one's past decisions, the Greek verb *brycho* (to gnash or grind teeth) is typically used to express rage or hatred. For instance, in the Septuagint[16] the verb invariably signals the desire for the destruction of another,[17] depicting, as Edward Fudge puts it, "someone so angry at another that he grinds his teeth in rage, like a mad animal straining at the leash."[18] Such is likewise the case in Acts 7:54 when Stephen's enemies gnash their teeth in rage. If so, then Jesus' warning depicts not a poor soul lamenting a string of bad decisions (i.e. someone who "goofed"), but rather the hardened heart of a dogged rebel continuing to shake his fist at God. But isn't it incredible to suppose that people could perpetually choose hell? Well perhaps not, for as psychologist Barry Schwartz observes, the emotions of pleasure and desire arise from different areas of the brain with the result that one can continue desperately to want something (i.e. a drug) even when that which is desired produces no pleasure.[19] So maybe the damned are like addicts whose insatiable desire for autonomy from God constrains their choice even as it perpetually increases their misery.

Finally, we come to what may be, from the free-will perspective, the most damaging misconception of all: the belief that God tortures people in hell. What else can be implied by the teaching that God punishes people eternally, consigning them to everlasting destruction (e.g. 2 Thes. 1:9)? It is on this point more than any other that the critics of the orthodox doctrine focus, as when Clark Pinnock states: "Everlasting torment is intolerable from a moral point of view because it makes God into a bloodthirsty monster who maintains an everlasting Auschwitz for victims whom he does not even allow to die."[20] Never one to mince words, Pinnock asks how there can be "a deity of such cruelty and vindictiveness whose ways include inflicting everlasting torture upon his creatures, however sinful they may have been? Surely a God who would do such a thing is more nearly like Satan than like God, at least by any ordinary moral standards, and by the gospel itself."[21] Here again the free will defender defuses the problem with the claim that God doesn't torture people; rather, people torture themselves by choosing to reject God. Thus, the torture is imposed not by God but rather by the self as the phrase "he is his own worst enemy" finds a final, tragic expression. If we accept the point that people can continue to reject God, then we can likewise accept that in doing so they ensure their own torment. Again, psychological reflection reinforces the credibility of the claim. As Lewis observes, "Ye see it easily enough in a spoiled child that would sooner miss its play and its supper than say it was sorry and be friends."[22] Indeed, how often people stubbornly deny themselves happiness, thereby setting themselves on a continuing spiral of misery. In the same way that self-destructive behavior is often rationalized in this life, so it may continue to be rationalized eternally. The number of potential rationalizations is without limit: "One will say he has always served his country right or wrong; and another that he has sacrificed everything to his Art; and some that they've never been taken in, and some that, thank God, they've always looked after Number One, and nearly all, that, at least they've been true to themselves."[23] Hell thus represents God's recognition that the will has been eternally set and that the spiral will never

end. As Lewis would have it, God is none other than the eternally jilted lover: " 'What are you asking God to do?' To wipe out
their past sins and, at all costs, to give them a fresh start, smooth-
ing every difficulty and offering every miraculous help? But He
has done so, on Calvary. To forgive them? They will not be forgiven. To leave them alone? Alas, I am afraid that is what he
does."[24]

This picture of hell as the final concession to self-destructive
human free will does much to alleviate the objections raised by
Russell and Ingersoll. As such, it is all the more disappointing that
the scriptural evidence does not support the claim that God's role
in damnation is limited to a passive ratification of the choices of
interminable free agents. Consider first the claim that human
beings send themselves to hell. While this has an air of truth, it
must be balanced against two additional points. The first is restric-
ted to the Calvinist (or Augustinian) theologian who believes that
God determines the choices of free agents.[25] On the Calvinist's
double causation view, Dave accepts Christ freely because God
determined his will to choose Christ freely while Shauna rejects
Christ freely because God determined her will to reject Christ
freely.[26] But here is the question: if God *could* have determined
Shauna (and indeed all people) to accept Christ freely like Dave,
why didn't he do so? Why does God determine some creatures to
choose damnation? In Romans 9 Paul seems to suggest a rather
straightforward reason: God simply loves some people and hates
others: "Just as it is written: 'Jacob I loved, but Esau I hated'"
(Rom. 9:13). Hence those God loves he determines to choose him
while those God hates he determines to reject him. It is important
to emphasize that there is nothing in individuals *per se* that makes
God love some and hate others (as if the Jacobs of the world are
inherently more loveable than the Esaus), for it is God that first
determines their wills either to be in accord with his or to rebel
against it. And so it follows that God elects to save some and to
damn others.[27] Whatever one might say for this view, it cannot be
reconciled with the free will defense of hell.

But what if one rejects the Calvinist view? Could one then
claim that hell is simply a self-imposed choice? This brings us to
our second problem: the biblical data suggest that God's role in
sending people to hell is more involved than the ratification of a

prior human decision. For instance, when Jesus describes the separation of the sheep and goats into their respective groups we discover that some goats thought they were sheep while some sheep thought they were goats. At face value this active divine judgment is very different from the passive ratification of a human decision. Further, the hellish end of judgment is not as passive as the free will response suggests: God does not pronounce on the fate of the goats by saying "Depart from me, you who are cursed, into the self-imposed torment of your own distorted wills." Rather, he proclaims "Depart from me, you who are cursed, into the eternal fire prepared for the devil and his angels" (Mt. 25:41). That is, the same God who actively judges the goats has *personally prepared* a place of torment for them.

Not only does God have an active role in sending people to hell, but scripture suggests that he has an equally active role in *keeping* them there and visiting his holy wrath upon them, that is, *torturing* them. While theologians are loathe to admit that God tortures people in hell,[28] this is really just a definitional issue. The *Oxford English Dictionary* defines torture as "the infliction of severe pain as a punishment or a forcible means of persuasion."[29] Not only does this mean hell is torture, but God, as the inflictor of this pain, is the torturer. And if one attempts to contend the point, there is ample biblical evidence to support God's role in visiting punishment. Take for instance the rich man in the Lazarus parable (Lk. 16:19–31) who awaits judgment in the interim state. Far from gnashing his teeth in rebellion, he appears anguished and fearful (v. 24), and even surprisingly altruistic in his concern for his siblings (vv. 27–28). Perhaps the relevance of this passage can be disputed because it is both parabolic and concerned with the interim (rather than final) state, but the same cannot be said of the profoundly disturbing portrayal of God's active punishment of the unregenerate in Revelation 14. In verses 9–11 we read of God pouring out the wine of his divine fury on the damned. As if this image were not shocking enough, John then describes the winepress of God's wrath into which damned humanity is cast in order to be pummeled by the divine judgment until their blood flows for a distance of 300 kilometers (vv. 14–18). And what may be most disturbing of all, this punishment is not tucked off in a corner of the new creation out of the sight and mind of the redeemed; rather, the unregenerate are tortured *in the presence of Christ and the angels*. Clearly the damned are *not* the agents of their own suffering here as if they were burning and crushing themselves while God helplessly watched! On the contrary, they are the anguished recipients of every blow of divine wrath.

But even if hell is in part self-imposed, it is difficult to see how the punishment fits the crime. Pinnock charges that eternal conscious torment flouts the justice of equivalency (an eye for an eye) taught in Exodus 21:24: "Did the sinner visit upon God everlasting torment? Did he cause God or his neighbors everlasting pain and loss?"[30] Indeed, how could the finite sins of even the most debauched life ever merit an infinite punishment? The apparent injustice is evident in Abraham's terse response to the rich man's plea for a reprieve: "Son, remember that in your lifetime you received your good things, while Lazarus received bad things, but now he is comforted here and you are in agony" (Lk. 16:25). Isn't God's judgment of eternal torment grossly excessive for the crime of neglecting the poor? (We may frown upon the selfish rich man, but surely he's no Hitler!)

Theologians have responded to this problem in a number of ingenious ways. To begin with, it has been argued that all sin is ultimately against God (as Psalm 51:4 implies). Anselm then adds that a sin against an infinitely great individual is itself infinite and thus requires an infinite payment.[31] But the operative principle here—the so-called "status principle" that an offense against a greater being requires greater punishment—is controversial.[32] And even if there is such a principle which dictates that such suffering is moral, must a merciful God *require it*?[33] Jonathan Kvanvig summarizes the dilemma: "To many—even to many who would declare their allegiance to the revelation of God in Christ—hell is the paradigm of truly pointless, gratuitous suffering."[34] Others have suggested that hell may exist to provide an eternal, smoldering deterrent to keep any regenerate citizens from falling into sin.[35] But this cannot work, for since in eternity the regenerate will be fully in Christ's image, it would seem that sin is no more possible for them at that point than it is for Christ (i.e. not at all). Hence, hell as deterrent would simply be redundant. Further, this claim depends upon an implausible premise that the effectiveness of a deterrent is dependent upon it being actualized but surely this is erroneous. Instead, every time someone was about to sin, God could simply give him/her a vision of the hellish consequences of capitulating to the sin: surely that would be deterrent enough. Finally, one might object that it is wrong to use some individuals as object lessons for others.

Before we leave the free will defense behind we must scrutinize an essential premise that lies at its heart: the absolute inviolability of free will. The assumption seems to be that God must respect human free will at all times which means he is constrained to allow people to do the most self-destructive actions if they so choose. But is this assumption so obvious? Parents benevolently frustrate the desires of their children all the time. Why mightn't God do the same? For instance, if an individual truly was hell-bent for destruction, why couldn't God temporarily determine his/her free will in a way that brings that individual to appreciate the error of his/her ways? The free will defender's response is predictable: what if the moment God lifts his control, the person were to fall right back into sin? What if it were the case that certain individuals just will not choose the good no matter how many times God intervenes to set them right? Perhaps God is forced to choose either to create an automaton or recognize that individual's prerogative to rebel in a way that will ultimately lead to damnation. In response I would offer two scenarios and ask us to reflect on which we find preferable. In the first scenario ten billion people choose salvation and ten billion people choose damnation: the first group experiences ineffable joy while the second group experiences unutterable agony, yet all have chosen freely. In the second scenario all twenty billion people choose salvation though 10 billion do so freely and 10 billion do so by God overriding their freedom and determining their choice. Note that in this second scenario the subtlety of God's action is such that nobody would or could know whether their choices had been determined. (Phenomenologically, the interior life of the determined would be indistinguishable from the non-determined.) Now imagine that you have the choice of which world to be born into knowing that in the first you have a fifty percent chance of damning yourself to hell, while in the second you have a fifty percent chance of being determined to heaven. I know which world *I* would choose! At this point it seems to me that philosophers and theologians who argue for the absolute inviolability of free will improperly weigh the abstract metaphysics of freedom over the visceral desire to avoid incredible suffering.[36] But if we would choose blissful determination over freely chosen damnation, then wouldn't God choose it for us as well?

The View From Above

Some time ago my wife and I watched the riveting documentary *One Day in September* which chronicles the 1972 Summer Olympics kidnappings in Munich. I shall never forget one haunting aerial shot looking down on the Olympic village. The scene begins with athletes serenely playing ping pong and lounging at poolside, but then it slowly pans to the horror of the Israeli hostage site a few hundred meters away. The scene affected me deeply as the casual leisure of the athletes spoke volumes on the callous depth of human fallenness. And yet that scene, forever etched in my mind, fades in comparison to that most shocking of all juxtapositions: the bliss of the saints of heaven even as the unregenerate hordes in hell are subjected to unspeakable agony. Here we face the problem raised by Ingersoll, one which the free will defense, whatever its success at defending the justice of hell, is unable to address. That problem, in short, is that it would seem for heaven to exist, its occupants would have to be inconceivably callous, a quality hardly indicative of perfectly Christ-like beings.

Traditional theologians will protest what they see as a deeply misleading illustration for heaven and hell are not bordering territories like the two sections of the Olympic Park! Not only are they not geographically contiguous, but neither are they ontologically parallel. C.S. Lewis made the point eloquently in *The Great Divorce* which opens in a shadowy and drizzly city that, as it turns out, is purgatory for some and hell for others. A number of people in the city board a flying bus which soars up above the vast city and continues in the clouds for many hours until it scales the face of a massive cliff and touches down in an incredible land of such vivid reality that even the grass hurts one's feet:

they have arrived at the borderlands of heaven. The narrator spends some time in this land watching the other denizens of the city—ghostlike personas like himself—refuse the entreaties of their angelic and redeemed greeters to surrender their commitment to the city and begin to adapt to a fully redeemed world. Then the guide, George MacDonald, points out that the great chasm up which they traveled to arrive at the land has shrunk down to a barely perceptible crack in the ground. Or rather, he points out that it *always was* a crack from the perspective of heaven, even as it is a dizzying chasm from the perspective down below. As he puts it, "Hell is smaller than one pebble of your earthly world: but it is smaller than one atom of *this* world, the Real world. Look at yon butterfly. If it swallowed all Hell, Hell would not be big enough to do it any harm or to have any taste."[37]

Is Lewis, with his minimization of hell, on to something? Theologians have long puzzled about the ontological status of evil, with Augustine famously arguing that it is not a thing in itself, but rather the absence of good in the same way that darkness is but the absence of light. Thinking in these terms, if heaven is the fullness of being, then hell is the privation of being, or at least something *just this side* of absolute privation: "The whole difficulty of understanding hell is that the thing to be understood is so nearly Nothing."[38] When the narrator in *The Great Divorce* lodges a modest protest that the sins of a particular woman are insufficient to warrant hell since she is just a "grumbler," MacDonald responds: "The question is whether she is a grumbler, or only a grumble. If there is a real woman—even the least trace of one—still there inside the grumbling, it can be brought to life again. If there's one wee spark under all those ashes, we'll blow it till the whole pile is red and clear."[39] Lewis' primary point seems to be that those who take up permanent residence in hell lose their "ontological substantiality" in inverse proportion to the deepened ontological substantiality gained by the redeemed. And once we understand the contrast, we will have shrunk both hell and with it the emotional pull of Ingersoll's protest, down to a relative crack in the renewed creation.

The essence of the point—that heaven and hell are radically different states—is surely correct. But it seems to me doubtful that this observation really addresses the present concern. Frankly, Lewis appears to be hiding behind an equivocation on the grumbler/grumble distinction. No doubt if hell is only populated by "grumbles" then the moral objection to the enduring existence of the state is effectively eliminated. After all, a grumble is no more liable to suffering than is a burp or a gnash. It seems to me that the continued existence of these effects as something like echoes of a completed final judgment would not be particularly troubling to us.[40] The real concern is with the *producer* of the effect, the one who grumbles, burps or gnashes. Lewis seems to be saying that once the grumbler becomes a permanent resident of hell, *there is no longer a grumbler at all*. If this really is his claim, then he has adopted the position of annihilationism. Lewis is free to take that position, but then he should be clear that it is not an ontological contrast of states *per se* that really explains hell, but rather the cessation of the rebels' existence. If, on the other hand, he believes that grumblers continue to exist, then the problem remains. And what can be said of the grumblers in hell can be said of hell itself: even if you shrink it down to a crack relative to heaven, you still must consider how it relates to heaven. Shrinking the *size* of hell does not shrink the *significance* of it, or the agony of those within it. Ingersoll's problem cannot be avoided by referring vaguely to ontological disparity or grumbles without grumblers.

It is time to look inside the crack in order to consider what sort of relation the regenerate might have to the damned. What are our options for construing the relationship between the saved and lost? Perhaps the easiest answer is to deny that the saved have any knowledge of the damned at all. Sure, they may see the crack in the ground, but they don't know what is going on inside (nor do they ever have the mind to inquire). On this view Ingersoll's young Presbyterian would simply be oblivious to the suffering of his mother. Millard Erickson proposes this position of "blissful ignorance": "we may infer that we will not recollect past failures and sins and missing loved ones, since that would introduce a sadness incompatible with 'He will wipe every tear from their eyes. There will be no more death or mourning or crying or pain, for the old order of things has passed away' (Rev. 21:4)."[41] One can certainly appreciate Erickson's motivation: to be aware of the incredible suffering of the unregenerate does not seem to *fit* into a blissful, redeemed state. But can we really live with this suggestion? It seems to me that all such ivory tower claims must be tested in the light of our most intimate relations, so I will put it into a personal context with the scenario that (*God forbid!!!*) I should be saved and my daughter eternally lost. How then is our ignorance of "missing loved ones" cashed out? Does it mean that I would be resurrected unaware that I even *had* a daughter? Or would I have a memory of her, but it would be such that every time she were to come to mind (say, whatever happened to . . . ?) the angels would strum their harps harder and faster so as to divert my attention? Frankly, this "out of sight, out of mind" response seems to reduce heaven to a "matrix" whose pleasures can only be enjoyed insofar as the horrors of hell are shielded from us. I dare say, this is a far cry from Paul's promise that "we shall see face to face. Now I know in part; then I shall know fully, even as I am fully known" (1 Cor. 13:12).[42] Take the example of a pagan who converts to Christianity while all of his family members and friends reject the faith. After he dies and enters eternity, are we really to suppose that he will remain forever *unaware* of any of those damned family members and friends? Wouldn't that involve virtually the complete eradication of his personal history? And even if we could leave these familial relations forever behind, we would still have to contend with the issue of *God's* knowledge of the suffering of the unregenerate, for certainly we cannot claim that *he* is unaware. Wouldn't the God of inestimable love and mercy suffer upon knowing of the suffering of the lost? Wouldn't he lament the anguish of my daughter, the Presbyterian's mother, and countless others? But then does this reduce God to putting on a "stiff upper lip" for his heavenly guests?[43]

While the ignorance position faces significant practical and moral difficulties, it also stands in tension with biblical passages which imply that the regenerate have awareness of the eternally lost. We begin by returning to the parable of the rich man and Lazarus (Lk. 16:19–31) and its depiction of communication between Abraham and the rich man. Though the parable concerns the interim state, it is reasonable to infer from the awareness of this state that awareness will continue into the eternal state (especially since the suffering of the rich man is of no concern to Lazarus). The second case is found in Isaiah 66:24 which describes the redeemed going out and looking on the bodies of the rebels whose "worm will not die, nor will their fire be quenched." Here we have a reference to awareness by the regenerate of those who have been judged even after their final judgment has been completed. Finally, we come back to the terrifying image of Revelation 14 noted above where those who accept the mark of the beast "will be tormented with burning sulfur in the presence of the holy angels and of the Lamb." We must take in the full, awesome implications of this spectacle. While there is no explicit mention of redeemed human beings, it seems plausible to conclude that they too would be aware of the judgment. As such, it is simply disingenuous to suggest that hell might be reduced to an insignificant atom, a barely noticeable crack, or perhaps a forgotten locked door concealed behind pleasant shrubbery.

Once we concede that the redeemed will be aware of the lost, we have three possible ways to construe that relationship. The first and second are rather weak and can be dealt with fairly quickly. The first position suggests that the bliss of the saved will be somewhat muted because of their knowledge of the lost, that glorification will include suffering with the lost. As Ted Peters puts it, if the redeemed "love sympathetically, they too would feel the pain of the damned."[44] The problem with this option is that there just is no room in the eternal blessed state for such sadness (Rev. 21:4), and so while it is psychologically plausible, it is biblically impossible.[45] Second, we might consider that the saved, though aware of the lost, will be indifferent to their suffering—a view which is implied by Lewis' depiction of the wife unmoved by her husband's rebellion. While this position might seem to some an attractive golden mean, to me it is rather the paradigm case of an unworkable compromise. If hell is the outworking of God's perfect justice upon the most belligerent rebel, how could the redeemed possibly remain indifferent? This sounds about as plausible as rabid English football fans remaining indifferent to England defeating Argentina for the World Cup.

So how would England react to the humiliated Argentinians? With inexpressible triumph and joy of course! And that brings us to what seems to be both the most powerful and worrisome option: the regenerate will be both aware of and satisfied in the punishment visited upon the damned.[46] Indeed, they will *delight* in the suffering of the damned and praise God the more for it. As unthinkable as this suggestion may sound, it has been defended with impeccable logic by some of Christianity's greatest minds. Hence, Thomas Aquinas argued:

> Nothing should be denied the blessed that belongs to the perfection of their beatitude. Now everything is known the more for being compared with its contrary, because when contraries are placed beside one another they become more conspicuous. Wherefore in order that the happiness of the saints may be more delightful to them and that they may render more copious thanks to God for it, they are allowed to see perfectly the sufferings of the damned.[47]

> It is written (Psalm lvii.11): The just shall rejoice when he shall see the revenge.[48]

Thomas' opening premise is unassailable: if heaven is to be heaven, then the regenerate cannot suffer in any way, including through compassionate suffering for the damned. He then goes further by arguing that in fact, the state of the damned *intensifies* the pleasures of the redeemed. Jonathan Edwards likewise expostulates on the suffering of the damned and our subsequent joy in it in his aptly titled "The End of the Wicked Contemplated by the Righteous: or, The Torments of the Wicked in Hell, No Occasion of Grief to the Saints in Heaven":

> The miseries of the damned in hell will be inconceivably great. When they shall come to bear the wrath of the Almighty poured out upon them without mixture, and executed upon them without pity or restraint, or any mitigation . . .[49]
>
> The saints in glory will see this, and be far more sensible of it than now we can possibly be. They will be far more sensible how dreadful the wrath of God is, and will better understand how terrible the sufferings of the damned are ; yet this will be no occasion of grief to them. They will not be sorry for the damned; it will cause no uneasiness or dissatisfaction to them; but on the

contrary, when they have this sight, it will excite them to joyful praises.[50]

One certainly must admire Edwards for not mincing his words. No half-hearted, mumbled speculation of how the loud fairway of the heavenly carnival might drown out the screams of the damned. No, here the suffering of the damned becomes one of the main attractions under the big top: not a scene for horror and anguish but rather one for cheering and praise.

One finds confirmation of this phenomenon of deriving pleasure from the misfortune of others in daily experience. You are dissatisfied with your $200,000 home . . . until you visit a third-world shanty town. And your complaint at the lazy drizzle outside your window is put into perspective by watching the latest hurricane wallop the Gulf coast on the news. Psychologists describe this phenomenon as the *contrast effect* wherein the contrast with someone else's worse condition intensifies one's pleasure or satisfaction in his/her present state.[51] It is not that you find pleasure in the sufferings of others *simpliciter* (as would a sadist), but rather that the sufferings of others unwittingly illustrate that you too could be much worse off than you are. And that is a great way to gain perspective and buoy up one's outlook.[52] Hence, Aquinas contends that against the backdrop of eternity, our pleasure will be greatly intensified as we see God's wrath visited justly upon others knowing that, but for his grace, we too could have been included in this sorry lot.

I wish I could dismiss these expostulations as the misdirected products of a bookish Italian misanthrope and a psychologically disturbed New England misfit. But the fact is that Aquinas and Edwards stand in the rarified air of the very greatest theologians and their arguments flow out of pious devotion, philosophical and psychological reflection, and yes . . . biblical exegesis. One might begin with the imprecatory psalms, so-called because they express the desire to see the destruction of the wicked. One such example is Psalm 139, a psalm which begins with a familiar paean to the sovereignty and intimate providential care of God, but ends with a less familiar curse on God's enemies: "Do I not hate those who hate you, Lord, and abhor those who are in rebellion against you? I have nothing but hatred for them; I count them my enemies" (vv. 21–22).[53] If one ought to *hate* the enemies of God, and the eternally lost are enemies of God, then one ought to *hate* the eternally lost. (And in eternity what ought to be will be.) And thus we will experience joy as they receive their deserved suffering as Revelation 14 seems to imply. In Romans 9 Paul seems to assume the contrast principle when he argues that the saved will have a fuller sense of the divine mercy by seeing the fate of the lost: "What if God, although choosing to show his wrath and make his power known, bore with great patience the objects of his wrath—prepared for destruction? What if he did this to make the riches of his glory known to the objects of his mercy, whom he prepared in advance for glory" (vv. 22–23). (Lazarus pointing at the rich man with relief: "Look at that bloke down there. That could have been *me*!") As we realize how well off we are and how merciful God has been to us, we have yet more reason for praise for we see his wrath and justice being dealt with meticulous precision upon these pitiless objects. To see God's inscrutable mercy *for us* and his righteous judgment *for them* is thus a double cause for praise. ("Look at that rich man getting his comeuppance! *Praise God!!*")[54] Reformed theologian Daniel Strange pushes the logic even further by claiming that "in their very punishment of hell, God is *giving a privilege* to the lost—the privilege of displaying his justice and his victory in the spiritual war (cf. Rom. 9:17)."[55] The damned, it would seem, are not even decent enough to appreciate the honor of being damned! (The picture is reminiscent of a fraternity initiation in which the candidate is expected to reply to each drubbing: "Thank you sir, may I have another?!") And if you find yourself distressed (or even repulsed) by this suggestion, Strange warns: "Those who find no benevolence in this privilege might be advised to consider whether their standards of goodness are sufficiently theocentric."[56]

It may be helpful at this point to provide a succinct summary of the reasoning that has led us to our incredible conclusion:

(1) Either the redeemed will be aware of the suffering of the damned or they will be unaware of it.

(2) The redeemed will not be unaware of the suffering of the damned.

(3) Therefore, the redeemed will be aware of the suffering of the damned.

(4) The redeemed will either be indifferent to the suffering of the damned, suffer themselves because of it, or take pleasure in it.

(5) The redeemed will not be indifferent to the suffering of the damned or suffer themselves because of it.

(6) Therefore, the redeemed will take pleasure in the suffering of the damned.

Ouch! As much as it hurts even to write down the conclusion of this argument, it appears to surpass the other options in biblical warrant and logical coherence. The only problem: *it appears positively inhumane.* And even the proponents of the view admit as much. So while J.I. Packer believes that we will derive satisfaction in God's judgment on the wicked, he admits, "That sounds appalling; how can it be?" In response, Packer admonishes us to "Remember, in heaven our minds, hearts, motives, and feelings will be sanctified, so that we are fully conformed to the character and outlook of Jesus our Lord."[57] Again he admits that "this sounds to us more like hard-heartedness than Christlikeness, yet Christlikeness is precisely what it will be."[58] Hence, we seem to be forced to interpret our present agony for the finally lost (including, perhaps, my daughter) as misdirected pity arising from an insufficiently holy character. Conversely, we are told that Packer's view of Christ-likeness appears counterintuitive (even repulsive) because we are sinful and "insufficiently theocentric." We are thus promised that when full Christlikeness comes, we will await God's punishing our loved ones with all the anticipation of a young boy waiting for his favorite wrestler to pummel his arch rival.

As one might expect, this claim that conformity to Christ will transform our moral revulsion into perfect joy has been met with a significant degree of skepticism. John Stuart Mill famously retorted: "I will call no being good who is not what I mean when I apply that epithet to my fellow creatures, and if such a being can sentence me to hell for not so calling him, to hell I will go."[59] Many Christians share this response, but instead of rejecting Christianity they reinterpret it. Hence, Thomas Talbott asserts that "the same God who commands *us* to love *our* enemies loves his own enemies as well."[60] It is just incomprehensible to demand that we love our enemies now, only to hate them later, that we are to grieve for their rebellion and suffering now, only to rejoice in it later. And how much more horrifying is the claim when declared of those we love and cherish most.

If we are to appreciate the radical nature of the Aquinas-Edwards proposal, we must carry this reasoning through to its final conclusion. Here again I insist that we make things personal, for the difficulties multiply exponentially when I move from an ill-defined collective mass of the damned to particular individuals, including (in that unthinkable alternate future) my beloved daughter. We begin by adding a plausible premise:

(7) The pleasure of the redeemed in the suffering of the damned includes awareness of the suffering of particular individuals.[61]

The point of (7) is that if I know a particular individual who is damned, I will derive joy not only from knowing that the total number of damned is being punished, but in addition from the *particular* knowledge that *that* specific person is being punished. Similarly, citizens of a society may take pleasure knowing that those in prison are being punished for their crimes, but those who personally know a criminal that offended them will take an additional personal satisfaction in knowing of the justice visited upon that individual. From there we can draw out the unthinkable consequences:

(8) Possibly, Randal is redeemed and Randal's daughter is damned.

(9) Therefore, possibly, Randal's pleasure in the suffering of the damned includes awareness of the suffering of his daughter.

And what might the horror of a damned child look like? Victorian child evangelist Father John Furniss painted many vivid descriptions of children facing eternal damnation including this account of a child locked in the "red-hot oven" of hell: "Hear how it screams to come out! See how it turns and twists itself about in the fire! It beats its head against the roof of the oven. It stamps its little feet on the floor. You can see on the face of this little child what you see on the faces of all in hell—despair, desperate and horrible."[62] That *could* be my daughter. And so I could have every tear wiped from my eyes even as I look on in delight at my daughter stamping her feet in rebellious agony? Shall I accept Packer's assurance that someday I shall appreciate how this horror manifests God's adorable justice? No. I could sooner believe with Ignatius Loyola that black is white and white is black than that a loving father should delight in his daughter's damnation.

I would anticipate the Aquinas-Edwards advocate providing a two-fold rebuttal. First, I could be accused of insufficient theocentricity. After all, God warned us to have no gods before him, and that includes family (Lk. 9:61–62). When the poet Ben Jonson was faced with the death of his young child, he could have cursed God, but instead he wrote "On My First Son" in which he gratefully thanked God for the time he had with his child: "Seven years thou wert lent to me." There is no bitterness here, but rather the recognition that human life is God's alone: the Lord graciously gives and sovereignly takes away. And if you don't like it, then Paul warns: "who are you, a mere human being, to talk back to God?" (Rom. 9:20) And then there is Job who, after losing everything proclaimed, "The LORD gave and the LORD has taken away; may the name of the LORD be praised" (Job 1:21). Could it be that my whole problem with (9) is rooted in idolatry? Have I placed my daughter ahead of the sovereign glory of God?

The sovereignty of God is a powerful trump card, but it does have limits. Nicolas Malebranche used it in the seventeenth century to argue for divine omnicausality, that is, the view that God is the sole cause of everything. Malebranche reasoned: if there were any other causal agency, then God's glory would be denigrated. However, as we saw in chapter three, the vast majority of Christians today would repudiate such an argument as erroneous: it is wholly God-like to grant creation its own proper being, including causal ability. But by the same token, I cannot buy the argument for divine glory. How can it be that I could be so "transformed" that I would delight in my daughter's inconceivable suffering?[63] Call me an idolater if you will, but when I make my best attempt to introspect my own motives I find a wholly self-giving love for my daughter that flows out of my love for God, rather than standing in idolatrous competition with it. And in that respect at least I may share a point with Paul who even wished for his own damnation if it could be the means to save his people (Rom. 9:3). Shall the one who wished to damn himself to save lost Jews one day rejoice in their damnation?[64]

The objector also might object to my appeal to my daughter's fate as an emotive red herring. J.I. Packer thus advocates replacing emotionally charged descriptions of hell with the neutral descriptor "divinely executed retributive process" since this phrase "is not emotionally loaded, and it should not cloud discussion by evoking prejudicial attitudes."[65] If he is against emotional language in this debate, then he would probably decry my appeal to my daughter's fate as cheap manipulation. But I would ask, which one of us is more in danger of manipulating the situation, of failing to grasp truly what is at stake. To be frank, Packer's sanitized nomenclature reminds me of the pro-choice description of the fetus as a "product of conception" and the taking of its life as the "evacuation of uterine contents." On the traditional view, hell is not an impersonal divinely executed retributive process, but rather the divine wrath poured out on individuals (perhaps including my daughter) to the delight of the elect (perhaps including me). And so again I ask, *shall we really delight in this*? Am I not shaken by Ingersoll's protest?

> The consolations of a doctrine that makes a father say, "I can be happy with my daughter in hell"; that makes a mother say, "I can be happy with my generous, brave boy in hell"; that makes a boy say, "I can enjoy the glory of heaven with the woman who bore me, the woman *who would have died for me*, in eternal agony." And they call that tidings of great joy.[66]

Conclusion

One ultimately must choose to embrace the traditional conception of hell with all its great mysteries, or to reject it. For those who deem the burden of orthodoxy too great to bear, there are other options short of apostasy. Some Christians have argued for annihilationism, the view that after the general resurrection the wicked face ultimate destruction that leads to the cessation of being.[67] Another minority has defended universalism, the view that though the unregenerate will experience incredible suffering in hell, ultimately everyone will be saved.[68] While both of these positions have powerful arguments in their favor, one must approach them with great caution as they stand outside the historical bounds of orthodox opinion.[69]

If we cannot quite agree on the nature of hell, is there anything on which we can agree? Ironically, for this I turn back to Robert Ingersoll, noting that he dedicated himself to denouncing the doctrine of damnation, vowing to speak against it "as long as there is one little red coal left in the bottomless pit. As long as the ashes are warm I shall denounce this infamous doctrine."[70] It is precisely here that I find a common ground, not with Ingersoll's repudiation of hell, but rather with his unyielding dissatisfaction that there could be such a reality. Oh that we would have the same passion to warn people away from hell that Ingersoll demonstrated in denouncing it. But instead of finding the church anguished we find apathy, and instead of passion we find passivity. It is almost enough to conclude that the greatest mystery of hell may not concern the doctrine itself, but rather our own inscrutably casual attitude toward it.

Afterword

Amen

The final word of the Creed is so small as to be easily missed. And yet when it is forgotten, as has often been the case in Christian history, the results are a cataclysmic rending of doctrine from practice. Put it this way: the demons may confess with impeccable theology the entire Creed . . . but when they come to this final word they must fall silent, for it is here that we not only confess the truth of the Creed, but we commit ourselves to *living* it. Our "Amen," our "So Let it BE!" stakes a claim that not only do we believe these truths, but we believe *in* them. Not only do we know them, but we *will* them. But if that is true, then why do we live otherwise? Why is Bertrand Russell so terribly correct to observe that "the teaching of Christ, as it appears in the Gospels, has had extraordinarily little to do with the ethics of Christians"?[1] Very simply, if we believe in the Creed then why do we not live it out? The question is indeed a simple one, but the answer plunges into the very depths of the fallen human heart and resolving it may prove to be the most difficult mystery of all.

Endnotes

One – On Not Understanding Belief

1. W.C. Placher, "Why Bother with Theology?: An Introduction," in *Essentials of Christian Theology* (ed. W.C. Placher; Louisville, KY: Westminster John Knox Press, 2003), 1.
2. "The Apostles' Creed," in *The Creeds of Christendom* Vol. 2, *The Greek and Latin Creed* (ed. P. Schaff , rev. ed. D.S. Schaff; Grand Rapids, MI: Baker, 1983), 45.
3. E.L. Mascall, *The Christian Universe* (The Boyle Lectures, 1965; London: Darton, Longman & Todd, 1966), 26.
4. M. Erickson, *Introducing Christian Doctrine* (ed. L. Arnold Hustad; 2nd edn; Grand Rapids, MI: Baker, 2001), 16.
5. G.K. Chesterton, *Orthodoxy* (1908; reprint; London: Hodder & Stoughton, 1996), 146.
6. "Paradox" derives from the Greek *"para"* (contrary to) and *"doxa"* (opinion or belief) via the Latin *"paradoxumi."*
7. N. Rescher, *Paradoxes: Their Roots, Range, and Resolution* (Chicago and La Salle, IL: Open Court, 2001), 10.
8. D. Baillie, *God was in Christ* (London: Faber and Faber, 1948), 109.
9. W. Hodges, *Logic: An Introduction to Elementary Logic* (London: Penguin Books, 1977), 15.
10. C.S. Lewis, *Miracles: A Preliminary Study* (New York: HarperCollins, 2001), 109.
11. See E.O. Wilson, *Consilience: The Unity of Knowledge* (New York: Knopf, 1998), 8.
12. Cited in Clifford Morris, "A Christian Gentleman," in *Remembering C.S. Lewis: Recollections of Those who Knew Him* (ed. J.T, Como; San Francisco: Ignatius, 2005), 320.

[13] J.I. Packer, "What did the cross achieve? The logic of penal substitution," in *The J.I. Packer Collection* (ed. Alister McGrath; Downers Grove, IL: InterVarsity Press, 1999), 101–102.

Two – On Not Understanding the Trinity

[1] K. Rahner, *The Trinity* (trans. J. Donceel; Great Britain: Burns and Oates, 1970), 10.

[2] P. Fiddes, *Participating in God: A Pastoral Doctrine of the Trinity* (Louisville, KY: Westminster John Knox Press, 2000), 4–5.

[3] R. Ingersoll, *Ingersoll's Lectures and Essays* (The Three series in One volume; third series; London: Watts & Co., 1926), 95.

[4] W. Placher, *Narratives of a Vulnerable God: Christ, Theology and Scripture* (Louisville, KY: Westminster John Knox Press, 1994), 65.

[5] See, for instance, Leonardo Boff, T*rinity and Society* (trans. Paul Burns; New York: Orbis Books, 1988); D.S. Cunningham, *These Three are One: The Practice of Trinitarian Theology* (Challenges in Contemporary Theology; Oxford: Blackwell, 1998); C. Gunton, *The One, the Three, and the Many: God, Creation, and the Culture of Modernity* (Cambridge: Cambridge University Press, 1993); C. Mowry LaCugna, *God For Us: The Trinity and Christian Life* (Chicago: HarperSanFrancisco, 1993).

[6] One of the exceptions among theologians is M. Erickson, *God in Three Persons: A Contemporary Interpretation of The Trinity* (Grand Rapids, MI: Baker, 1995), ch. 5.

[7] F. Kerr, "The Trinity and Christian Life," available [online] at http://www.atf.org.au/index.php?type=page&ID=1346

[8] A.W. Tozer, *The Knowledge of the Holy: The Attributes of God: Their Meaning in the Christian Life* (New York: Harper Collins, 1963), 20.

[9] R. Cartwright, "On the Logical Problem of the Trinity," *Philosophical Essays* (Cambridge, MA: MIT Press, 1987), 193.

[10] This is a standard argument which asserts that Christian trinitarianism derives from one or more of the "pagan" triads to be found in non-Christian religions, philosophies and cultures (e.g. the Hindu triad of Brahman, Shiva, and Vishnu). For a defense of this thesis see J. Gwyn Griffiths, *Triads and Trinity* (Cardiff: University of Wales Press, 1996).

[11] This argument is widely repudiated because the resemblances are superficial and no causal connection has ever been established. And

even if the resemblance was significant, a Christian could simply interpret the triads that predate Christianity as instances of general revelation that were fulfilled in the New Testament revelation.

12 See P. Enns, *Inspiration and Incarnation: Evangelicals and the Problem of the Old Testament* (Grand Rapids, MI: Baker Academic, 2005), 97–102.

13 Cf. Mt. 23:9; Mk. 10:18; 12:29; Jn. 17:3; Rom. 3:30; 1 Cor. 8:4.

14 G. O'Collins, *The Tripersonal God: Understanding and Interpreting the Trinity* (New York: Paulist Press, 2002), 44. In addition, "He invited his hearers to accept a new relationship with God as Father; yet it was a relationship that depended on his (Lk. 22:29–30) and differed from his" (45).

15 This title is attributed to Yahweh in Isaiah 44:6 and 48:12 and again in Revelation 1:8.

16 Hence, while the Old Testament warns of judgment in the "Day of the Lord" (e.g. Isa. 13:6; Ezek. 13:5) Jesus is judge of all (Mt. 25:31) such that we now await the Day of our Lord Jesus Christ. (1 Cor. 1:8).

17 A.W. Wainwright, *The Trinity in the New Testament* (London: SPCK, 1969), 42. Any attempt to avoid the impact by suggesting that Paul was using "Lord" merely as an honorific term fails to grapple with the context.

18 Wainwright comments: "The gospel seems to lead up to Thomas' final confession of the divinity of Christ. Since chapter 21 is probably an appendix to the original gospel, the story of Thomas may have concluded the earlier version of the gospel. The evangelist began and ended his work with a confession that Christ is God." *Trinity*, 63.

19 Recognizing this problem, Jehovah's Witnesses have interpreted Thomas' confession as an expletive of surprise tantamount to "Omigod!"

20 In addition we find devout monotheistic Jews offering prayers to Jesus Christ (Acts 7:59–60; 1 Cor. 16:22; 2 Cor. 12:8–10; Rev. 22:20) as well as astounding doxological utterances as in 2 Peter 3:18: "But grow in the grace and knowledge of our Lord and Savior Jesus Christ. To him be glory both now and forever! Amen." (Cf. Rom. 9:5; Heb. 13:20–21; Rev. 1:5). While utterly inconceivable within a Jewish worldview, these statements were natural consequences of the emerging theology of the early Christians.

21 T. Oden, *The Living God: Systematic Theology* Vol. 1 (Peabody, MA: Prince Press, 1998), 200.

22 Cited in Oden, *The Living God*, 202.

[23] "Athanasian Creed," in P. Schaff (ed.), *The Creeds of Christendom With a History and Critical Notes* (Grand Rapids, MI: Baker Books, 1983), 66.

[24] Cartwright, "On the Logical Problem of the Trinity," 193.

[25] Very often theologians distinguish between "Latin" approaches that begin with the divine unity (i.e. the psychological analogy) and "social" approaches that begin with the trinity (plurality) of persons. The WPA manifests characteristics of both. Thus Dale Tuggy aptly refers to it (specifically the Craig and Moreland model that we will consider below) as "a theory that sort of straddles the social/Latin divide." [online] available at http://trinities.org/blog/archives/92

[26] Not every major theoretical option is being considered here. One of the most promising attempts to explain the Trinity currently on offer draws upon relative identity and the problem of material constitution. See M. Rea, "Relative Identity and the Doctrine of the Trinity," *Philosophia Christi* 5 (2003), 431–46; Jeffrey Brower and Michael Rea, "Material Constitution and the Trinity," *Faith and Philosophy* 22 (2005), 487–505.

[27] J. Thompson, *Modern Trinitarian Perspectives* (New York: Oxford University Press, 1994), 7, emphasis added.

[28] A.W. Tozer, *The Knowledge of the Holy*, 23, emphasis added.

[29] Creedal statements prior to the Athanasian Creed tend not to specify whether the is of attribution or the is of identity is intended. Such is the case with the key term homoousion in the Creed of Nicaea (AD 325). For a good discussion of these issues see D. Allen, *Philosophy for Understanding Theology* (Atlanta: John Knox Press, 1985), 96–105.

[30] See B. Leftow, "Anti Social Trinitarianism," in S. Davis and D. Kendall (eds), *The Trinity* (New York: Oxford University Press, 1999), 203–49.

[31] D. Brown, *The Divine Trinity* (London: Duckworth, 1985), 291.

[32] We know it is false because of the indiscernibility of identicals, the law that says any two things that are identical (that are actually one thing) will have all the same properties. As such, any two things that do not share at least one property cannot be the same thing.

[33] Tertullian, "Against Praxeas," sec 5, in Tertullian's *Treatise Against Praxeas* (ed. and trans. Ernest Evans; London: SPCK, 1948), 135–36.

[34] L. Rosten, *The Power of Positive Nonsense* (New York: McGraw-Hill Book Company, 1977), 116–17.

[35] Origen argues that the Divine Word's relation to God is analogous to human introspection (*On First Principles*, 1.2.3) while Gregory

Nazianzen compared Christ's relation to the Father as the word (or idea) to a mind (*The Five Theological Orations*, 4.30.20).

[36] St. Augustine, *The Trinity* (ed. J.E. Rotelle; trans. E. Hill; New York: New City Press, 1991), 9.1.7, 274–75.

[37] Augustine, *The Trinity*, 9.1.8, 275.

[38] For a discussion see J.L. Bermúdez, *The Paradox of Self-Consciousness* (Cambridge, MA; London: MIT Press, 1998).

[39] Brown, *The Divine Trinity*, 273.

[40] W.L. Craig and J.P. Moreland, *Philosophical Foundations for a Christian Worldview* (Downers Grove, IL: InterVarsity Press, 2003), 586–87.

[41] Craig and Moreland, *Philosophical Foundations*, 589, emphasis added.

[42] Craig and Moreland, *Philosophical Foundations*, 591.

[43] Craig and Moreland, *Philosophical Foundations*, 594.

[44] For a fuller critique of this model see D. Howard-Snyder, "Trinity Monotheism," in *Philosophia Christi*, 5.2 (2003), 375–403.

[45] Craig and Moreland, *Philosophical Foundations*, 593.

[46] There has been some controversy regarding the historical antecedents of the social analogy. Cornelius Plantinga Jr. argues that Gregory of Nyssa was a forerunner to social trinitarianism. See "Gregory of Nyssa and the Social Analogy of the Trinity," *The Thomist* 50 (1986), 325–52. Others contest that claim. See L. Ayres, "On Not Three People: The Fundamental Themes of Gregory of Nyssa's Trinitarian Theology as Seen in *To Ablabius: On Not Three Gods*," *Modern Theology* 18.4 (2002), 445–73.

[47] *The Trinity*, 2.20. For a discussion see T. McCall, "Social Trinitarianism and Tritheism Again: A Response to Brian Leftow," *Philosophia Christi* 5.2 (2003), 411. This interpretation has been influential in eastern Christianity where it provided iconographers with a means to circumvent the proscription against "graven images" of God: instead of depicting God *in se*, they could depict Abraham's three visitors. The most famous such icon is Rublev's "Holy Trinity" (ca. 1410).

[48] C. Plantinga Jr., "Social Trinity and Tritheism," in *Trinity, Incarnation and Atonement: Philosophical and Theological Essays* (ed. R.J. Feenstra and C. Plantinga, Jr.; Notre Dame: University of Notre Dame, 1989), 22.

[49] Craig and Moreland, *Philosophical Foundations*, 583.

[50] D. Macleod, *The Person of Christ* (Contours of Christian Theology; Downers Grove, IL: InterVarsity Press, 1998), 126.

[51] Fiddes, *Participating in God*, 43.

52 See T. Nagel, "What is it like to be a bat?" *Philosophical Review* 83.4 (1974), 435–50. Nagel uses the example of a bat to argue that we could learn everything about a bat's brain and still not know what it is like to *be* a bat. As such, there is an irreducible dimension of conscious life.

53 Many other passages imply a distinction in the consciousness of Father, Son, and Spirit such as Jesus' reference to the glory he had *with* the Father (Jn. 17:5).

54 Craig and Moreland observe: "The most pressing task of contemporary social trinitarians is to find some more convincing answer to why, on their view, there are not three Gods." *Philosophical Foundations*, 584.

55 L. Hodgson, *The Doctrine of the Trinity* (Digswell Place: James Nisbet and Co., 1943), 94. Hodgson adds: "Approximation to the ideal of mathematical unity is measured by a scale of degrees of absence of multiplicity; but approximation to the ideal of organic unity is measured by a scale of intensity of unifying power." *The Doctrine of the Trinity*, 94.

56 Plantinga, "Social Trinity or Tritheism?," 31.

57 Plantinga, "Social Trinity or Tritheism?," 22. Plantinga, adds: "the primal unity of Father, Son, and Paraclete is revealed, exemplified, and maybe partly constituted by common will, work, word, and knowledge among them, and by their reciprocal love and glorifying." "Social Trinity or Tritheism?," 25.

58 Plantinga, "Social Trinity or Tritheism?," 27.

59 Certain texts can be read this way including 1 Corinthians 8:6 and 15:28.

60 B. Leftow, "Anti Social Trinitarianism," in *The Trinity: An Interdisciplinary Symposium on the Trinity* (eds S.T. Davis, D. Kendall and G. O'Collins; Oxford: Oxford University Press, 1999), 232.

61 This illustration is based on a similar one developed by T. Merricks in "Split Brains and the Godhead," in *Knowledge and Reality: Essays in Honor of Alvin Plantinga on His Seventieth Birthday* (eds T. Crisp, M. Davidson, and D. Vander Laan; Dordrecht: Kluwer Academic Publishers, 2006), 299–326.

62 Similarly, those who are fans of Uncle John's Bathroom Reader may be disillusioned to learn that "Uncle John" is actually a team of editors and writers.

63 Of course, we could still use personal language of the one God as a *facon de parler* in the same way that we say "Manchester United

played brilliantly." Technically speaking, however, it was not the *club* that played brilliantly, but rather the members of it.

[64] See D. Tuggy, "Divine Deception, Identity, and Social Trinitarianism," *Religious Studies* 40 (2004), 269–87.

[65] Hodgson, *The Doctrine of the Trinity*, 89.

Three – On Not Understanding the Creation

[1] B.E. Olson, *Bruchko* (Carol Stream, IL: Creation House, 1978), 132–33.

[2] C. Raymo, *Skeptics and True Believers: The Exhilarating Connection Between Science and Religion* (London: Vintage, 1999), 94–95.

[3] Raymo, *Skeptics*, 95.

[4] W. Pollard, *Chance and Providence: God's Action in a World Governed by Scientific Law* (New York: Charles Scribner's, 1958), 7.

[5] As Aubrey Moore observed, "The one absolutely impossible conception of God in the present day, is that which represents Him as an occasional Visitor." Cited in R.J. Berry, "Divine Action: Expected and Unexpected," *Zygon* 37.3 (2002), 724.

[6] Gerhard May argues that the doctrine of creation out of nothing is not found in scripture but developed in the second century as a theological reflection on scripture. See *Creatio ex Nihilo: the Doctrine of "Creation out of Nothing" in Early Christian Thought* (trans. A.S. Worrall; Edinburgh: T&T Clark, 1994). In contrast, Paul Copan and William Lane Craig argue that it is scripturally rooted. See *Creation Out of Nothing: A Biblical, Philosophical, and Scientific Exploration* (Leicester: Apollos; Grand Rapids, MI: Baker Academic, 2004).

[7] As Charles Bradlaugh put it, "either something existed or nothing; but something must have existed, for out of nothing nothing can come." "A Plea for Atheism," in *Champion of Liberty: Charles Bradlaugh* (London: C.A. Watts and Co. Ltd., 1922), 123.

[8] Robert Ingersoll thus posed this mocking line of questioning to Christians: "Of what did he make it? If matter had not existed through eternity, then this God made it. Of what did he make it? What did he use for the purpose?" *Ingersoll's Lectures and Essays* (The Three series in One volume; second series; London: Watts & Co., 1926), 119.

⁹ Jastrow, *God and the Astronomers* (2nd edn; New York: W.W. Norton & Company, 2000), 107.

¹⁰ J. Polkinghorne, *Belief in God in an Age of Science* (The Terry Lectures; New Haven, CT and London: Yale University Press, 1998), 49.

¹¹ See M. Wiles, *God's Action in the World* (The Bampton Lectures for 1986; London: SCM Press, 1986).

¹² W. Drees, "Gaps for God?" in *Chaos and Complexity: Scientific Perspectives on Divine Action* (eds R.J. Russell, N. Murphy and A.R. Peacocke; 2ⁿᵈ edn; Vatican City State: Vatican Observatory Publications; Berkeley, CA: Center for Theology and the Natural Sciences, 1997), 223.

¹³ Robert Ingersoll presented the problem of providence and evil as follows: "Only the other day a gentleman was telling me of a case of special Providence. He knew it. He had been the subject of it. A few years ago he was about to go on a ship, when he was detained. He did not go, and the ship was lost with all on board. 'Yes!' I said, 'do you think the people who were drowned believed in special Providence?' Think of the infinite egotism of such a doctrine." *Ingersoll's Lectures and Essays*, second series, 117.

¹⁴ A few theologians believe that miracles ceased with the apostolic age. See for instance B.B. Warfield, *Counterfeit Miracles* (New York: Charles Scribner's, 1918). At the opposite extreme, some charismatics believe that miracles should be frequent, even normative for the Christian. John Wimber and Kevin Springer, *Power Healing* (London: Hodder and Stoughton, 1986).

¹⁵ C. Zimmerman, "Suffering from aplastic anemia, Oregon girl's bone marrow returns to normal—on its own," in *The Daily News*, Aug. 11, 2006 [online] available at http://www.tdn.com/articles/2006/08/11/top_story/news01.txt

¹⁶ Cited in "Cancer Gone from Little Girl after Much Prayer," Aug. 14, 2006 [online] available at http://www.aplastic-anemia.org/aplastic-anemia-news/aplastic-anemia-news–0106.htm

¹⁷ See D. Hume's famous essay "On Miracles," in *An Inquiry Concerning the Human Understanding*.

¹⁸ N. Murphy, "Divine Action in the Natural Order: Buridan's Ass and Schrödinger's Cat," in *Chaos and Complexity: Scientific Perspectives on Divine Action*, 325.

¹⁹ T. Nichols, "Why Miracles?" *Zygon* 37.3 (2002), 702.

²⁰ As such, the criteria William Dembski argues warrant a design inference could be employed to identify miracles. See *The Design Inference:*

Eliminating Chance Through Small Probabilities (Cambridge: Cambridge University Press, 1998).

21 C. Humphreys, *The Miracles of Exodus: A Scientist's Discovery of the Extraordinary Natural Causes of the Biblical Stories* (New York: HarperSanFrancisco, 2003); cf. W. Keller, *The Bible as History: Archaeology Confirms the Book of Books* (trans. W. Neil; London: Hodder and Stoughton, 1956).

22 Thomas Tracy observes, "Even if God's providential activity is understood entirely as the outworking of the potentialities that God builds into the universe in creation, we can still identify the particular events as special divine acts in the sense that (1) these events play a distinctive causal role in advancing God's purposes for the world's history, or (2) these events play a distinctive epistemic role in disclosing God's purposes to us." "Divine Action and Quantum Theory," *Zygon* 35.4 (2000), 894.

23 A.S. Tune, "Quantum Theory and the Resurrection of Jesus," *Dialog: A Journal of Theology* 43.3 (2004), 169.

24 Though this does not seem to be Peter's understanding (Acts 2:24).

25 Lewis, *Miracles: A Preliminary Study* (New York: HarperCollins, 2001), 94.

26 J. Calvin, *Institutes of the Christian Religion* (ed. J.T. McNeill; trans. F.L. Battles; Philadelphia: Westminster Press, 1960), 1.16.4, p. 202. Systematic theologians commonly recognize (b), (c) and (d) in their accounts of providential divine action, with (d) commonly referred to as "concurrence."

27 J. Miles, *God: A Biography* (London: Simon and Schuster, 1995), 33.

28 Miles, *God*, 35.

29 For instance, since God is not literally embodied, the description of God walking in the garden must be symbolic.

30 C. Spurgeon, *Sermons Preached and Revised by the Rev. C.H. Spurgeon* (fifth series; New York Sheldon, 1859), 201; cf. Calvin, *Institutes*, 1.16.2.

31 D. Bodanis, $E=MC^2$: *A Biography of the World's Most Famous Equation* (London : Macmillan, 2000), 19–20.

32 For one thing, this seems to make God's divine action *measurable*. We first calculate the universe's total energy at $T-1$, and then measure it again at $T-2$; the difference between the two is the energy God added to realize his providential will between $T-1$ and $T-2$. While such experiments may remain forever beyond human technical ability, their mere *possibility* may be sufficient to reject the proposal.

[33] Murphy, "Divine Action," 328.

[34] J. Polkinghorne, "The Metaphysics of Divine Action," in *Chaos and Complexity*, 151.

[35] See R. Chisholm, *Person and Object: A Metaphysical Study* (La Salle, IL: Open Court, 1976), 69–72.

[36] K. Ward, "Divine Action in the World of Physics: Responses to Nicholas Saunders," *Zygon* 35.4 (2000), 903.

[37] Polkinghorne, *Belief in God*, 59.

[38] Cited in M.W. Worthing, *God, Creation, and Contemporary Physics* (Theology and the Sciences Series ed. K. Sharpe; Minneapolis: Fortress Press, 1996), 115.

[39] Tracy, "Divine Action and Quantum Theory," 896.

[40] Pollard, *Chance and Providence: God's Action in a World Governed by Scientific Law*, 52.

[41] K. Tanner, "Is God in Charge?" *Essentials of Christian Theology* (ed. W. Placher; Louisville, KY and London: Westminster John Knox Press, 2003), 117.

[42] N. Saunders, "Does God Cheat at Dice? Divine Action and Quantum Possibilities," *Zygon* 35.3 (2000), 522.

[43] We can fine-tune this notion of causation counterfactually: had the world been exactly the same except that the butterfly had not fluttered its wings, there would have been no thunderstorms.

[44] Saunders, "Does God Cheat at Dice?," 522.

[45] Murphy also maintains that God acts through human action and intellect. "Divine Action," 339–40.

[46] Occasionalism is the doctrine that there are no efficient causes within creation while theological occasionalism views God as the sole efficient cause.

[47] Murphy, "Divine Action," 341.

[48] Murphy, "Divine Action," 342.

[49] R.P. Crease and C.C. Mann, *The Second Creation: Makers of the Revolution in Twentieth Century Physics* (London: Quartet Books, 1997), 9.

[50] D. Bonhoeffer, *Letters and Papers from Prison* (ed. E. Bethge, enlarged edn; New York: Macmillan, 1979), 311.

[51] Murphy, "Divine Action," 343.

[52] Saunders, "Does God Cheat at Dice? Divine Action and Possibilities," 532.

[53] Miles, *God*, 35.

54 Calvin, *Institutes*, 1.13.1.

55 A. Marsden Farrer, *Faith and Speculation* (Deens Lectures, 1964; New York: New York University Press; London: Adam and Charles Black, 1967); K. Tanner, *God and Creation in Christian Theology: Tyranny or Empowerment?* (Oxford: Basil Blackwell, 1988).

56 Tanner, "Is God in Charge?," 121.

57 W. Stoeger, "Describing God's Action in the World in Light of Scientific Knowledge of Reality," in *Chaos and Complexity: Scientific Perspectives on Divine Action*, 242.

58 Stoeger, "Describing God's Action," 247.

59 See Thomas Aquinas, *Summa Theologica*, 1.105.

60 Tanner, "Is God in Charge?," 128.

61 According to compatibilism, the criteria necessary for a free action include desire and absence of constraint but *not* the ability to have done otherwise. And so, my action of eating chocolate cake for dinner is free if I desired the chocolate cake and I was able to eat it, even if I could not have done otherwise than eat it. It thus follows on this view that freedom is compatible with determinism.

62 I. Kant, *The Critique of Practical Reason* (trans. L.W. Beck, 1788: Indianapolis, IN: Bobbs-Merril, 1956), 189–90.

63 F. Turretin, *Institutes of Elenctic Theology* Vol. 1 (ed. J.T. Dennison, trans. G.M. Giger, Jr.; Phillipsburg, NJ: P&R Publishing, 1992), 1.6.10, p. 493. Cf. Thomas Aquinas, *Summa Theologica*, 1.49.2.

64 Polkinghorne, "Metaphysics," 150.

65 Polkinghorne, *Belief in God*, 58.

66 Polkinghorne, "Metaphysics," 150.

67 P. Clayton, *God and Contemporary Science* (Edinburgh Studies in Constructive Theology; Edinburgh: Edinburgh University Press, 1997), 196.

Four – On Not Understanding the Incarnation

1 B. Robinson, *The Best Christmas Pageant Ever* (New York: Harper Collins, 1972), 1.

2 Robinson, *Pageant*, 61.

3 Robinson, *Pageant*, 82.

4 As Raymond Brown puts it, "it may well be that most Christians tolerate only as much humanity as they deem consonant with their

view of the divinity." *An Introduction to New Testament Christology* (New York: Paulist Press, 1994), 27.

[5] See the telling passages in Elaine Pagels, *Beyond Belief: the Secret Gospel of Thomas* (London: Macmillan, 2003), 34, 68.

[6] John Hick, "Jesus and the World Religions," in *The Myth of God Incarnate* (ed. John Hick; London: SCM Press, 1977), 178.

[7] "The Symbol of Chalcedon," in *Creeds of Christendom* Vol. 2, *The Greek and Latin Creed* (ed. P. Schaff; rev. D.S. Schaff; Grand Rapids, MI: Baker, 1983), 62.

[8] See "theism, classical," in D.J. Hill and R.D. Rauser, *Christian Philosophy A–Z* (Edinburgh: Edinburgh University Press, 2006), 182–83.

[9] Hick, "Jesus and the World Religions," 178; cf. Karl Rahner's influential reassessment of Chalcedon in "Current Problems in Christology," *Theological Investigations* Vol. 1, *God, Christ, Mary and Grace* (trans. Cornelius Ernst; New York: Seabury Press, 1961), 149–200.

[10] For instance, is impassibility really essential to being divine? Or is peccability really essential to being human?

[11] It is worth pointing out that we would face the problem of incompossible attributes even if God was not omniscient, for so long as he knew *at least one* true proposition essentially that would still conflict with the fact that Jesus was once a zygote which did not know anything.

[12] See for instance D.J. Hill, *Divinity and Maximal Greatness* (London: Routledge, 2005), ch. 2.

[13] Among the few exceptions are some process and openness theists.

[14] One way to justify this conclusion is through the reasoning of so-called "perfect being theology" according to which God is the most perfect being and, as such, exemplifies the maximal set of compossible perfections. Since knowledge is a good, God has perfect knowledge and has it essentially. For an introduction to perfect being theology see T.V. Morris, "God of Abraham, Isaac, and Anselm," *Anselmian Explorations: Essays in Philosophical Theology* (Notre Dame, IN: University of Notre Dame Press, 1987), 10–25.

[15] "The Westminster Confession of Faith," in *The Creeds of Christendom* Vol. 3, *The Evangelical Protestant Creeds* (ed. P. Schaff; rev. D.S. Schaff; Grand Rapids, MI: Baker, 1983), II.2.

[16] See Brown, *New Testament Christology*, 37–38.

17 Athanasius, "Orations Against the Arians," in *The Christological Controversy* (ed. R.A. Norris Jr.; Philadelphia: Fortress Press, 1980), 97.

18 Cited in H. Heppe, *Reformed Dogmatics* (rev. and ed. E. Bizer; trans. G.T. Thomson; London: Wakeman Great Reprints, nd.), 438.

19 R. Jenson, "How Does Jesus Make a Difference?" in *Essentials of Christian Theology* (ed. W. Placher; Louisville, KY: Westminster John Knox Press, 2003), 201. To be sure, in principle WP theologians are also anxious to affirm one acting subject. So Douglas Macleod: "whenever we look at the life of Christ and ask, Who did this? Who suffered this? Who said this? the answer is always the same: 'The Son of God!' We can never say, 'The divine nature did this!' or 'The human nature did this!' We must say 'He did this: he, the Son of God!'" *The Person of Christ* (Contours of Christian Theology; Downers Grove, IL: InterVarsity Press, 1998), 189.

20 The picture is actually a bit more complicated because Apollinaris was a trichotomist—that is, he believed that human beings are composed of three parts: body, soul and spirit. As such, he actually argued that Christ took the place of the human spirit and united to a human body/soul. However, since most WF proponents have been dualists, I have glossed over this nuance.

21 Apollinaris of Laodicea, "On the Union in Christ of the Body with the Godhead," in *The Christological Controversy*, sec. 6, p. 104.

22 T. Oden, *The Word of Life, Systematic Theology* Vol. 2 (Peabody, MA: Prince Press, 1998), 125.

23 A. Strong, *Systematic Theology* (Valley Forge, PA: Judson Press, 1907), 671.

24 "3. So that those things which pertain to man are rightly said of God, and, on the other hand, those things which pertain to God are said of man. 4. It is true to say: This man created the world, and this God suffered, died, was buried, etc." Martin Luther, "Disputation on the Divinity and Humanity of Christ," trans. Christopher B. Brown, [online] available at http://www.ctsfw.edu/etext/luther/divinity/divinity.asc.

25 As Louis Berkhof observes, Lutherans teach "that the attributes of one nature are ascribed to the other on the basis of an actual transference, and feel that it is only by such a transference that the real unity of the person can be secured." *Systematic Theology* (Edinburgh; Carlisle, PA: Banner of Truth, 1958), 325.

26 Hence Theodore Beza warns against the Lutheran approach: "these, therefore, are most false, 'the Godhead was crucified,' or 'The Godhead died; the flesh of Christ is infinite.'" *Questions and*

Responses, in Reformed Reader Vol. 1 *Classical Beginnings: 1519–1799* (ed. W.S. Johnson and J.H. Leith; Louisville: Westminster/John Knox Press, 1993), 209.

[27] Craig and Moreland, *Philosophical Foundations for a Christian Worldview* (Downers Grove, IL: InterVarsity Press, 2003), 603. Similarly, Macleod warns that "It is . . . difficult to avoid the conclusion that the Lutheran doctrine involves the destruction of the human nature." *The Person of Christ*, 197.

[28] See C. Welch (ed.), *God and Incarnation in Mid-nineteenth Century German Theology* (New York: Oxford University Press, 1965).

[29] Kenoticism notably flourished in England between 1890 and 1910. For an excellent example from this period see F. Weston, *The One Christ: An Enquiry into the Manner of the Incarnation* (London: Longmans Green, 1907).

[30] Cited in R.J. Feenstra "Reconsidering Kenotic Christology," in *Trinity, Incarnation, and Atonement* (eds R.J. Feenstra and C. Plantinga, Jr.; Notre Dame, IL: University of Notre Dame Press, 1990), 136.

[31] Cited in Feenstra, "Reconsidering Kenotic Christology," 139–40.

[32] "Necessarily, any divine person is omniscient unless voluntarily surrendering his attribute of omniscience and necessarily at least one divine person is always omniscient." Feenstra, "Reconsidering Kenotic Christology," 140.

[33] D Brown, *The Divine Trinity* (London: Duckworth, 1985), 257.

[34] Brown, *Divine Trinity*, 257.

[35] Or he reinterprets the two natures *diachronically*: Christ was both divine and human . . . *but not at the same time.*

[36] Craig and Moreland, *Philosophical Foundations*, 607.

[37] Craig and Moreland, *Philosophical Foundations*, 607.

[38] "Belgic Confession," in *The Creeds of Christendom* Vol. 3, *The Evangelical Protestant Creeds*, 18, p. 403.

[39] Specifically at the fifth ecumenical council (553).

[40] Theodore of Mopsuestia, "On the Incarnation, Bk. VIII, fragment 3," in *The Christological Controversy*, 117.

[41] Eustathius, an older contemporary of Athanasius, explained that the indwelling of the Word in Christ was different from the indwelling in the prophets because it was continuous. Theodore rather unhelpfully added that the Word's indwelling in Christ is different than his presence in the prophets because he indwells Christ *as a Son*. See "On the Incarnation," Book VII, in *The Christological Controversy*, 116–17.

[42] J.N.D. Kelly, *Early Christian Doctrines* (New York: Harper Collins, 1978), 285.

[43] Nestorianism is the heresy that there are two persons in the incarnation.

[44] For further discussion on this point see chapter six.

[45] Calvin, *Institutes*, 2.13.4, p. 481.

[46] Johnson and Leith, *Reformed Reader*, 202. While Athanasius appears to anticipate the WF approach, aspects of his Christology also are amenable to the WP model, including his own anticipation of Calvin's extra. See Athanasius, *De Incarnatione Verbi Dei*, 17.

[47] The mid-fifth-century Nestorian debate erupted over a related issue: whether it was appropriate to speak of Mary as Mother of God (as the WF advocates stressed) or only as Mother of Christ. Even today Calvinists remain uncomfortable with the confession of Mary as Mother of God.

[48] Oden, *Word of Life*, 77. Pope Leo wrote: "the human being who is Jesus Christ, can at one and the same time die in virtue of the one nature and, in virtue of the other, be incapable of death." "Letter to Flavian," in *The Christological Controversy*, 148.

[49] Macleod, *Person of Christ*, 165.

[50] Pope Leo, "Letter to Flavian," 150.

[51] W. Grudem, *Systematic Theology: An Introduction to Biblical Doctrine* (Leicester: InterVarsity Press; Grand Rapids, MI: Zondervan, 1994), 539.

[52] Grudem, *Systematic Theology*, 539.

[53] T. Morris, *The Logic of God Incarnate* (Ithaca, NY: Cornell University Press, 1986); "The Metaphysics of God Incarnate," in *Trinity, Incarnation, and Atonement*, 110–27.

[54] Morris, "Metaphysics," 121.

[55] Macleod, *Person of Christ*, 193.

[56] Morris, "Metaphysics," 121.

[57] Morris, "Metaphysics," 122.

[58] I confess to finding this example unhelpful. While I have had lucid dreams, I have never had one where I was simultaneously unaware of my awareness of dreaming.

[59] Morris, "Metaphysics," 123.

[60] Morris, "Metaphysics," 124.

[61] Morris, "Metaphysics," 125; cf. 121.

[62] Jenson, "How Does Jesus Make a Difference?" 200.

63 P. Geach, *Providence and Evil* (Cambridge: Cambridge University Press, 1977), 26–27. Thanks to Daniel Hill for this reference.

64 Geach, *Providence and Evil*, 27.

65 This should not be surprising since adoptionism is usually construed as a type of degree Christology.

66 See J. Macquarrie, *Jesus Christ in Modern Thought* (London: SCM Press; Philadelphia: Trinity Press International, 1990), 209–11.

67 Morris recognizes the point: "any divine person stands in a direct, immediate, and complete asymmetric accessing relation to the mind of every human being." "Metaphysics," 125.

68 "Information flow by itself does not constitute mental, metaphysical ownership. So, what does?" Morris, "Metaphysics," 125–26.

69 The best Morris can do is to suggest that "The complete human mental system of Jesus was not intended alone to define a person. It was created to belong to a person with a divine mind as well, as the ultimate, hierarchically maximal mental system." "Metaphysics," 126.

70 Morris, *The Logic of God Incarnate*, 183.

71 J. Hick, *The Metaphor of God Incarnate: Christology in a Pluralistic Age* (2nd edn; Louisville and London: Westminster John Knox Press, 2005), 94.

72 Hick, *Metaphor*, 96.

73 While it seems to me that multiple incarnations of Christ are impossible, Thomas Aquinas would disagree. See *Summa Theologica*, 3.3.7.

74 B. Hebblethwaite, "The Impossibility of Multiple Incarnations," *Theology* 104 (2001), 327.

75 Hebblethwaite writes: "we do not, in the eschaton, expect to be encountered by a group of divine incarnations, themselves in theory capable of interpersonal relation." "Impossibility," 328.

76 Macleod, *Person of Christ*, 225.

77 As John Hick observes, "the more philosophically ingenious Christologies have become the less religiously realistic they seem to be." *Metaphor*, 104.

78 Robinson, *Pageant*, 90.

Five – On Not Understanding the Atonement

1 J. Rosenbaum, "The Passion of the Christ," *Chicago Reader* [online] available at http://onfilm.chicagoreader.com/movies/capsules/ 25486_PASSION_OF_THE_CHRIST.

² D. Edelstein, "Jesus H. Christ, The Passion, Mel Gibson's Bloody Mess," (Feb. 24, 2004) [online] available at http://www.slate.com/id/2096025/

³ J. Bernard, "GORE'S THE CRIME OF 'PASSION' Over-the-top brutality saps movie's power," *New York Daily News* (Feb. 24, 2004), 5.

⁴ R. Groen, "The Greatest Gory Every Told," *Globe and Mail* (Feb. 25, 2004) [online] available at http://www.theglobeandmail.com/servlet/ArticleNews/movie/MOVIEREVIEWS/20040225/PASS25

⁵ As I will note below, the critic's indignation is not directed at a particular *theory* of atonement (e.g. penal substitution) but rather at the claim that this horrific event of torture and execution could be a divinely orchestrated event which is intended to be an object of religious devotion.

⁶ R. Nozick, *The Examined Life: Philosophical Meditations* (New York: Simon and Schuster, 1990), 236–37.

⁷ Nozick, *Examined Life*, 239.

⁸ As Charles Bradlaugh put it, "Are you poor in spirit, and are you smitten ; in such case what did Jesus teach?—'Unto him that smiteth thee on the one cheek offer also the other.' Surely better to teach that 'he who courts oppression shares the crime'; and if smitten once to take careful measure to prevent a future smiting." "What did Jesus Teach?" in *Champion of Liberty: Charles Bradlaugh* (London: C.A. Watts and Co. Ltd., 1922), 154.

⁹ G. O'Collins, *Interpreting Jesus* (London: Geoffrey Chapman, 1983), 95.

¹⁰ Not all theories of atonement fit into these three categories. Among the other theories are the Eastern Orthodox theory of recapitulation and Hugo Grotius' governmental theory which combines elements of satisfaction/substitution with elements from the example/influence view.

¹¹ Most theories of atonement recognize the link between atonement and Christ's life. For instance, ransom/victory sees the battle as *culminating* in the cross rather than being limited to it. Similarly, example/influence sees the *entire* life of Christ as a model for emulation (again, culminating in the cross). Even the satisfaction/substitution theory, which is often critiqued for focusing on the cross alone, views the resurrection as God's acceptance/ratification of Christ's sacrificial and propitiatory work. As such, it is interesting to note that John Milton's sequel to *Paradise Lost*, entitled *Paradise Regained*,

did not focus on the cross but rather on Christ's temptations in the desert.

[12] This brings us to the "New Perspective on Paul" debate. See for instance N.T. Wright, *What Saint Paul Really Said: Was Paul of Tarsus the Real Founder of Christianity?* (Grand Rapids, MI: Eerdmans, 1997).

[13] Among these are the themes of recapitulation (*Against Heresies*, 3.18.1) and ransom (*Against Heresies*, 5.1.1) found in Irenaeus.

[14] Aulén, *Christus Victor* (trans. A.G. Hebert; 1931; New York: Macmillan, 1969).

[15] R. Gaffin, "Atonement in the Pauline Corpus," in *The Glory of the Atonement: Biblical, Historical and Practical Perspectives* (eds C.E. Hill and F.A. James; Downers Grove, IL: InterVarsity Press, 2004), 140–41.

[16] "Rufinus of Aquileia on the 'Mousetrap' Theory of the Atonement," in A.E. McGrath (ed.), *The Christian Theology Reader* (Oxford: Blackwell, 2005), 180.

[17] R. Bultmann, "New Testament and Mythology," in *New Testament and Mythology and Other Basic Writings* (ed. and trans. S.M. Ogden; Philadelphia: Fortress Press, 1984), 4.

[18] As Alvin Plantinga points out, "Many physicists and engineers . . . understand 'electrical light and the wireless' vastly better than Bultmann or his contemporary followers, but nonetheless hold precisely those New Testament beliefs Bultmann thinks incompatible with using electric lights and radios." *Warranted Christian Belief* (New York; Oxford: Oxford University Press, 2000), 405.

[19] O'Collins, *Interpreting Jesus*, 137.

[20] See, for instance, Joel Bakan's analysis of the pathology of the corporate form which looks surprisingly like an institutional form of total depravity. *The Corporation: The Pathological Pursuit of Profit and Power* (Toronto: Penguin, 2004).

[21] Anselm's actual words: "But since neither the devil nor man belong to any but God . . . what should he do but punish his servant, who had seduced his fellow-servant to desert their common Lord." *Cur Deus Homo*, ch. 7, in *St. Anselm, Proslogium; Monologium; An Appendix in Behalf of the Fool by Gaunilon; and Cur Deus Homo* (trans. S. Norton Deane; reprint: Eugene, OR: Wipf and Stock, 2003), 187.

[22] To illustrate, why couldn't I forgive your debt if I so chose instead of going to the trouble of transferring the correct sum from one of my accounts to another?

[23] Aulén, *Christus Victor*, 9–10.

²⁴ Session 3, "Why Did Jesus Die?" This session provides the Prodigal Son (Lk. 15) as the supplementary Bible study, a point that is of interest given the use of this text among moral influence theorists to marginalize the implications of satisfaction and substitution.

²⁵ The concept is first found in Tertullian's writing, though he did not apply it to the atonement. See C. Gunton, *The Actuality of Atonement* (Edinburgh: T&T Clark, 2000), 86.

²⁶ Sinclair Ferguson, a defender of penal substitution, repudiates the notion of a clinical economic transaction: "we do not believe we are saved by a mere mathematical equation (or by a theological 'theory'), but by the all-demanding, all-consuming, Son-in-the-flesh forsaking activity of the God of grace." "Preaching the Atonement," in *The Glory of the Atonement*, 436.

²⁷ M.D. Baker and J.B. Green, *Recovering the Scandal of the Cross: Atonement in New Testament and Contemporary Contexts* (Downers Grove, IL: InterVarsity Press, 2000), 24–25.

²⁸ E. Black, *IBM and the Holocaust: The Strategic Alliance Between Nazi Germany and America's Most Powerful Corporation* (New York: Crown Publishers, 2001).

²⁹ Ingersoll, *Ingersoll's Lectures and Essays*; third series, 99.

³⁰ As D.A. Carson notes, the judge is not the source of the moral order but merely a participant within it. See "Atonement in Romans 3:21–26," in *The Glory of the Atonement*, 132.

³¹ M. Luther, *St. Paul's Epistle to the Galatians* (Westwood, NJ: Fleming H. Revell Co., nd), 272.

³² J. Stott, *The Cross of Christ* (Leicester: Inter-Varsity Press, 1986), 158.

³³ D. Edwards and J. Stott, *Evangelical Essentials: A Liberal – Evangelical Dialogue* (Downers Grove, IL: InterVarsity Press, 1988), 152.

³⁴ Edwards and Stott, *Evangelical Essentials*, 166.

³⁵ James Packer admits that rational objections to penal substitution "made the word of the cross sound more like a conundrum than a confession of faith—more like a puzzle, we might say, than a gospel." "What did the cross achieve?," 100.

³⁶ T.S. Giesel, *The Cat in the Hat Comes Back!* (New York: Beginner Books, 1958).

³⁷ Giesel, *The Cat in the Hat Comes Back!* 55–57.

³⁸ As Boso puts it, "it is a strange thing if God so delights in, or requires, the blood of the innocent, that he neither chooses, nor is able, to spare the guilty without the sacrifice of the innocent." *Cur Deus Homo*, 1.10, p. 200.

[39] Edwards and Stott, *Evangelical Essentials*, 149.

[40] S.C. Guthrie, *Christian Doctrine* (rev. edn; Louisville, KY: Westminster/John Knox Press, 1994), 250–251.

[41] Bultmann, "New Testament and Mythology," 7.

[42] "The Penal Substitution Debate," (Oct. 11. 2004), [online] available at http://www.surefish.co.uk/faith/features/2004/111004_chalke_edwards_debate.htm. Anselm anticipated this response in Boso's comment: "when God commands us in every case to forgive those who trespass against us, it seems inconsistent to enjoin a thing upon us which is not proper for him to do himself." *Cur Deus Homo*, 1.12, p. 204.

[43] Cited in D.A. Carson, *Becoming Conversant with the Emergent Church: Understanding a Movement and its Implications* (Grand Rapids, MI: Zondervan, 2005), 166. While Carson points out that the character of Kerry is an unbeliever, he observes that McLaren never refutes the charge. This charge of child abuse is an oft repeated theme in feminist theology as well. For instance, Joanne Carlson Brown and Rebecca Parker describe Christ's death by torture as "divine child abuse" which is "paraded as salvific." And this ensures the abusive status quo for "Any sense that we have a right to care for our own needs is in conflict with being a faithful follower of Jesus." "For God so Loved the World," in *Christianity, Patriarchy and Abuse: A Feminist Critique* (eds J.C. Brown and C.R. Bohn; New York: Pilgrim Press, 1989), 2.

[44] Ferguson, "Preaching the Atonement," 431.

[45] Stott, *Cross of Christ*, 174. Similarly, Guthrie writes: "The holy God thunders that a sacrifice must be made to atone for human sin—then makes a self-sacrifice." *Christian Doctrine*, 261.

[46] Gunton, *Actuality*, 92.

[47] Edwards and Stott, *Evangelical Essentials*, 153.

[48] Cited in D. Baillie, *God was in Christ: An Essay on Incarnation and Atonement* (London: Faber and Faber, 1961), 172.

[49] Collins, "Understanding Atonement: A New and Orthodox Theory," [online] available at http://home.messiah.edu/~rcollins/AT7.HTM

[50] Ingersoll, *Ingersoll's Lectures and Essays*, third series, 99.

[51] Abelard, "Peter Abelard on the Love of Christ in Redemption," in *The Christian Theology Reader*, 184.

[52] According to Rene Girard, the cross is a non-violent revelation of human complicity in violence which God uses to break the cycle of

violence and usher in a non-violent society See *Things Hidden Since the Foundation of the World* (Stanford, CA: Stanford University Press, 1987); cf. W.M. Swartley (ed.), *Violence Renounced: René Girard, Biblical Studies, and Peacemaking* (Telford, PA: Pandora Press, 2000).

53 D. Tomlinson, *The Post Evangelical* (rev. North America edn; El Cajon, CA: emergent/ys; Grand Rapids, MI: Zondervan, 2003), 101.

54 In a reflection on the suffering of an individual named Sam, David Kelsey refers to the notion of God as fellow sufferer as "well intentioned but terminally ineffectual." He then adds, "Sam and his family would be fully justified in saying to the God who works in and through what Jesus does and undergoes, 'Sir, we really appreciate your concern and your understanding. It does strengthen us to survive. But couldn't you help change things a little?" "Redeeming Sam," *Christian Century* (June 28, 2005), 24.

55 L. Van Dyk, "How Does Jesus Make a Difference?" in *Essentials of Christian Theology* (ed. W. Placher; Louisville, KY and London: Westminster John Knox Press, 2003), 212.

56 H. Boersma, *Violence, Hospitality, and the Cross: Reappropriating the Atonement Tradition* (Grand Rapids, MI: Baker Academic, 2004), 117.

57 Boersma, *Violence*, 118.

58 Among its other problems, the example/influence theory loses the uniqueness of Christ insofar as the life of a Mother Teresa or Maximillian Kolbe could in principle inspire people as much or more than did Christ.

59 Van Dyk, "How Does Jesus Make a Difference?" 216.

60 G. Green, "The Gender of God and the Theology of Metaphor," in *Speaking the Christian God: The Holy Trinity and the Challenge of Feminism* (ed. A. Kimel; Grand Rapids, MI: Eerdmans; Leominster: Gracewing, 1992), 51.

61 Green, "Gender of God," 57.

62 Boersma, *Violence*, 107–108.

63 In seeking to identify root metaphors, we need to be careful not to marginalize certain voices in scripture, for elevating one particular metaphor as most central could be a way of doing violence to those we do not like.

64 See, for instance, Roger Nicole, "Postscript on Penal Substitution," in *The Glory of the Atonement*, 445–52.

65 R.G. Gruenler, "Atonement in the Synoptic Gospels and Acts," in *The Glory of the Atonement*, 95.

66 The fact that we can isolate the particular conceptual content of metaphors does not undermine their irreducible participatory nature, as if once the concepts had been identified, the metaphor could be dispensed like a wrapper.

67 In addition, while I readily understand the concept of *imputation* in economic terms (you owe me $5000; I credit [or *impute*] it to your account thereby removing your debt), one may puzzle at the claim that the guilt of Adam's sin was imputed to us, our sin and guilt were imputed to Christ and his righteousness was imputed to us.

68 See C.H. Dodd, *The Bible and the Greeks* (London: Hodder & Stoughton, 1935), 93.

69 See R. Nicole, "CH. Dodd and the Doctrine of Propitiation," *Westminster Theological Journal* 17 (1955), 117–57; Leon Morris, *The Apostolic Preaching of the Cross* (3rd edn; Grand Rapids, MI: Eerdmans, 1965), chs. 5 and 6.

70 R. Ebert, "The Passion of the Christ," (Feb. 24, 2004), [online] available at http://rogerebert.suntimes.com/apps/pbcs.dll/ article? AID=/20040224/REVIEWS/402240301/1023

Six – On Not Understanding the Ascension

1 J.G. Williams, *Christian Faith and the Space Age* (Cleveland and New York: World Pub. Co., 1968), 50.

2 B. Russell, "The Theologian's Nightmare," in *Bertrand Russell on God and Religion* (ed. Al Seckel; Buffalo: Prometheus, 1986), 337.

3 Russell's parable predates personal computers; otherwise the search would have been a lot quicker!

4 Russell, "The Theologian's Nightmare," 339.

5 The intuition is reflected in Steven Weinberg's much quoted statement that "The more the universe seems comprehensible, the more it also seems pointless." *The First Three Minutes: A Modern View of the Origin of the Universe* (2nd edn; London: Flamingo, 1983), 148–49. Stephen Crane famously captured the godless universe in this poem:

> A man said to the universe:
> "Sir, I exist!"
> "However," replied the universe,
> "the fact has not created in me
> A sense of obligation."

6 It is perhaps this incredulity that leaves many theologians reluctant to discuss the personal return of Christ. For example, see T. Peters, R.J. Russell and M. Welker (eds), *Resurrection: Theological and Scientific Assessments* (Grand Rapids, MI: Eerdmans, 2002).

7 Williams, *Christian Faith*, 50.

8 See, for instance, G. Gonzalez and J.W. Richards, *The Privileged Planet: How Our Place in the Cosmos is Designed for Discovery* (Washington, DC: Regnery Pub. 2004).

9 The "Book of Abraham" is a sacred Mormon text allegedly written by Abraham, translated by Joseph Smith, and published by Smith as a part of *The Pearl of Great Price*, one of the four principle sacred LDS texts.

10 Some Mormon scholars believe that the "star" is in fact a planet while a few interpret the passages symbolically. For a critical discussion see J. Gee, W.J. Hamblin and D.C. Peterson, "'And I Saw the Stars': The Book of Abraham and Ancient Geocentric Astronomy," *Astronomy, Papyrus, and Covenant* (eds J. Gee and B.M. Hauglid; Studies in the Book of Abraham, no. 3; Utah: Brigham Young University Press, 2006), 1–16.

11 One Mormon theory places God's throne at or near the centre of the Milky Way.

12 "Session" derives from the Latin *sessionem*, an act of sitting, and refers to Christ sitting with the Father after the completion of his mission.

13 Ingersoll, *Ingersoll's Lectures and Essays*, second series, 147. For a similar characterization of the Hebrew mindset see Harry Emerson Fosdick's reconstruction cited in B. Ramm, *The Christian View of Science and Scripture* (Grand Rapids, MI: Eerdmans, 1956), 97–98. Peter Enns reproduces an excellent diagrammatic depiction of the Hebrew worldview in *Inspiration and Incarnation: Evangelicals and the Problem of the Old Testament* (Grand Rapids, MI: Baker Academic, 2005), 54.

14 Ramm, *Science and Scripture*, 98; cf. T. Oden, *The Word of Life* Vol., 508.

15 Cardinal J.H. Newman, "Galileo, Revelation, and the Educated Man," in *Philosophical Readings on Cardinal Newman* (ed. J. Collins; Chicago: H. Regnery Press, 1961), 285.

16 R. Jenson, *Systematic Theology* Vol. 1, *The Triune God* (Oxford: Oxford University Press, 1997), 202.

17 Jenson, *Systematic Theology* Vol. 1, 202.

18 Williams, *Christian Faith*, 25–26.
19 Cited in Williams, *Christian Faith*, 28.
20 Rich Buhler shrewdly observes that "No one had bothered to ask . . . what kind of microphone they used that could withstand 2,000 degrees." "Scientists Discover Hell in Siberia," *Christianity Today* (July 16, 1990), 28. In his article Buhler traces the fictive origins of the story.
21 The story apparently originated in a Finnish newspaper which quoted one of the workers, a "Dr. Azzacov," as recounting: "We could hardly believe our own ears. We heard a human voice, screaming in pain. Even though one voice was discernable, we could hear thousands, perhaps millions, in the background, of suffering souls screaming." Cited in "Not Frozen Over. Hell Found Under Siberia: Screams Scientists," *Biblical Archaeology Review* 16.6 (1990), 6.
22 Ingersoll, *Ingersoll's Lectures and Essays*, second series, 132–33.
23 R. Clements, *Introducing Jesus* (rev. ed.; Eastbourne: Kingsway Publications, 1992), 123–24.
24 M. Harris, "Power point," *Christian Century* (May 3, 2005), 20.
25 Bultmann, "New Testament and Mythology," 3.
26 Lewis, *Miracles*, 108.
27 Bultmann, "New Testament and Mythology," 4.
28 Bultmann, "New Testament and Mythology," 8.
29 C. Brown, *Miracles and the Critical Mind* (Grand Rapids, MI: Eerdmans; Exeter: Paternoster, 1984), 252. If Bultmann's modern man is not an atheist, he should specify which modern man he is listening to and why.
30 See J.I. Packer, "Incarnate Forever," *Christianity Today* (March 1, 2004), 72.
31 C. Hodge, *Systematic Theology* Vol. 2 (USA: Hendrickson, 2003), 631. The Reformed scholastic theologian Riissen provides a helpful contrast: "Did Christ's ascension take place strictly by a local movement from lower places to the highest heaven of the blessed or metaphorically by disappearing? The former is affirmed, the latter denied, [by the Reformed] against the *Lutherans*." Cited in H. Heppe, *Reformed Dogmatics* (rev. and ed. E. Bizer; trans. G.T. Thomson; London: Wakeman Great Reprints, nd.), 500.
32 The teaching is also assumed in Peter's early preaching in Acts 2:33.
33 D. Farrow, *Ascension and Ecclesia: On the Significance of the Ascension for Ecclesiology and Christian Cosmology* (Edinburgh: T&T Clark, 1999), 16.

34 There is likewise abundant evidence for the session and second coming of Christ. The session begins at the completion of the ascension when Christ is seated at the right hand of the Father (Mk. 16:19; Acts 2:33, Eph. 1:20; Heb. 10:12–14). The word "session" both refers to the completion of Christ's work and the advent of his kingly office, as well as his ongoing priestly office as intercessor: (Heb. 8:1). After the session we have the expectation of the visible return of Christ on the clouds of heaven (Mt. 24:30; 26:24; 1 Thes. 4:17), an expectation that prompts prayers for Christ's return (1 Cor. 16:22; Rev. 22:20).

35 Ludwig Ott comments: "The Fathers give unanimous testimony of Christ's Ascension. All the ancient rules of Faith mention it together with the Death and the Resurrection." *Fundamentals of Catholic Dogma* (ed. J.C. Bastible; trans. P. Lynch; Rockford, IL: Tan Books, 1974), 194.

36 W. Kasper, *Jesus the Christ* (trans. V. Green; London: Burns and Oates, 1976), 148.

37 Augustine, "29. Is there an 'Above' and a 'Below' in the Universe?" in *The Fathers of the Church* Vol. 70, *St. Augustine, 83 Different Questions* (trans. D.L. Mosher; Washington DC: Catholic University of America Press, 1982), 54.

38 See "Ascension," in K. Rahner and H. Vorgrimler, *Theological Dictionary* (ed. C. Ernst; trans. R. Strachan; Montreal: Palm Publishers; Freiburg: Herder, 1965), 37.

39 According to the Westminster Larger Catechism (A. 5) Christ's exaltation includes resurrection, ascension, session and second coming.

40 Cited in Oden, *The Word of Life*, 512.

41 Jansen, "The Ascension, the Church, and Theology," *Theology Today* 11.1 (1959), 26.

42 No doubt the doctrine has additional functions as well. For instance, K.M. Kapic has argued that the ascension should be viewed as a priestly benediction. See "Receiving Christ's Priestly Benediction: A Biblical, Historical, and Theological Exploration of Luke 24:50–53," *Westminster Theological Journal* 67 (2005), 247–60.

43 A. Strong, *Systematic Theology* (Valley Forge, PA: Judson Press, 1907), 709.

44 "Earth" in this context is synecdochic for the entire physical universe.

45 Grudem, *Systematic Theology: An Introduction to Biblical Doctrine* (Grand Rapids, MI: Zondervan; Leicester: Inter-Varsity Press, 1994), 617.

46 Berkhof, *Systematic Theology*, 350

47 Hodge, *Systematic Theology* Vol. 2, 630.

48 "Strictly he [Christ] could not be received at God's right hand in this place, since God is Spirit and consequently does not have flesh and bones. But it is taken metaphorically for that highest degree of glorification to which Christ was raised by the Father." "Leiden Synopsis," cited in Heppe, *Reformed Dogmatics*, 503.

49 Jansen observes that "Calvinistic theologians, properly concerned to lay stress on the Holy Spirit, increasingly do what Calvin did not do—insist that the ascension is a local transfer from place to place, a 'third heaven' where Christ exists spatially in some circumscribed way. Yet these same theologians do an about-face by insisting that 'the right hand' is a metaphorical expression." "Ascension," 27.

50 Heppe, *Reformed Dogmatics*, 500, emphasis added.

51 Heppe, *Reformed Dogmatics*, 501.

52 Cited in Heppe, *Reformed Dogmatics*, 501.

53 Even Captain Kirk's being beamed on board the Starship Enterprise requires a physical pathway through which the dissembled physical elements of his body may travel.

54 Hodge apparently believes that heaven is located within *our* universe (*Systematic Theology* Vol. 2, 630). While this is certainly *possible*, I find the notion of heaven being a separate universe more plausible (or perhaps less implausible). If heaven is a separate universe, then John's description of God coming to live among people (Rev. 21:2–4) could represent the cosmic merging of these two universes.

55 By one estimate the technical requirements for creating a traversable wormhole would be phenomenally high, with fine-tuning to the point of one part in ten to the sixtieth power. See Paul Rincon, "Wormhole no use for time travel," [online] available at http://news.bbc.co.uk/2/hi/science/nature/4564477.stm Presumably God would not find that technical challenge insurmountable.

56 M. Erickson, *Christian Theology* (2nd edn; Grand Rapids, MI: Baker, 1998), 796.

57 Grudem, *Systematic Theology*, 617.

58 J.O. Buswell, *A Systematic Theology of the Christian Religion*, Part IV, Eschatology (Grand Rapids, MI: Zondervan, 1962), 315.

59 Buswell, *A Systematic Theology*, Part IV, 315.

60 See Michio Kaku, *Hyperspace: A Scientific Odyssey Through Parallel Universes, Time Warps, and the 10th Dimension* (New York and Oxford: Oxford University Press, 1994). Other string theories posit even more spatial dimensions.

[61] H. Ross, *Beyond the Cosmos: The Extra-Dimensionality of God* (Colorado Springs, CO: NavPress, 1996). Part of the problem with Ross' prop-osal is that he seems to believe that God actually exists in the higher spatial dimensions as if God were physical (see *Beyond the Cosmos*, 49). However, this seems to be contradicted elsewhere (*Beyond the Cosmos*, 117).

[62] Ross, *Beyond the Cosmos*, 46–47.

[63] See, for instance, P. Woit, *Not Even Wrong: The Failure of String Theory and the Search for Unity in Physical Law* (New York: Basic Books, 2006).

[64] W.L. Craig, "Hugh Ross's Extra-Dimensional Deity: A Review Article," *Journal of the Evangelical Theological Society* 42.2 (1999), 299. For Ross' response to this and other criticisms see "Response to the Panel," *Philosophia Christi* 21.1 (1998) : 49–58.

[65] D. Farrow, "Confessing Christ Coming," in *Nicene Christianity: The Future for a New Ecumenism* (ed. C.R. Seitz; Grand Rapids, MI: Brazos Press, 2002), 136.

[66] B.A. Demarest and G.R. Lewis, *Integrative Theology* (Grand Rapids, MI: Zondervan, 1996), 472.

[67] As Hodge summarizes, "His ascension was his entering on their full enjoyment and exercise. He passed from the condition of an ordinary man to being as a man (as to his soul and body) everywhere present, and everywhere the supreme ruler. The heaven He entered is immensity." *Systematic Theology*, 631.

[68] Jenson, *Systematic Theology* Vol. 1, 202.

[69] Erickson comments that "This [passage] gives every indication that Jesus currently is a human who mediates between God and us." *Christian Theology*, 796.

[70] Dan. 7:14; Mt. 24:30; Mk. 13:26.

[71] Also see the Augsburg Confession, article 3.

[72] Jansen, "Ascension," 27.

[73] Luther, "That These Words of Christ, 'This is my Body,' Etc., Still Stand Firm Against the Fanatics," *Luther's Works* Vol. 37, *Word and Sacrament III* (ed. R.H. Fischer; trans. R.H. Fischer; gen. ed. H.T. Lehman; Philadelphia: Fortress Press, 1961), 46–47.

[74] M. Luther, "That These Words of Christ," 48.

[75] See R.H. Fischer, "Introduction to Volume 37," *Luther's Works* Vol. 37, *Word and Sacrament III*, xii.

[76] In P. Schaff, *The Creeds of Christendom* Vol. III, *The Evangelical Protestant Creeds* (Grand Rapids, MI: Baker, 1983), Ans. to Q. 47, p. 322.

Seven – On Not Understanding Final Judgment

[1] C.S. Lewis would agree in part with Russell's claim: if Jesus was not God then, in light of his teaching, he must have been either evil or insane. *Mere Christianity* (New York: HarperCollins, 2001), 52.

[2] B. Russell, "Why I am Not a Christian," in *Why I am not a Christian and Other Essays on Religion and Related Subjects* (ed. Paul Edwards; New York: Touchstone, 1957), 17–18. Charles Darwin made a similar observation in his autobiography: "I can hardly see how anyone ought to wish Christianity to be true ; for if so the plain language of the text seems to show that the men who do not believe, and this would include my Father, Brother and almost all my best friends, will be everlastingly punished. And this is a damnable doctrine." In *The Autobiography of Charles Darwin* (ed. N. Barlow; New York: W.W. Norton & Co., 1958), 87.

[3] Ingersoll, *Ingersoll's Lectures and Essays* (The Three Series in One Volume; London: first series; Watts & Co., 1926), 83–84.

[4] C. Pinnock, "The Conditional View," in *Four Views of Hell* (ed. William Crockett; Grand Rapids, MI: Zondervan, 1992), 136. Similarly, Richard Neuhaus observes: "'Go to hell.' That's a very rude thing to say, but relatively few people today would think themselves solemnly cursed were they on the receiving end of it. There is very little thinking about hell, solemn or otherwise, these days." "The Logic of Damnation," *First Things* (April 1994), 60.

[5] D. Sayers, *A Matter of Eternity: Selections from the Writings of Dorothy L. Sayers* (ed. R.K. Sprague (Grand Rapids, MI: Eerdmans, 1973), 86.

[6] J. Walvoord, "The Literal View," in *Four Views of Hell*, 11–28.

[7] Paul R. Coleman-Norton published an article some decades ago in which he claimed to have discovered a previously unknown saying in which Jesus is asked how the toothlessly damned will gnash their teeth. Jesus purportedly replied, "O thou of little faith, trouble not thyself, if haply they will be lacking any, teeth will be provided...." See S. Carlson, *The Gospel Hoax: Morton Smith's Invention of Secret Mark* (Waco: Baylor University Press, 2005), 17. While it turns out the article was an elaborate practical joke, the exchange highlights the absurdity of taking these passages literally.

[8] See W. Crockett, "The Metaphorical View," in *Four Views of Hell*, 43–81; cf. Crockett, "Response to John F. Walvoord," in *Four Views of Hell*, 29–31.

⁹ J.I. Packer, "The Problem of Eternal Punishment," in *The J.I. Packer Collection* (ed. Alister McGrath; Downers Grove, IL: InterVarsity Press, 1999), 225; Crockett, "The Metaphorical View," 45; Pinnock, "The Conditional View," 141.

¹⁰ Lewis depicts the city as purgatory for those who ultimately leave and hell for those who opt to stay there.

¹¹ Lewis was a great fan of this nineteenth century fantasy novelist, and thus honored him in the narrator's role in this novel.

¹² C.S. Lewis, *The Great Divorce: A Dream* (London: Fount, 1990), 111.

¹³ J.T. Chick, *Somebody Goofed*, [online] available at http://www.chick.com/reading/tracts/0003/0003_01.asp.

¹⁴ C.S. Lewis, *The Problem of Pain* (New York: Collier Books, 1962), 119.

¹⁵ Lewis, *Problem of Pain*, 127; "There are only two kinds of people in the end: those who say to God, 'Thy will be done,' and those to whom God says, in the end, '*Thy* will be done.'" Lewis, *Great Divorce*, 66–67.

¹⁶ This is a Greek translation of the Old Testament that predates Christianity. The relevant passages here include Job 16:9; Ps. 35:16; 37:12; Lam. 2:16.

¹⁷ See "βρυχω" *Theological Dictionary of the New Testament* Vol. 1 A–I (ed. G. Kittel, trans. and ed. G.W. Bromiley; Grand Rapids, MI: Eerdmans, 1964), 641.

¹⁸ E. Fudge, "The Final End of the Wicked," *Journal of the Evangelical Theological Society* 27.3 (1984), 330.

¹⁹ B. Schwartz, *The Paradox of Choice: Why More is Less* (New York: Harper Perennial, 2005), 115.

²⁰ C. Pinnock, "The Destruction of the Finally Impenitent," *Criswell Theological Review* 4 (1990) : 253. Cf. Pinnock, "The Conditional View," 149–50.

²¹ Pinnock, "The Destruction of the Finally Impenitent," 246–47.

²² Lewis, *Great Divorce*, 64.

²³ Lewis, *Great Divorce*, 62–63.

²⁴ Lewis, *Problem of Pain*, 128.

²⁵ This is congruent with the TA model critiqued in chapter three.

²⁶ For a biblical defense of Calvinism see J. Piper, *The Justification of God: an Exegetical and Theological Study of Romans 9:1–23* (Grand Rapids, MI: Baker, 1983). For a theological and philosophical defense see P. Helm, *The Providence of God* (Contours of Christian Theology; Downers Grove, IL: InterVarsity Press, 1994).

27 As Calvin put it, God "has barred the door of life to those whom he has given over to damnation." *Institutes*, 3.21.7, p. 931.

28 See for instance Packer, "The Problem of Eternal Punishment," 219.

29 *The Oxford American Desk Dictionary and Thesarus* (2nd edn; New York: Berkley Books, 2001), 886.

30 Pinnock, "The Conditional View," 152.

31 See O. Crisp, "Divine Retribution: A Defence," *Sophia* 42 (2003), 35–52.

32 See W. van Holten, "Can the Traditional View of Hell Be Defended? An Evaluation of Some Arguments for Eternal Punishment," *Anglican Theological Review* 85.3 (2003), 468–69; Pinnock, "The Conditional View," 152–53.

33 Another approach to justify eternal punishment is to claim that once in hell, people keep sinning such that while their individual sins are finite, there is an ever increasing (potentially infinite) number of sins and this is sufficient to keep the perpetrators damned for eternity. But this seems to contradict such passages as Colossians 1:20 and Philippians 2:10–11 which teach universal submission to Christ. Moreover, even if God *could* justifiably torture someone eternally, the salient question is *would he?*

34 Kvanvig, *The Problem of Hell* (New York and Oxford: Oxford University Press, 1993), 12.

35 Van Holten, "Can the Traditional View of Hell be Defended?' 475.

36 When I asked my wife which world she would prefer she put it rather bluntly: "I don't care about free will, as long as I go to heaven."

37 Lewis, *Great Divorce*, 113.

38 Lewis, *Great Divorce*, 68. The theme likewise appears in Tolkien's *Lord of the Rings* where the ring wraiths fade to nothing but a shadow due to their bondage to the ring.

39 Lewis, *Great Divorce*, 68.

40 I'm giving Lewis the benefit of the doubt here, but on reflection it seems to me that I might very well be disturbed by the echoing screams of an annihilated loved one.

41 Erickson, *Christian Theology*, 1241.

42 Perhaps Paul's concern is primarily with theocentric knowledge, but it would be strange indeed if this perfect knowledge of God only came at the cost of blotting out vast portions of the past and present.

[43] As Ingersoll put it, "No good man can be perfectly happy while he knows that even one being is in torment. No good god can be perfectly happy while misery inflicted by him exists." *The Letters of Robert G. Ingersoll* (ed. Eva Ingersoll Wakefield; New York: Philosophical Library, 1951), 239.

[44] T. Peters, "Where are We Going?" in *Essentials of Christian Theology* (ed. W. Placher; Louisville, KY and London: Westminster John Knox Press, 2003), 363.

[45] As Peters adds, "So anxious would they be to see the sufferings of the damned stopped and their souls released from agony that they would find heaven a miserable place." "Where are We Going?" 363.

[46] If this is not explicitly stated in Revelation 14, it is a justifiable inference. Further, in Revelation 6:10 the martyrs call out to the Lamb to have their blood avenged and then are entreated "to wait a little longer" (v. 11). The text surely implies that they will be satisfied when their pleas are finally met.

[47] Aquinas, *Summa Theologica* Vol. 3 (trans. Fathers of the English Dominican Province; New York: Benziger Brothers, 1948) suppl., 94.1, p. 2972.

[48] Aquinas, *Summa Theologica*, suppl., 94.3, p. 2973.

[49] J. Edwards, "The End of the Wicked Contemplated by the Righteous," *The Works of Jonathan Edwards* Vol. 2 (rev. E. Hickman; Edinburgh: Banner of Truth Trust, 1988), 208.

[50] Edwards, "End of the Wicked," 208. Pinnock comments: "Reading Edwards gives one the impression of people watching a cat trapped in a microwave squirm in agony, while taking delight in it." "The Conditional View," 140.

[51] Schwartz, *Paradox of Choice*, 156.

[52] Schwartz illustrates this with a cartoon of a man driving by a fellow parked on the side of the road talking in a phone booth in the pouring rain. The caption reads "I was sad because I had no on-board fax until I saw a man who had no mobile phone." *Paradox of Choice*, 155.

[53] Other imprecatory psalms include 57, 69, 109 and 143 and 137 with the shocking image of verse 9: "Happy are those who seize your infants and dash them against the rocks."

[54] This contrastive view of divine glory is assumed by Packer when he claims that the absence of eternal conscious torment would mean that we would have a deflated understanding of divine justice and

lose the ability to praise God's righteous judgments fully. "The Problem of Eternal Punishment," 224.

[55] D. Strange, "A Calvinist Response to Talbott's Universalism," in *Universal Salvation?: The Current Debate* (eds R.A. Parry and C.H. Partridge; Grand Rapids, MI and Cambridge, UK: Eerdmans, 2003), 162, emphasis added.

[56] Strange, "A Calvinist Response," 162.

[57] J.I. Packer, "Hell's Final Enigma," *Christianity Today* (April 22, 2002), 84.

[58] Packer, "Hell's Final Enigma," 84.

[59] Cited in A. Millar, "Mill on Religion," in *The Cambridge Companion to Mill* (ed. J. Skorupski; Cambridge: Cambridge University Press, 1998), 186.

[60] Talbott, "Christ Victorius," *Universal Salvation? The Current Debate*, 27.

[61] Note that I am not speculating about the nature of that awareness but simply that some sort of awareness will exist.

[62] Cited in G.H. Smith, *Atheism: The Case Against God* (Amherst, NY: Prometheus Books, 1989), 300.

[63] One might think that such a transformation makes more sense if it includes little horns and a forked tail.

[64] Peters comments: "What is love like? One of the significant characteristics of love is sympathy. Combining *syn* ("with") with *pathos* ("feeling"), the word *sympathy* means feeling someone else's pain with him or her. The precedent begins with God. Yahweh, the God of Israel, saw the sufferings of the chosen people in Egypt and 'heard their cry' (Ex. 3:7)." Peters, "Where Are We Going?" 363.

[65] Packer, "The Problem of Eternal Punishment," 219.

[66] Ingersoll, *Ingersoll's Lectures and Essays,* first series, 84.

[67] Annihilationism is the historic position of some early General Baptists as well as the Seventh Day Adventists, and has attracted a number of recent theologians including Philip Hughes, John Wenham, Stephen Travis, Edward Fudge, Clark Pinnock, and John Stott as well as the Doctrine Commission of the Church of England for which see *The Mystery of Salvation: The Story of God's Gift* (Harrisburg, PA: Morehouse Publishing, 1995), 199.

[68] Notable universalists in the early church include Origen and Gregory of Nyssa. In the modern church the view has been defended by a number of theologians including William Temple, John Baillie, and

John Robinson while receiving sympathetic treatment (if not official endorsement) from Karl Barth and Hans Urs von Balthasar. For a discussion see R.A. Parry and C.H. Partridge (eds), *Universal Salvation?: The Current Debate* (Grand Rapids, MI; Cambridge, UK: Eerdmans, 2003).

[69] But see G. MacDonald, *The Evangelical Universalist* (Eugene, OR: Cascade Books, 2006).

[70] Ingersoll, *Ingersoll's Lectures and Essays*, second series, 136. Charles Spurgeon reflected the right kind of passion: "If sinners will be dammed, at least let them leap to Hell over our bodies. If they will perish, let them perish with our arms about their knees." *Sermons of the Rev. C.H. Spurgeon* (NP: Sheldon, Blakeman and Co, 1864), 333.

Afterword

[1] B. Russell, "Has Religion Made Useful Contributions to Civilization?" in *Why I am not a Christian and Other Essays on Religion and Related Subjects*, ed. Paul Edwards (New York: Simon and Schuster, 1957), 25.